The ABC's of dBASE III PLUS

The ABC's of dBASE III PLUS™

Robert Cowart

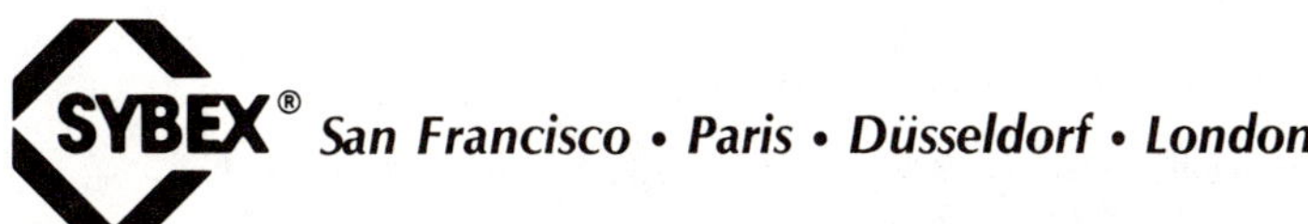

Cover art by Thomas Ingalls + Associates
Book design by Joe Roter

Library of Congress Card Number: 86-62263
ISBN 0-89588-379-1
Manufactured in the United States of America
20 19 18 17 16 15 14 13

To my parents, Jean and John, for their love and support, and encouragement of my curiosity

ACKNOWLEDGMENTS

I want to extend my humblest thanks to all those who participated in the process which has finally culminated in the printing of this book.

For the initial conception and support of my dBASE series for *A+ Magazine* over three years ago, I want especially to thank Steve Rosenthal and the people at *A+*. Many of the ideas in this book had their beginnings during that period.

Many heartfelt thanks also to the people at SYBEX, particularly my editor, David Kolodney, whose keen eye, calm demeanor, and seemingly infinite patience helped to sort out the wheat from the chaff—and then to make the whole thing read like English. To Dr. R. S. Langer, Editor-in-Chief; Chuck Ackerman, Acquisitions Editor; Karl Ray, Managing Editor; Dan Tauber, Technical Editor; Olivia Shinomoto, word processing; Donna Scanlon, typesetting; Adam Cardamon, proofreading; Joe Roter, book design, and Jannie Dresser, indexing—my appreciation for their collective ability to make a seemingly impossible schedule survivable. Thanks also to Carl Townsend for the use of his dBASE III PLUS command reference as the basis for Appendix C.

For her willingness to help resolve my technical questions, many thanks to The Answer Woman, Miriam Liskin. For general encouragement and help in the developmental stages of my writing and programming, special thanks to my friends George Hart and Alan Nelson.

Certainly not to be overlooked are my brother, Richard Cowart and my colleague, Robin Eckhardt, for their legal guidance in contractual matters.

And last but definitely not least, many thanks to Renée for putting up with a grouch, being my guinea-pig reader, and keeping my refrigerator stocked up.

CONTENTS

CHAPTER 14: Working with Logical Fields 171

CHAPTER 15: Working with Multiple Databases 179

CHAPTER 16: Creating Customized Data-Entry and Report Screens 199

INTRODUCTION

If you've never used dBASE III PLUS before and you want to learn how, this book is for you. If you already know dBASE III PLUS and someone else has asked you to teach it to them, this book is for them. (It will save you precious hours!)

Here's why. This book is a compact, direct, and practical introduction to dBASE III PLUS. Even though all the essentials of dBASE III PLUS are covered here in about 250 pages, the step-by-step instructions and breezy, down-to-earth style make learning dBASE III PLUS relatively painless. The sixteen chapters and three appendixes have been designed to take the dBASE novice from the first steps to such real-life applications as updating a permanent inventory database from a daily receiving-room database. And everything is presented in bite-sized chunks with lots of practical (and amusing) examples to make clear how the resources of dBASE III PLUS can be used in the actual work you do.

Of course, as you have probably already discovered, there are more books on the shelf about dBASE III PLUS than you can shake a stick at. And some of them are very good. But for a beginner, many of the books are too voluminous and cover a lot of advanced material you may not need to get into at this point. Others assume that you already know a lot about programming or about computers. Still others are beginners' books that prove to be a little bit too patronizing. And far too frequently, these books tell you how to use a feature of the program, but not when or why.

As a hands-on introduction for the novice, this book is meant to be read while you operate your computer. You will produce results while you learn, and you will be able to apply what you learn to your own work.

Of course, a set of manuals did come with the program, and this book is not meant to replace them. As reference materials they are well worth the considerable (!) shelf space they'll consume in your library. The manuals contain a great deal of information about the more than 260 commands which dBASE III PLUS now incorporates. They also cover the field of dBASE programming, which this book intentionally does not address. They are comprehensive, but they just don't serve as portable, convenient learning tools.

Having to become a dBASE programmer used to be part and parcel of learning dBASE. Now, with dBASE III PLUS, all that is history. The newly devised menu format of the dBASE Assistant renders dBASE less intimidating than ever before, while still extremely capable. For those tasks beyond the scope of the Assistant, typing commands directly at the dBASE "Dot prompt" is also useful. Both modes are covered in this book. dBASE programming is not.

How to use this book

If you're one of those folks who just bought dBASE III PLUS, looked at the manuals, and headed out for the book stores in hopes of rescue, chances are you haven't even gotten dBASE installed for your computer. So for starters, you should begin with Appendix A, which covers installation. Then move on to Chapter 1. Appendix A details all the steps necessary for making backup copies of your program disks, preparing blank data disks for storing your information, and even installing dBASE III PLUS on your hard disk, if you have one.

Beginning with Chapter 1, you'll start learning about databases—what they are, how they work, and what you can use them for. Then the next few chapters will take you through the steps of creating your first database—a telephone book/mailing list. You'll add data (names, addresses, and so on) to the list and learn how to reorder and select from your data using a variety of techniques. Editing the data to keep it up-to-date is covered too, as is arranging the data in your files for easier retrieval.

Then, beginning with Chapter 10, you'll create a business database (an inventory file), and you'll learn how to create professional-looking printed reports in a variety of styles. Building on that basis, you'll learn how to modify this database for different applications and we'll create a few other databases as well, for the purpose of building an integrated inventory-management system.

Chapter 11 will take you through the steps of printing mailing labels from the phone book/mailing list. Chapters 12, 13, and 14 will show you how to use the numbers, dates, and "logical" (yes/no) information in your databases for calculations and other purposes (with lots of exercise, of course).

Chapter 15 shows you a number of ways to link several databases together into a single application. To wind things down, Chapter 16 covers customizing you data-entry and editing screens. You'll actually design something almost artistic.

Appendix A, as mentioned, covers installation. Appendix B explains a variety of options for formatting printed reports of information from your database. Appendix C is a complete summary of all dBASE III PLUS commands and functions.

Conventions used in this book

To pack all this concisely into a book of this size, we've had to devise some rules for differentiating between the things you type, the things dBASE III PLUS itself displays, and the instructions you are being given by me. The rules are as follows:

- Explanatory notes or discussion are presented in standard paragraphs.
- When I want you to actually do something specific on your computer, I will tell you in a series of numbered steps:

  1.

  2.

  3.

  etc.

- When dBASE shows something on the screen in response to something you have done, I will generally say "dBASE responds with:" and then show you the response printed in blue letters, like this:

  dBASE response

- When I ask you to type something in from the keyboard, I will show you what to type in lighter letters, like this:

  What you type

1 What Is a Database?

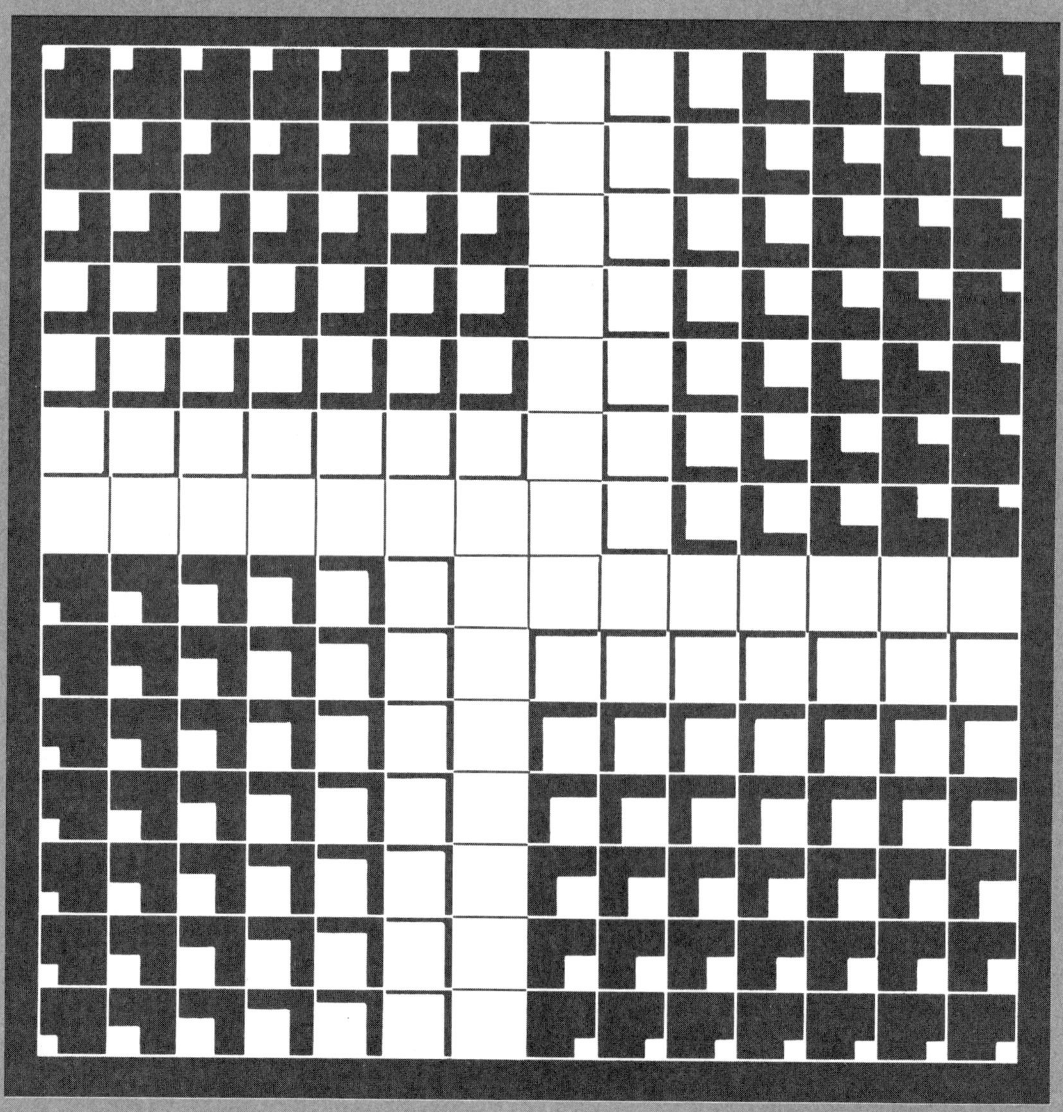

FEATURING:

database systems; the keyboard; saving your work

"Databases" are nothing new, but as it often occurs in the computer world, a cryptic pseudonym has replaced a common term.

Databases probably made their first appearance as pictures on the walls of Cro-Magnon caves to assist people in remembering (and avoiding) the migration routes of mastodons, or maybe they were used for keeping track of all of those collected berries. Nowadays it's likely that most of us use databases even more frequently. But like the Cro-Magnons, we just don't think of them as databases.

Actually, an encyclopedia, a dictionary, a phone book, or even a shopping catalog are common examples of household databases. Basically, these are all just lists of information. But what qualifies these lists as databases? Why isn't a novel or a magazine a database too?

What Is a Database?

A database provides a way of finding information quickly and easily based on a chosen reference point. An unorganized collection of information, like a novel, does not. The entries in an encyclopedia are arranged in alphabetical order. The paragraphs in a novel aren't.

The most common databases are really nothing but a series of rows and columns filled in with information. In addition, these rows and columns are laid out in such a way that any specific piece of information is easily available. Typically, each column has a heading that describes the type of information in it, and each row contains the information itself. In database terminology, the columns are called *fields* and the rows are called *records.* For example, consider another common household database—a checkbook register. Yours is probably laid out something like this:

Field # 1	2	3	4	5
check no.	description	charges	credits	balance
(record) # 1 # 2 # 3				

You could think of each of these familiar columns as a database field, with each check entry constituting one record. Should you need to look up the details of a particular check, it's relatively easy to do it by referring to the check number, since they are in numerical order.

Here's another example. Suppose you want to look up the phone number of your friend, Karen, in the telephone book. Your reference point (sometimes called a *key* in database circles) is, in this case, her last name. From this one piece of information you should be able to find Karen's phone number, and possibly even her address (if it is listed). Conceptually, it would probably look something like this:

name	address	city	phone
Davies, Karen	8071 Claremont	Berkeley	555-1212

Why Use a Computer?

The next question, obviously, is "So, who needs a computer? I can make lists like this easier and cheaper on paper!" A good point. In some cases, it would be foolish to use a computer. Let's take the telephone book example. As long as you want to look up Karen's phone number based on her name, you are better off with a book rather than a computer. However, what if you already knew Karen's phone number but had forgotten her last name? Or you needed a list of everyone whose phone number started with "527"? With its inexhaustible capacity for drudgery, a computer is the perfect tool for this type of work.

Not only does a computer allow you to find the desired information easily, it also allows you to add more people to the phone book, and keep the listings up-to-date as phone numbers and addresses change. Another advantage is the ease with which a computer can combine several existing databases into one larger database *system*. Large business systems will often consist of numerous subdatabases such as receivables, payables, inventory, or general ledger all linked together.

Of course, all this could be (and sometimes still is) done by hand, particularly the actual collection of data. But as we all know, collecting exorbitant amounts of information is a cinch. Most of us have more facts, figures, dates, prices, memos, and so on, than we know what to do with already. The real question is, once you've got them, what do you do with them? Where do you keep them? How do you find them later? Even—What do they mean? Are there some trends, or patterns, in the data which have escaped your eye? And so on. Computers can help with most of these questions.

In a world already caught up in a serious case of "information overload," computers offer a means of efficiently and constructively managing the masses of information we have created, discovered, or collected, leaving people more time to do what they do best—creative and intuitive endeavors.

The class of computer tools designed for this task is called *Database Management Systems* (DBMS). A good computerized database system serves not only as a repository for data, but it allows for selective extraction of data meeting specific criteria. That is, you can search even huge databases relatively quickly—a little like looking for a needle in a haystack, only with success.

What Is dBASE III PLUS?

Sophisticated database management systems have been available on large (that is, expensive) computers for at least a decade now. But, until recently, squeezing much capacity or flexibility out of a *microcomputer* has been like trying to get blood from a stone. This is precisely where dBASE III PLUS comes in. With dBASE III PLUS, you can:

- Easily create a wide variety of databases.
- Add to and edit your databases by simply "filling in the blanks" on your computer's screen.

- Search out and display information in an almost endless variety of ways, either on screen or on paper.
- Easily generate printed reports and mailing labels in a variety of sizes and formats.
- Automatically perform mathematical calculations on numerical data in your database. dBASE III PLUS can incorporate the results of calculations in printed reports, and it can actually store the results in a database for future use in applications such as balance sheets, sales transactions, accounts receivable reports, and the like.

Many of these capabilities result from the flexible design of dBASE III PLUS. For instance, say you did decide to create a telephone directory database. Maybe to start with, you want to search for people's phone numbers based only on their names. Later, if you want to use another key for the search (perhaps the company they work for), you can. With some less flexible types of database management systems, all of this must be totally prearranged, with no afterthoughts allowed. With dBASE III PLUS, modifications are easily made. Of course there are many more features of dBASE III PLUS—and of its predecessors, dBASE II and dBASE III—which have made them among the most popular DBMS systems today (one recent estimate suggests close to 500,000 copies of dBASE are in use). We'll be covering many of dBASE's attractive features in the following chapters.

Computer Basics

Before we get started, though, there are a few topics you will have to know about in order to work through the examples and exercises in this book.

The keyboard

This book uses the IBM PC, PC/XT, and Compaq personal computers as its standard for labeling keys and displaying the keyboard layout in figures. Chances are that your computer's keyboard is very similar, if not identical, to this standard. If you have another kind of keyboard, including those supplied with the IBM AT and compatibles, or are using the new standard IBM keyboard similar to that found on the IBM Convertible computer, your key placement will differ. Please refer to the operations manual for your computer if you have trouble locating specific keys.

In general though, your computer's keyboard is essentially identical to that of a typewriter (see Figure 1.1). All the letter and number keys are in exactly the same locations as you'd expect, though a few punctuation marks might be rearranged a bit. The only real difference between a typewriter and your computer keyboard is the *addition* of extra keys, each of which has its own purpose.

The Function keys On the far left side of the keyboard you will see 10 keys labeled F1 to F10. These are called *function* keys. The effect of pressing a given function key will vary, depending on which program you are running at the time (WordStar, Lotus 1-2-3, Sidekick, etc.). However, with many programs, including dBASE III PLUS, pressing the F1 key will display a Help screen providing useful information. Of the 10 function keys, this is the one you will use the most with dBASE III PLUS.

The Escape key Just to the right of the F2 key is a key labeled *Esc,* meaning *Escape.* Pressing this key generally lets you back out of, or escape from, a choice you have made in dBASE III PLUS. For example, when a submenu or prompt is displayed on the screen, pressing this key returns you to the previous step.

Figure 1.1: The computer keyboard

The Control key

The Ctrl or Control key, just to the right of the F6 key, is similar in operation to the Shift key on a typewriter, in that it is always used in conjunction with another key. To get a capital letter, you have to hold down the Shift key, and then press the letter you want capitalized. The Ctrl key is used the same way, only with different results. With dBASE III PLUS the Ctrl key is used mostly for moving the cursor (the blinking pointer) around the screen and for editing (changing) data in your database. The important thing to remember is that for the Ctrl key to work, you must press it first, and keep it down. Then you press the second key, as indicated in whichever exercise you are working on. Also, be careful not to press the Ctrl key when you mean to press the Shift key. They are close to each other, and easily confused.

The Shift keys

The Shift keys work much as they do on a typewriter. They are located at the right and left of the bottom row of letter keys, and they are labeled with outlined, upward-pointing arrows.

The Underscore key

dBASE III PLUS makes extensive use of the underscore (underline) key. The underscore key is located just above the P key. You must press the Shift key to produce an underscore.

The Enter key

The Enter key, represented in this book by the symbol it is generally labeled with, ↵, has several effects, depending on what you are doing. In general, it tells the computer to accept or act on what you have typed in and to respond accordingly. Think of it as the *Go Ahead* key.

If a menu is displayed, pressing ↵ confirms that you want to select the menu option you have highlighted.

If you are entering data into a field, ↵ moves you down to the next field. In some operations, ↵ may move you to the next record.

In a few operations, ↵ acts like an on/off switch. Pressing it once selects an option, pressing it again deselects the option. This will become clearer in the exercises.

Your Enter key may be labeled ENTER, RETURN, or CR (Carriage Return), if it is not labeled ↵.

The Cursor keys

To the right side of the keyboard, there is a block of number keys. The 2, 4, 6, and 8 keys have arrows on them. These keys control the movement of the cursor, letting you move around on your computer's screen to highlight menu options, type in commands, or enter data into databases. These keys will be referred to in this book using the same arrows you see on the keys: →, ←, ↑, and ↓.

The Backspace key

Not to be confused with the ← key is the Backspace key, located at the upper right of the keyboard. This key often has a similar ← mark on it, or sometimes it has a larger arrow on it, though still pointing to the left. In any case, this key does more than just move the cursor to the left. It also erases the letters you backspace over! It's just like a self-correcting typewriter. Be careful with this key because it can erase valuable information in your database if you use it unintentionally.

End, Home, PgUp, and PgDn

Notice that the 1, 7, 9, and 3 keys on the numeric keypad say *End, Home, PgUp,* and *PgDn,* respectively. Like the ↵ key, the effect of these keys differs depending on what you're doing in dBASE III PLUS. In general, they move the cursor in larger "jumps" than the arrow keys do. Instead of moving one letter at a time, they may move a whole word or a whole screen at a time. The Ctrl key is used with both Home and End to enter data or to save your work in dBASE III PLUS.

If you find that your cursor keys do not work properly—printing numbers instead of having the expected effect—press the key labeled *NumLock* once. This activates the cursor keys.

One final note about the keyboard. Almost all the keys on the keyboard are *repeating* keys. If you hold down a key more than about one second, it will begin to repeat continually. When entering data, you want to be careful not to accidentally press down a letter for too long, otherwise unpredictable results can occur, such as the name John Doooooooe showing up in a database.

Saving your work

As is the case with most computer programs, and dBASE III PLUS is no exception, your work at any given point is actually being done inside the computer's memory chips, called RAM (for Random Access Memory). Using RAM enables the computer to work with your data more quickly than if it worked only with your disk drives. The disadvantage is that RAM "loses its memory" once your computer is turned off. As a friend of mine once remarked, your computer's a bit like a classroom blackboard. Once the lecture is over, someone is bound to come in and erase the whole board, so you'd better take down some notes first.

Your floppy-disk drive or hard-disk drive is used by your computer to store the information which would otherwise be lost when the power is shut off. But the computer does not do this automatically! It's up to you to remember to *save* your work onto a disk before you turn off your computer.

There are several ways to do this in dBASE III PLUS, but the surest one is to select the *Quit dBASE III PLUS* option from the Set Up menu. If you are using a floppy-disk drive to store your data, you must make sure not to switch disks between the time you begin work with dBASE III PLUS and the time you Quit. (There are other ways to save your work. They are covered in Chapter 5.)

Getting Oriented 2

bringing up dBASE III PLUS; using the dBASE Assistant

Now that you have acquired the necessary background understanding, you're ready to get down to some useful work. The first step is to start the program, also called "bringing the program up." How you bring up dBASE III PLUS on your computer depends on whether you have a hard-disk or floppy-disk computer system.

How to Bring Up dBASE

Follow the instructions that fit your computer system, floppy or hard.

If you have a hard-disk system

1. If you are using a hard-disk system and your computer is not on, turn it on. If your system is already running, reset the computer by pressing the Ctrl, Alt, and Del keys simultaneously (see Figure 2.1). This gets the computer to properly reset for use with dBASE.
2. Enter the date and time if prompted. Use a format like this:

   09/28/86

Figure 2.1: The Ctrl, Alt, and Del keys

for September 28, 1986, and

08:30

for 8:30 A.M. (For 2:30 P.M. use 14:30)

3. When the C> prompt appears, get into the dBASE subdirectory by typing

   CD DBASE (or whatever the name of your dBASE subdirectory is, if any)

   and pressing ↵.

4. Then simply type

   DBASE

   and press ↵. The dBASE copyright information appears on your screen.

5. Press ↵ again to bring up dBASE. Your screen will look like Figure 2.2. You are now ready to start working with the program.

If you have a floppy-disk system

1. If you are using floppies and your computer is not on, place your dBASE III PLUS System Disk #1 in drive A and turn the machine on.

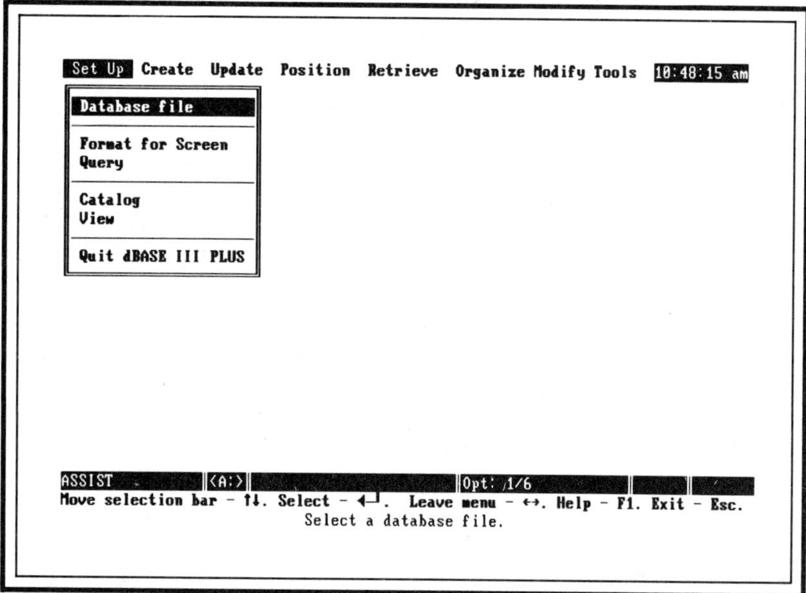

Figure 2.2: The dBASE III PLUS main screen: the Assistant

2. If your system is already running, then simply place System Disk #1 in drive A and reset the computer by pressing the Ctrl, Alt, and Del keys simultaneously (see Figure 2.1). This gets the computer to reset properly for use with dBASE.

3. Enter the date and time if prompted. Use a format like this:

   09/28/86

   for September 28, 1986, and

   08:30

   for 8:30 A.M. (For 2:30 P.M. use 14:30)

4. When the A> prompt appears, type

   DBASE

   and press ↵.

5. After several seconds, the dBASE copyright notice appears. Press Enter.

6. A message appears on the screen prompting you to put System Disk #2 into drive A. Do so, and press Enter again.

7. The main dBASE screen appears, as in Figure 2.2 above.

This is dBASE III PLUS' main screen, called the Assistant. The Assistant screen lets you control dBASE III PLUS by making selections visually from a number of *menus*. A menu is a list of options shown on the screen from which you can select. For example, notice that the screen now shows a list enclosed in a large box in the upper left corner. These are the options you can select while this particular menu, called the Set Up menu, is showing on the screen. Altogether, there are eight menus on the Assistant screen, each containing its own list of options. The names of the menus appear across the top of the screen.

Try the following exercises to become comfortable with the Assistant screen and its menus.

How to Make Menu Selections

1. First we'll take a look at the Create menu. Notice that there are four arrow keys on the numeric keypad at the right of the keyboard (see Figure 2.3). One of the functions of these keys is to move the highlighting around the menus so you can indicate your selections. Press → once. The Create menu now appears, replacing the Set Up menu. (If nothing happened, try pressing the NumLock key located above the arrow keys. This will activate the arrow keys.) Pressing → or ← is one way to select from the eight menu names across the top of the screen. Instead of moving the highlighting with the arrow keys, though, you can also select a menu by pressing the first letter of its name on the typewriter part of the keyboard.

2. Type the letter S. Notice that the Set Up menu appears. Type the letter C again to get back to the Create menu. You can choose menus by typing the first letter of the name, so you can use either arrow keys or letter keys to move from one menu to another.

3. Now press ↓ several times. Notice that a new option within the Create menu's box becomes highlighted with each press of the key.

Figure 2.3: The four arrow keys used for making menu selections

This is how you select a specific action for dBASE to perform. Once a desired option is highlighted, pressing ↵ finalizes the choice, telling dBASE to start working for you. But don't press ↵ just yet.

4. Try moving around through the various menus now, up and down within menus and across to new menus. (You can move across from anywhere within a menu.) You might notice that many menus do not seem to respond to ↓ at all, and on other menus, some options, which are displayed in dimmed letters on the screen, are skipped over. This is because certain options are not available to you until you start working with some actual databases. We'll get to that stage in just a bit.

5. In the meantime, select the Set Up menu and look at the bottom line of the screen. Notice that as you move up and down with the arrow keys, the message on the bottom line, the *Message Line,* changes. For example, highlight *Database File,* (the first option in the Set Up menu). The Message Line says "Select a database file," and your screen should look like the one in Figure 2.2. The Assistant gives you hints here, on the Message Line by showing a brief description of the menu choice you are on. It's good to keep an eye on the Message Line for instructions from the Assistant.

6. Look just above the Message Line. This is the *Navigation Line.* Here, you see instructions about what moves you can make next and how to make them. These instructions will change depending

on the task you and dBASE are working on. Look at it now. It appears as in Figure 2.2. Try selecting the *View* option in the Create menu, and press ↵. The screen should look like Figure 2.4. Notice that the Navigation Line information has changed to advise you how to make selections from this new small box.

7. We don't want to continue defining a View just now, so press the Esc (Escape) key once to back out of this option. The small box that popped up next to the menu disappears, and you are returned to the Create menu. It's good to remember that the Esc key lets you change your mind and simply "escape" from most dBASE operations. When using the Assistant, the Esc key always takes you back one step.

   However, if you press Esc too many times, the Assistant screen disappears, leaving only a dot (called the *Dot prompt*) down at the bottom left of the screen. If this happened to you, don't worry. If you find yourself at the Dot prompt, simply type

   Assist

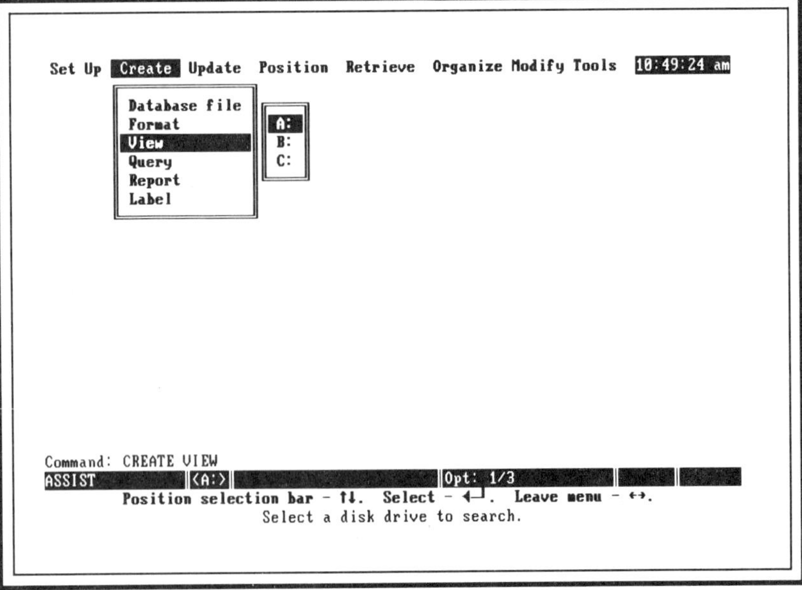

Figure 2.4: Notice the Navigation Line

and press ↵. The Assistant screen will then reappear. Then select the Create menu again and highlight *View*. More experienced dBASE users sometimes prefer to work with dBASE from the Dot prompt level rather than through the Assistant, though the novice is better off with the Assistant. At the Dot prompt you type in your commands instead of selecting them from menus. We will cover this in more detail later.

8. There are two more areas of the Assistant screen which we haven't talked about yet—the *Status Bar* and the *Command Line*. Looking at Figure 2.4, the Status Bar is the line just above the Navigation Line and is always highlighted in reverse video. The Status Bar indicates the state of various optional settings such as whether or not you are using the Assistant, which disk drive your database files are on, and which option you are chosing from a menu. We will come back to the Status Bar later on.

9. The Command Line, just above the Status Bar, is invisible now, but it appears when you actually begin building dBASE III PLUS commands. To see the beginning of a Command Line, press ↵. The Command Line says

   Command: CREATE VIEW

   Press the Esc key once to get back to the Create menu.

How to Get Help When You Need It

Sometimes you need more help than is provided by the Message and Navigation Lines. To see an example:

1. Press F1. Do not press the letter F and then 1. Actually press the key at the left of the keyboard labeled F1. The F stands for Function. On IBM PC style keyboards, there are ten Function keys labeled F1 through F10, as in Figure 2.5.
2. A window will appear on the screen with some information about the menu option that is currently highlighted. See Figure 2.6.
3. Don't worry if you don't understand everything on a Help screen. Some of the information is there for people typing dBASE commands from the Dot prompt. Other information on Help screens is

Figure 2.5: The Function keys

geared to advanced applications. But in general it's a good idea to sample the Help screens occasionally as you learn more about dBASE III PLUS.

4. Now press any key to keave the help screen and return to the Assistant.

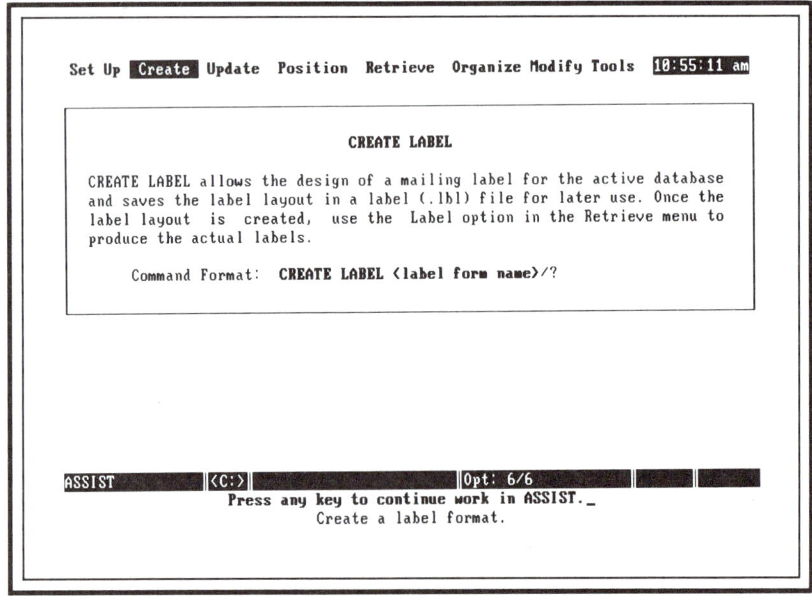

Figure 2.6: A typical Help screen

3

Creating Your First Database

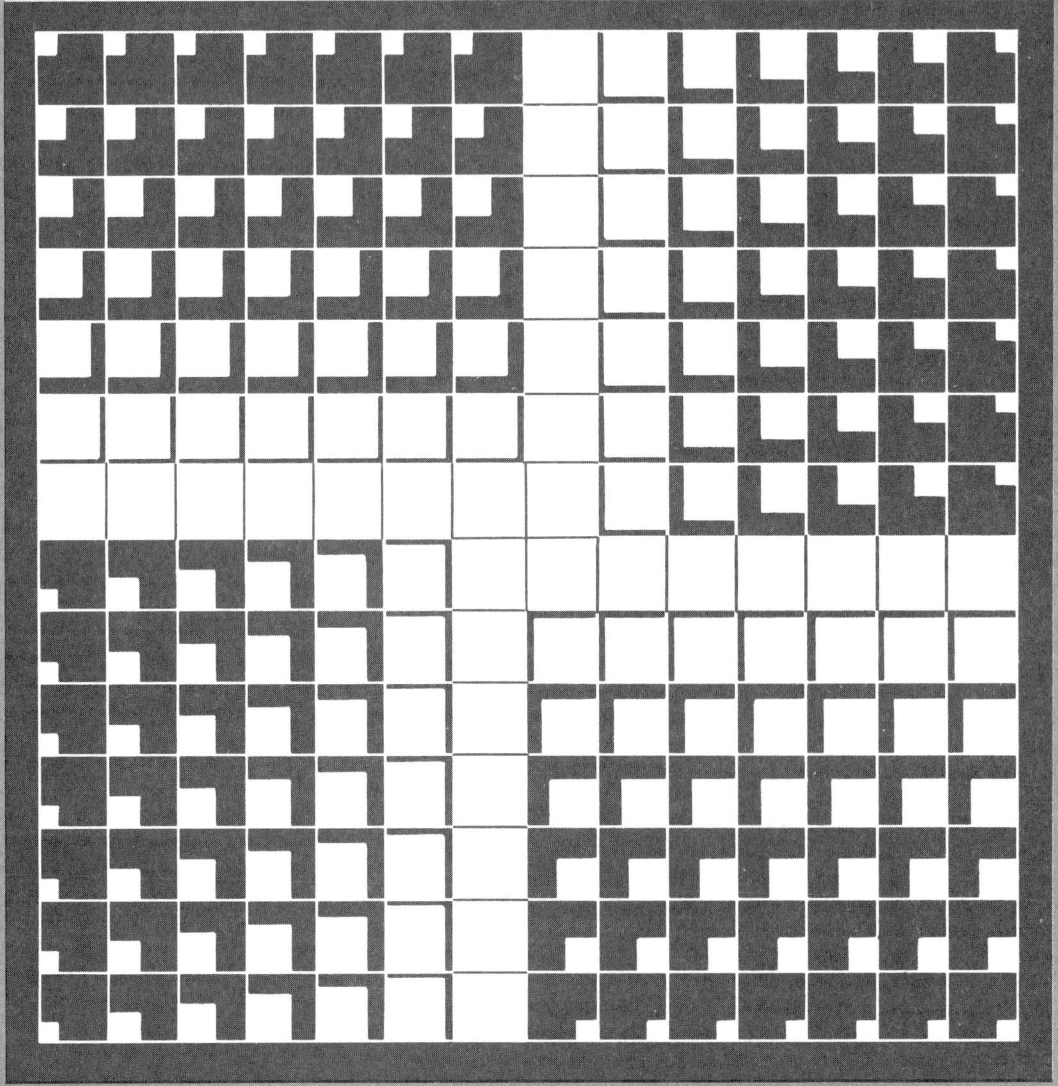

file names; the Create screen

Since the telephone book example referred to in Chapter 1 is something everyone is familiar with and can use, it's a good case study for our first database. You may even find it convenient enough for everyday use after this tutorial. Since addresses will be included in this database, you could even use it for creating mailing labels and form letters.

As mentioned in Chapter 1, a database is comprised of a list of information and the form into which that information is put. The information is called the *data,* and the form is called the *structure.* Defining a database's structure amounts to deciding how many fields your database will have, and what kind of information each field will hold. It's a little like drawing up an empty form which will later be filled in with data. Both the data and the database structure are stored by your computer on floppy-disk or hard-disk in a *file,* called a database file.

To distinguish one file from another, each file must have a unique name. Without it, your computer could not find your database on the disk next time you wanted to use it. The first step in creating a database, then, is assigning it a name. Next, you define its structure. Finally, you begin filling up the file with data, like filling a filing cabinet with papers.

How to Name the Database

1. From the Assistant screen, select the Create menu. (Since we want to create a new database from scratch, we use this menu, not the Set Up menu, which also has a Database option in it.)

2. Make sure that the first option in the Create menu, *Database,* is highlighted. Simply press ↵ to select this option, and you should see the screen in Figure 3.1.

3. Notice the new small box which appears to the right of the Create menu. Before the DBASE III PLUS Assistant can start creating a new database, it needs to know which disk drive you want to store the database on. This may seem a little backwards since we haven't done anything yet, but who ever said computers are logical?

   The box contains the letters A, B, and C, referring to the disk drives of the same name. If you are using a floppy-disk system, make sure you have an empty, formatted floppy-disk in drive B. Then highlight *B:* and press ↵. If you are using a hard disk system, highlight *C:* and press ↵.

4. In response, the Assistant now erases the box with the drive letters in it and a new, longer box appears (see Figure 3.2). The Assistant is now asking for the name of the database file you wish to create.

   In deciding on a name, it's a good idea to use one that will remind you of the file's contents. This will help to avoid confusion

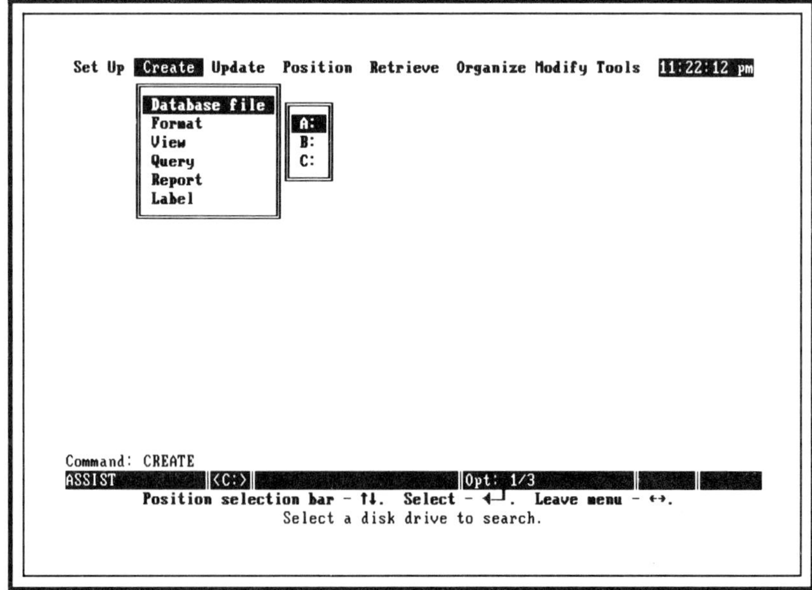

Figure 3.1: Selecting a disk drive for your new database

later, when you have a number of databases on your disk. So, obviously, something like PHONE BOOK would be the logical choice. Unfortunately, a database name cannot be longer than eight letters, and no spaces are allowed, so you have to be a little more crafty. Therefore, we'll have to go with a slight abbreviation. Let's call it PHONEBK.

You can type the file name in lowercase or uppercase letters. However dBASE always displays the names in uppercase and that is how they will appear when they are referred to in this book.

5. Type in the file name.

   PHONEBK ↵

How to Create the Database Structure

Good. Now dBASE III PLUS should have gone off for a second or two, and come back with a new screen—the Create screen, shown in

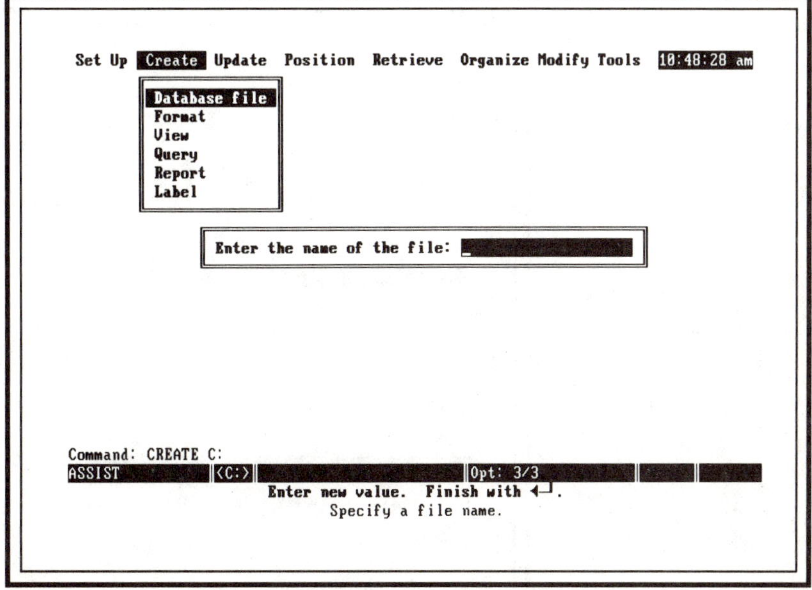

Figure 3.2: Naming your database

Figure 3.3. It may look a little confusing at first, but don't worry. It's really not that complicated. Let's pause here for a moment to consider what this screen's purpose is.

Essentially, the Assistant is now asking you to define the database structure. Recall from Chapter 1 that a *record* is the database term for one complete entry, like a card in a index card box or a listing in a phone book. Each record consists of *fields,* each of which stores one portion of the entry, such as name, address, and so on. So you now have to tell dBASE how many fields the records will have and what each field will contain.

1. Notice the boxed in area at the top of the screen. This merely tells you how to move the cursor around and make changes during the process of defining the structure. You will be seeing this box on many dBASE III PLUS screens, and we will discuss the various elements as they become important, in this chapter and later on.

2. Now look at the central part of the screen. This is where we will be defining the structure. Notice that there are two identical sets of column headings, one on the left and one on the right, which say

   Field Name Type Width Dec

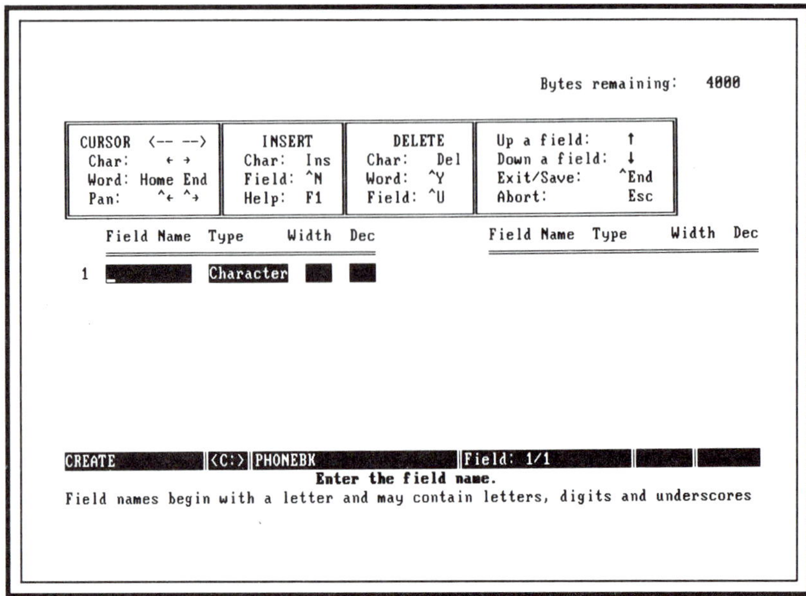

Figure 3.3: The Create screen

Under each of the four headings is a highlighted area. The number 1 appears to the left. dBASE is asking you to fill in the highlighted boxes with four pieces of information about the first field in your phone book database. Then you will move down and fill in the same four specifications for the second field, and so on for all the fields you wish to include in your database records. Although there is some help down on the message line, it's not fully explanatory. Here is a breakdown of what each of the four field specifications means and what your options are for each one.

Field Name What is the *name* you want to give to the field? The name can be up to ten letters long (either uppercase or lowercase), and may contain only letters, digits, and underscores (_).

Type What kind of information is going to be stored in this field? There are five choices, which you can select by pressing the space bar until your choice appears in the place where the choice "Character" is now displayed. You can also just type the first letter of the choice. Here are the five kinds of field type.

- Character type—this includes all letters, punctuation marks, and special symbols, as well as any numerals that are merely going to be printed, not used in any mathematical calculations (zip codes, for example).
- Numeric type—numbers that will later require mathematical calculation, such as dollar amounts.
- Logical type—this covers true/false or yes/no entries.
- Date type—such as 12/5/85.
- Memo type—used for storing varying amounts of text about each record. For example, for our phone book, we might want to have a Memo field to write a few notes about each person.

Width What is the maximum number of letters, numbers, etc. that you plan to put into the field? That is, how "wide" do you want it? Logical, Memo, and Date fields are automatically assigned a width by dBASE III PLUS, so you only have to decide this for Numeric and Character fields. If you make a field too small, then you will have to abbreviate long names or numbers to fit them in your database. If you make a field too long, you will waste space on your disk.

Dec If you enter N (meaning Numeric) as the field type, you must indicate the number of decimal places you want in the field. So for monetary figures you would type in 2 to indicate that there are two decimal places. You only have to do this for Numeric fields.

Planning the structure

Now, with the possible field types in mind, we can begin to plan our database structure. A little careful thinking at this stage will pay off in the long run, so let's revert to a bit of low technology for a minute by pulling out a piece of paper and a pencil. Imagining what your database would look like on paper simplifies the structuring process. Here's a layout of what we probably want the phone book database to store.

Field:	1	2	3	4	5	6	7
Field Name:	FIRST NAME	LAST NAME	PHONE NO	STREET	CITY	ST	ZIP

For the time being, we'll use this model for our structure. We'll modify it later on as part of the tutorial. That way you can practice adding your own finishing touches to meet any specific needs you might have. In the meantime, do the following steps, remembering that we will define the structure one field at a time, for each of the seven fields listed above.

Creating the structure

1. The cursor should be in the Field Name box for Field number 1. Notice that the Status Bar (at the bottom of the screen) says Field 1/1. This means that you are working on Field 1 and that there is only one field so far. Type in:

   FIRST_NAME

   The underscore is used here to separate the words. If you try using any other punctuation marks, dBASE III PLUS will beep at you. If you make a mistake, simply use the ← key to back up and correct it.

2. When you type the last letter in FIRST_NAME, you will hear a beep. This beep is O.K. It just tells you that the field name was the maximum length. The cursor skips to the next box, Type, which has the word Character already filled in. (If the field name had been shorter you would have had to press ↵ to move to the next box.) The Assistant always assumes, by default, that you want your fields to be Character fields. Since you will not be doing mathematical calculations on any of the fields in your phone book (such as asking dBASE to find the average of all your friend's zip codes), you can accept the default assumption and categorize all the fields as Character. (Both you and dBASE III PLUS will find it easier to use Character fields whenever possible, even though some of the fields, such as phone number and zip code actually will be used to store numerals.) So just press ↵.

   The cursor skips to the Width box. The Assistant wants to know how long the FIRST_NAME field should be.

Since you'll have to answer this question for each of the fields, this is a good time to do a little research. Pull out a phone book and get an idea of how long people's last names are. How long is the average street address? Count the letters in a few city names.

Of course, you can play it safe by making fields longer than they need to be, but keep in mind that blank spaces take up room on your disk, just as actual characters do. You want your fields to be long enough for all relevant data, such as phone numbers and zip codes, but don't make your fields so long that they end up being half filled with blank spaces. You know your field length is correct when only an occasional name or address won't fit in the field. You can usually abbreviate in these cases without ambiguity.

From experience, the lengths indicated below have been found to work best. The PHONE_NO field is 12 spaces long to allow room for an area-code and the two dashes between the numerals.

Field:	1	2	3	4	5	6	7
Field Name:	FIRST NAME	LAST NAME	PHONE NO	STREET	CITY	ST	ZIP
Type:	C	C	C	C	C	C	C
Size:	10	15	12	22	13	2	5

3. So, getting back to the screen, type

   10 ↵

   for the width of the FIRST_NAME field.

4. The cursor skips past the Dec box and moves down to prepare for defining the next field. This is because dBASE III PLUS is smart enough to know that character fields, being non-numeric, will not need decimal places. The screen should now look like Figure 3.4.

5. Good. You've created the first field in the structure. Now go ahead to fill in the rest of the fields, repeating the steps you just took, but using the names and sizes shown in Figure 3.5. Remember, if you get a beep, look at the message line at the bottom of the screen. Use the arrow keys to move around, and ↵ for advancing to the next box or field. When you are through, your screen should look like the one in Figure 3.5.

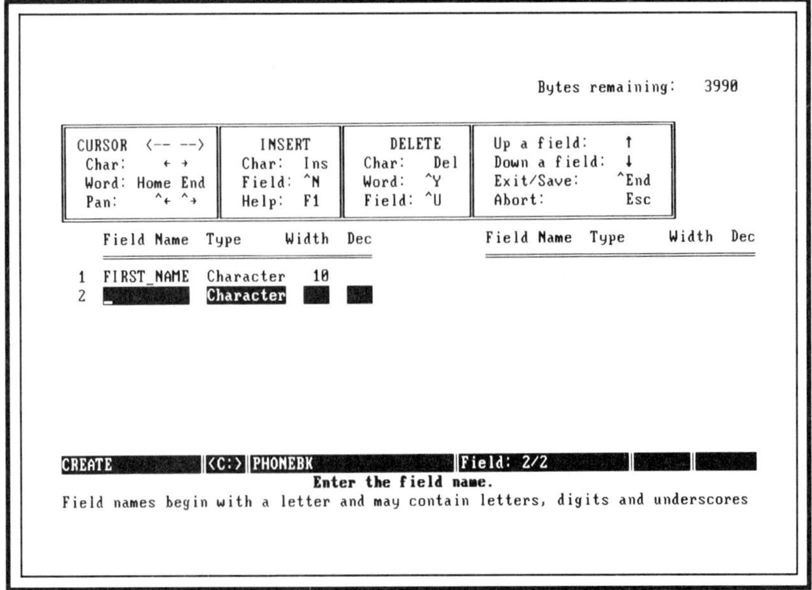

Figure 3.4: The first field is defined

6. After the cursor moves down to begin creating Field 8, look up towards the right of the Help box at the top of the screen. The third line down says EXIT/SAVE. Now that we are through defining all 7 fields, we'll use this command to save the structure on the disk and exit this part of dBASE III PLUS. The command listed next to EXIT/SAVE is ^End. The ^ means Ctrl, so press the Ctrl key and hold it down while pressing the End key (located on the number pad just below the ← key). Then press ↵. This saves the structure of the seven fields on your disk.

7. dBASE III PLUS now asks, down at the bottom of the screen, if you want to start typing data into your new database at this time.

   Input data records now? (Y/N)

8. Since we want to do a few other things first, just type N, and dBASE returns you to the Assistant screen. Congratulations! You have successfully created your first database structure.

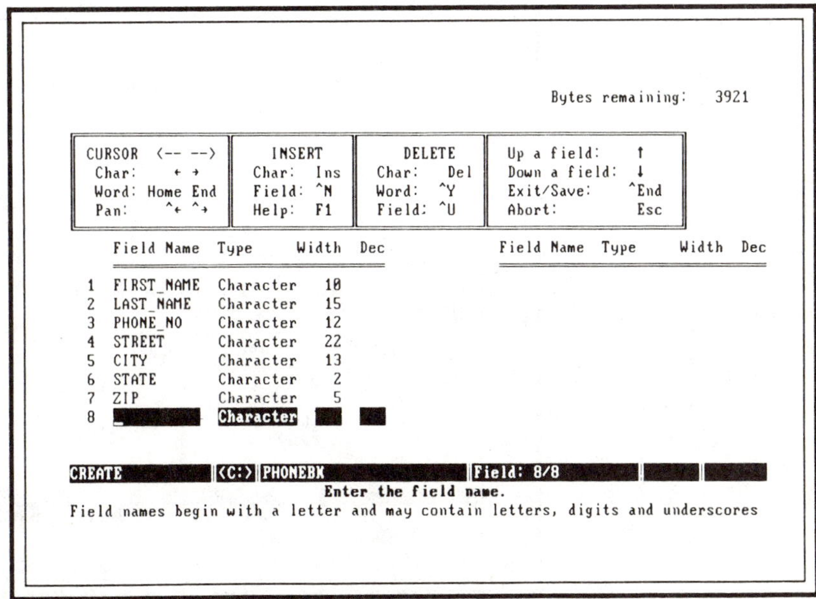

Figure 3.5: The completed PHONEBK structure

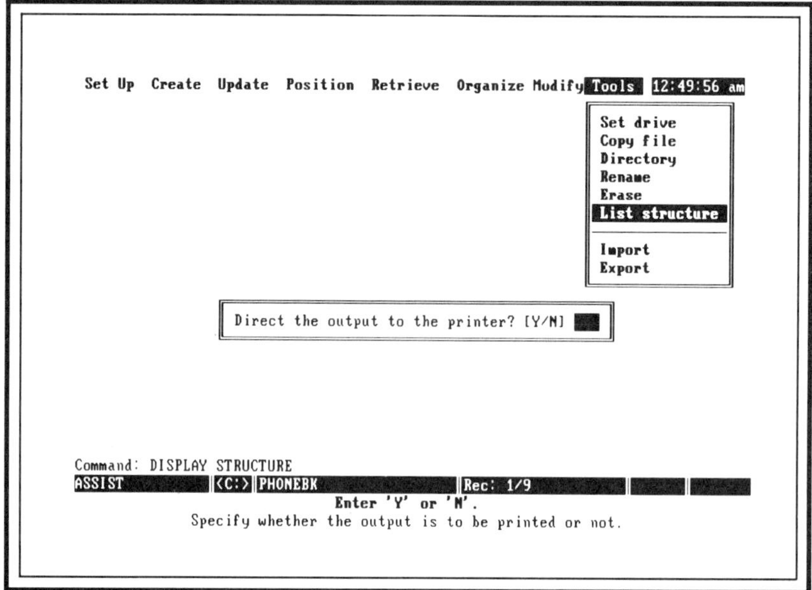

Figure 3.6: Checking the structure

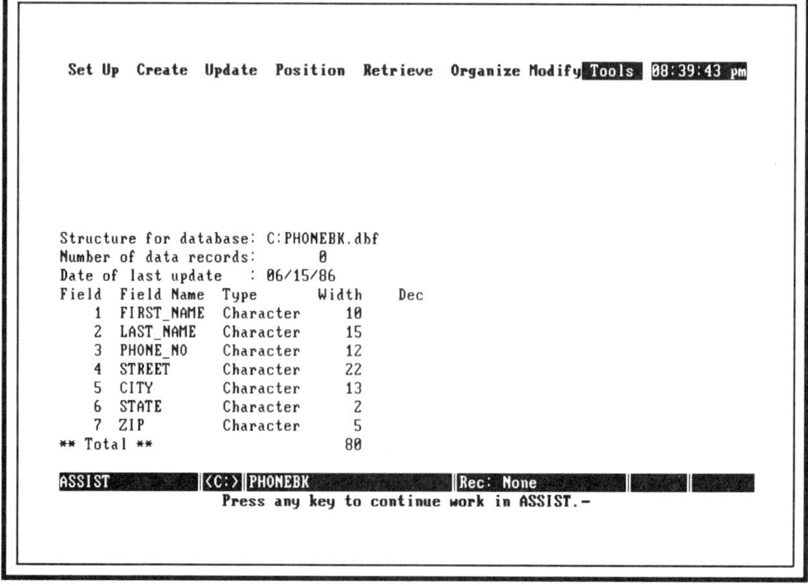

Figure 3.7: Listing the structure

Verifying the structure

Just to be safe, it is a good idea to verify that the structure is properly recorded on disk. This can be done using an option from the Tools menu:

1. Select the Tools menu.
2. Highlight *List Structure* and press ↵. The screen should look like Figure 3.6
3. The Assistant asks if you want to print the structure out on the printer. Type N.
4. The screen now lists the structure of the PHONEBK file for you, as shown in Figure 3.7. Notice that aside from the structure, you will also see some other information, including the date when your database was last updated and the number of records you have added thus far. Since no data has been added yet, this number should be 0.

   If your structure does not look exactly like Figure 3.7, don't worry. In the next chapter you will find out how to make changes to your database structure.
5. The Message Line now tells you to press any key to return to the Assistant. Do this now.

How to Take a Break

You now know how to create a new database structure and verify that it was properly recorded on the disk. You may well wish to take a break before going on to the next chapter. If you do want to take a break now:

1. Select the Set Up menu
2. Highlight the *Quit dBASE III* option at the bottom of the menu.
3. Press ↵.
4. You will see the familiar A> or C> prompt.

If you do not want to take a break just now, simply move on to Chapter 4.

Modifying the Structure 4

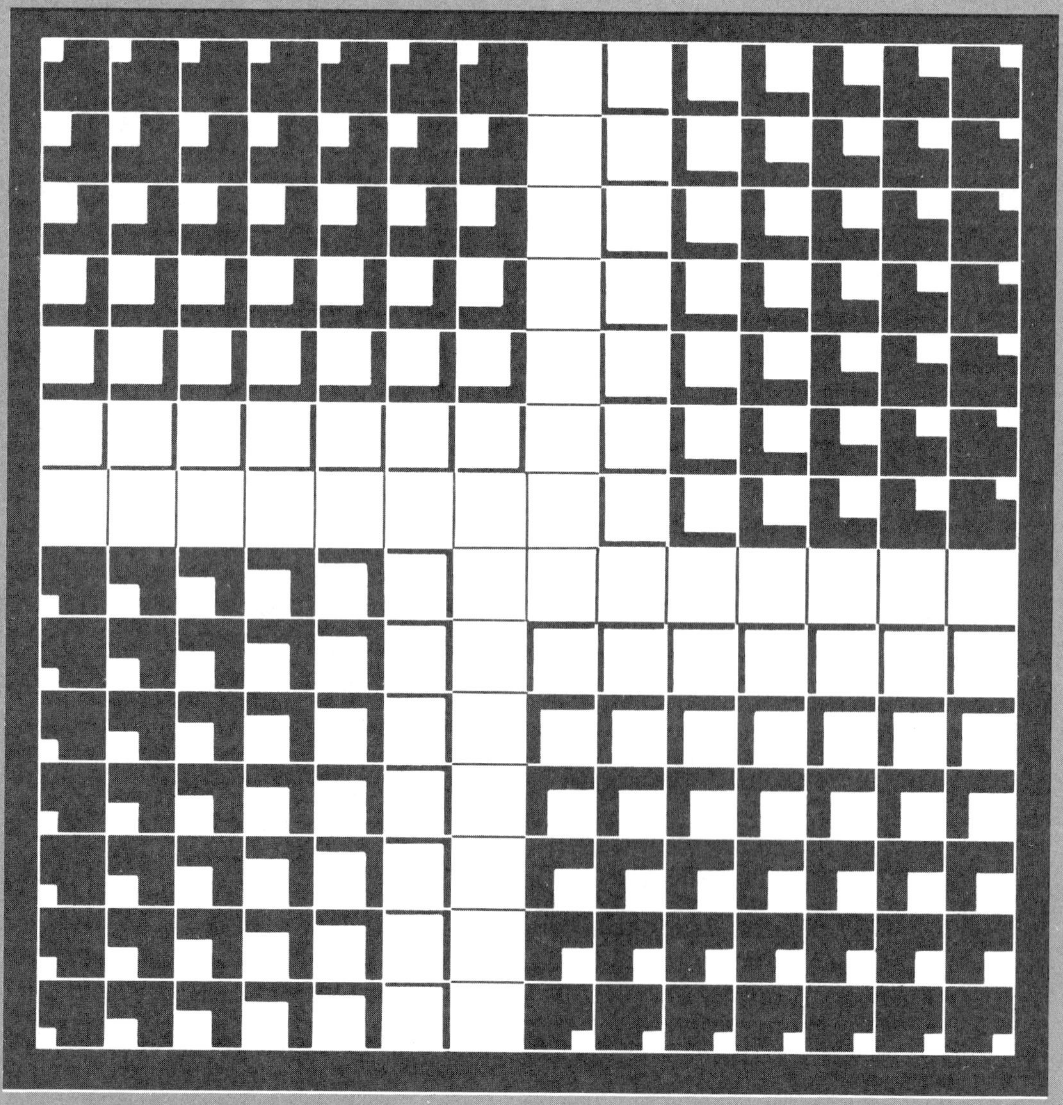

adding and deleting fields; changing fields

In the last chapter, you learned how to create and verify the structure of a dBASE III PLUS database. Using the dBASE Assistant, it's a relatively easy process.

However, even the best laid plans are sometimes shortsighted, and it's not an uncommon experience to find that your database's structure needs alteration, either to change the size of fields or to add or subtract a field. In fact, you may already have thought of a few things we've left out of the phone book structure.

For example, lots of people have a work phone number in addition to their home phone number, and we didn't include a place to put it. Also, maybe a slot for the name of each person's company would be a good idea. Finally, how about a Memo field to write some notes about each person as a sort of memory jogger. So, now what? Is it too late to change things, or do you have to start from scratch again?

Luckily, dBASE III PLUS accommodates 20/20 hindsight by allowing you to modify an existing database structure. It's even possible to change the structure after you have lots of data in the file, though at that stage there are some restrictions that we will get to later. In either case, the process is called *modifying the structure.*

How to Modify the Structure

1. For those of you who quit dBASE III PLUS to take a break after the last chapter, bring up dBASE again. You may refer to the instructions in Chapter 2.

If you are using a floppy-disk system, make sure you have the data disk containing your PHONEBK database in Drive B.

Use the *Set drive* option on the Tools menu to tell the Assistant which disk drive you will be using to save and retrieve files. For hard-disk users, it will probably be C. For floppy-disk users, it will be B.

2. Now, in order to start working on our phone book database, the first thing we have to do is *open* the file. Opening the file means telling dBASE III PLUS to read the file from the disk, and load it into the computer's internal memory. Regardless of whether you are going to add to the file's data, make changes to its structure, or perform any number of other activities, you must open the file first.

   a. So, regardless of whether you took a break or not, select the Set Up menu, make sure *Database file* is highlighted, and press ↵.

   b. A box appears asking you to specify the drive on which dBASE should look for the file you want to open. The drive you specified just now from the Tools menu should already be highlighted, so you shouldn't have to do anything except press ↵.

   c. Now a new box appears next to the menu and your screen should look like Figure 4.1. This box shows you the names of all the database files the Assistant found on the data disk. If you have more than the just the PHONEBK file on your disk, the box will have more than one name in it. Notice also that the name of our file is PHONEBK.*DBF*. The DBF part (called the *extension*) after the period stands for Data-Base File. This extension is added automatically by dBASE III PLUS to distinguish database files from other types of files that we will discuss later in this book.

      To select PHONEBK.DBF as the file you want to open, make sure it is highighted and press ↵.

   d. One more new box appears, asking

      Is the file indexed? [Y/N]

      The significance of this question will become clearer in later chapters, but for now, simply type the letter N.

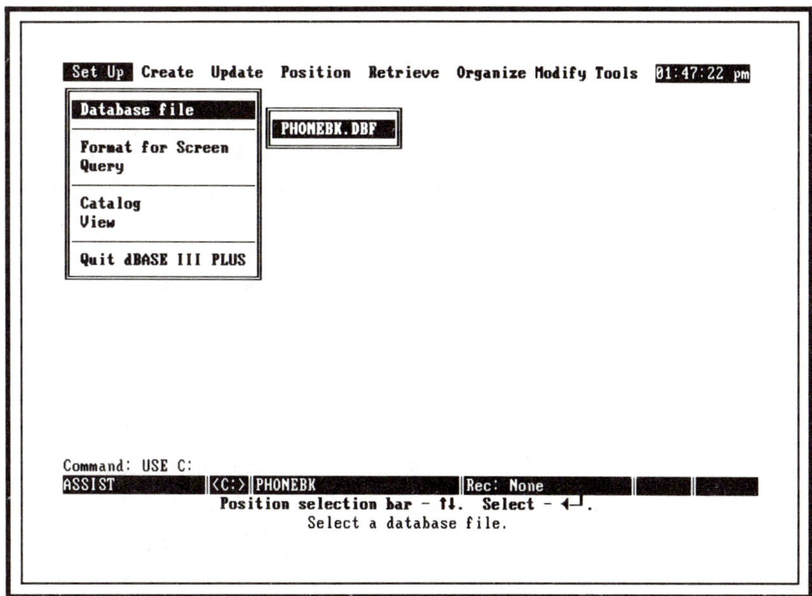

Figure 4.1: Opening the PHONEBK file

3. Good. Now you know how to open a database file. It will become almost automatic with just a little more practice. Now that the file is open, we can make those modifications to its structure. Select the Modify menu, see that *Database file* is highlighted, and press ↵.

4. The screen changes to something that should look familiar (see Figure 4.2). This is essentially the same screen we used to create the PHONEBK structure in the last chapter. There really isn't any difference between the Modify and the Create screens except that now we will use some additional keyboard commands to add new fields and to change a field's name.

How to Make the Changes

1. Press ↓ twice to highlight Field 3, PHONE_NO.

2. We want to insert a new field here, between Fields 2 and 3. This will be for the company name. The command for inserting a field

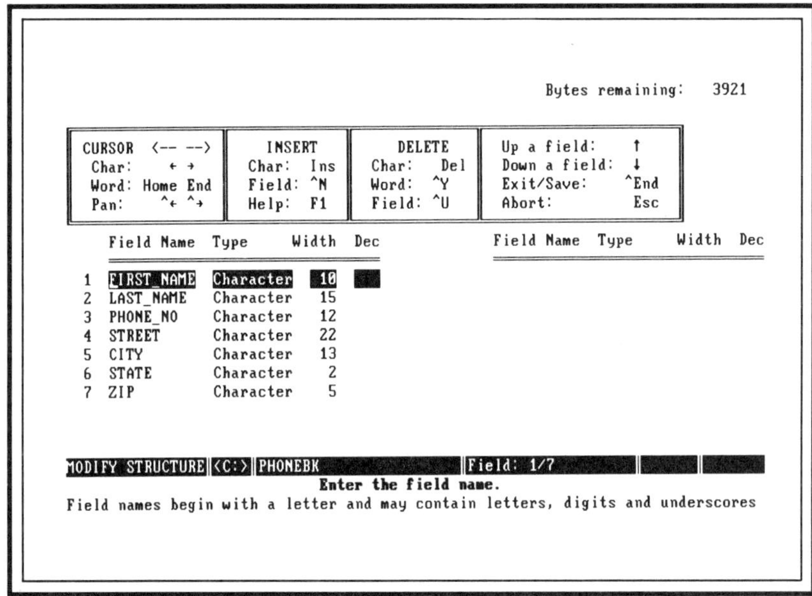

Figure 4.2: Modifying the structure

is ^N. Remembering that the ^ symbol means to press the Ctrl key while at the same time pressing the other letter, which in this case is N, press ^N. Field 3 moves down one line, leaving a new, empty Field 3 for you to define, as shown in Figure 4.3.

3. Now fill in the new field, which will hold a company name for each person in the phone book. Thus, this should be a Character field, with COMPANY as its name. Make the field 20 spaces wide, and press ↵. Notice that there are now eight fields in the structure.

4. Next, let's add a space for the work phone number. Since the highlighted bar dropped down a line when you last pressed ↵, it's now on the fourth field, PHONE_NO. Insert a field here (with ^N), and call it WORK_PHONE, using the same field size and type as PHONE_NO. When you are done, the screen should look like Figure 4.4, with the two new fields defined and the zip code field bumped over to the top of the second column.

5. Now, just for the sake of consistency, let's change the name of Field 5 from PHONE_NO to HOME_PHONE. The cursor happens to be just in the right place, so you can simply type the new name over the old one.

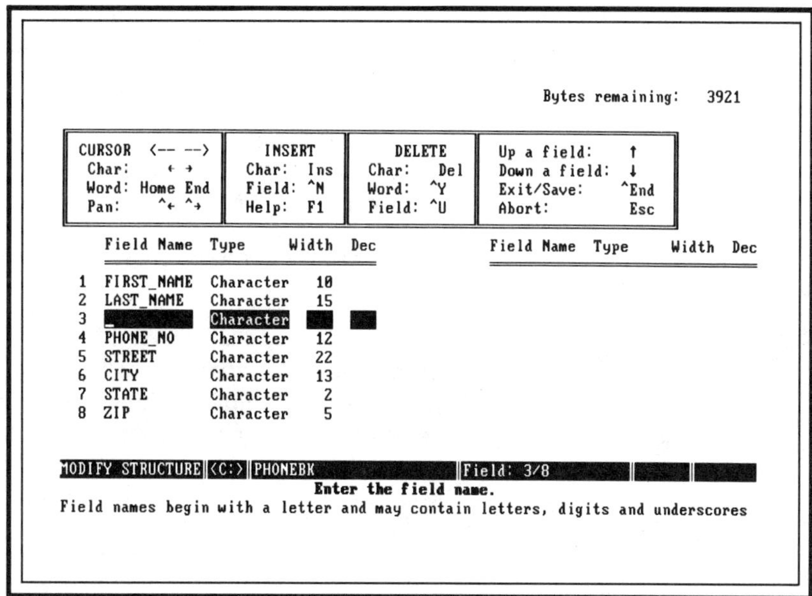

Figure 4.3: Inserting a new field

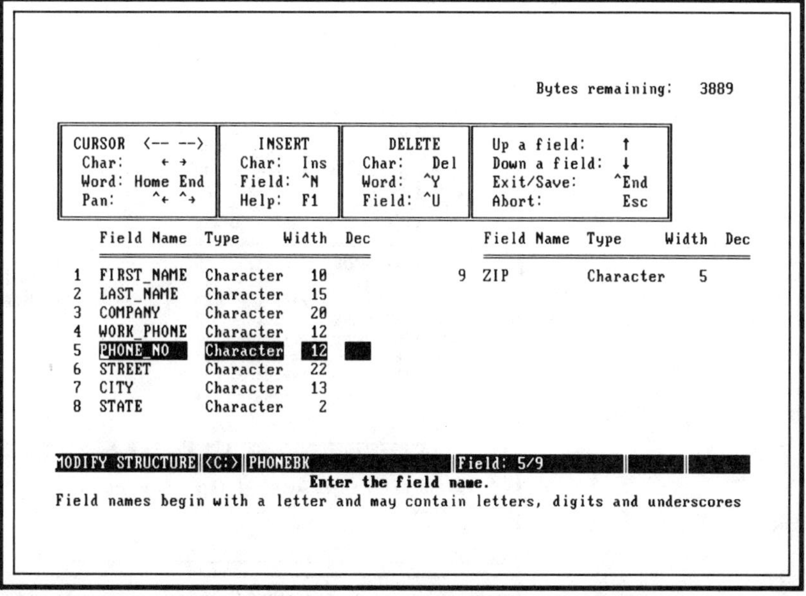

Figure 4.4: PHONEBK structure with company and work phone fields added

6. Finally, let's add a Memo field for jotting down notes about people. Move the cursor to Field 9 using ↓. Now press ↓ once again.

7. A new field space appears. Type in

   NOTES ↵

   as the field name. The cursor moves to the Type box.

8. Press the space bar four times. The word Memo will appear in the Type box.

9. Press ↵. Notice that dBASE III PLUS fills in the Width box with the number 10 automatically. Since all Memo fields take up ten spaces, dBASE simplifies things by typing the 10 for you. (Your memos can be much longer than ten characters, of course. What goes in the ten spaces merely "points" dBASE to your actual text. We'll talk more about how Memo fields work later on.) The screen should look like Figure 4.5.

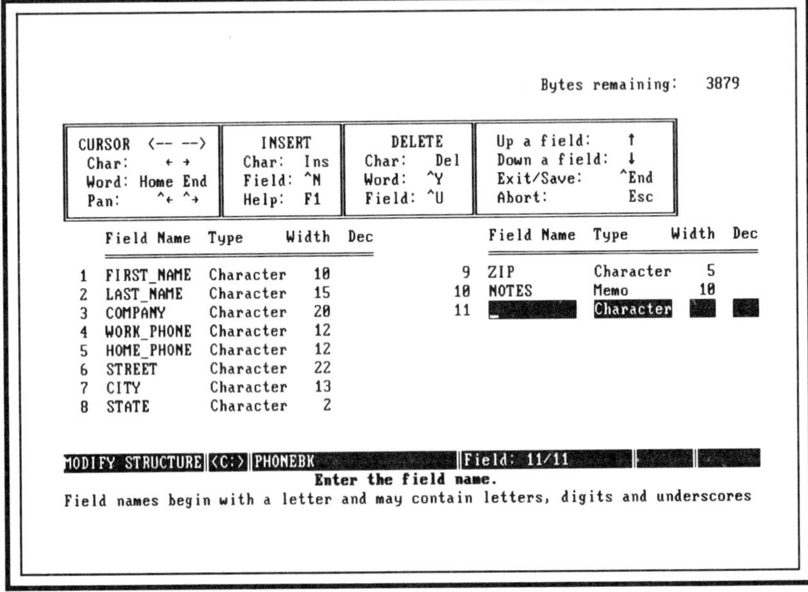

Figure 4.5: PHONEBK structure with Field 5 renamed and Memo field added.

10. Good. All modifications to the structure are now complete. Press ↵ again, and look at the Message Line. It says

Press ENTER to confirm. Any other key to resume.

"Confirm" means to save the changes you have made. "Resume" means to make some more changes. Since you are finished making the modifications, press ↵.

11. The screen goes blank for a minute, the disk drive light goes on, and then the Assistant screen appears again. The modifications are complete.

If you had already added data

As was mentioned at the beginning of this chapter, if you are careful, you can modify the structure of a database even after it is filled with data. The process is exactly the same except for a few restrictions.

1. If you change a field's name, do not change its position at the same time. Save the new structure first, with only the name change. Then select *Modify* again and change the position. (The reverse order will work too.)
2. If you change a field's length, do not change its name or position at the same time. Data will be lost.
3. Changing a field's type will cause data to be lost in that field.

In the next chapter, we'll begin entering some names and addresses into the phone book. If you'd like to take a break now select *Quit* from the Set Up menu. And as a general rule, be sure not to remove any floppy-disks from the computer before seeing the DOS A> or C> prompt, otherwise data may be lost.

5 Entering Data

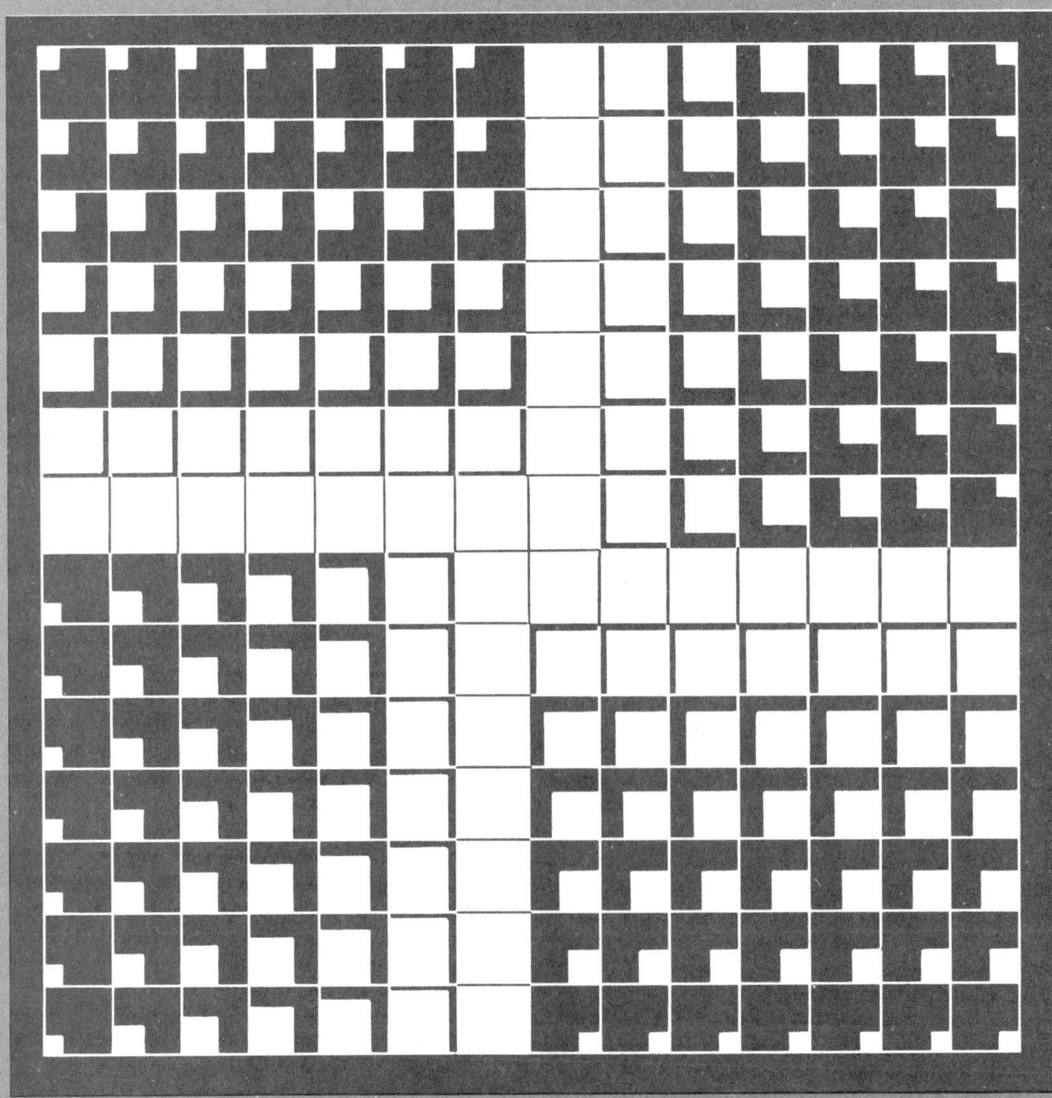

FEATURING:

entering and editing records; backup disks

It's time to enter some names into the database. If you took a break after the last chapter, bring up dBASE III PLUS again, and open the PHONEBK database, using the Set Up menu as we did in the last chapter. Remember to answer N to the question about the file being indexed.

How to Enter Your First Record

1. Select the Update menu. Notice that the first option on this menu, *Append,* is already highlighted.
2. Press ↵.
3. You have now told dBASE III PLUS, via the Assistant, that you wish to add, or *append,* records to the database file that is currently open, in this case PHONEBK. dBASE responds by presenting you with a blank form for the first record, waiting to be filled in, as shown in Figure 5.1.

   Notice the similarities between this screen and the screens we used to create and modify the database structure. Actually, working with the Append screen will be very similar to what you've already learned. The only difference is that from this screen we're adding or modifying the data itself, instead of the database structure.
4. Notice that the cursor is waiting for you in the FIRST_NAME field and that the highlighted area is the space that you will be filling in.

To the left of this area you see the names of the fields—the same names we typed into the structure in the last chapter. Each field name on the left goes with the blank field space to its right.

5. Now let's enter the first record, as listed below. (Be sure to capitalize as indicated.) Type in the first name, then press ↵. Continue the process, using ↵ in each case to move down to the next field, unless you hear a beep indicating the field has been filled and the cursor has moved ahead on its own. Don't forget to type in the dashes between the parts of the phone numbers and to use uppercase letters where they are shown. When you get to the last field, you'll notice that dBASE has already filled in the word "memo." This is just a reminder that this is a Memo type field. We will discuss later how to enter your own notes in these fields. For our sample database entries, just press ↵ when you get to this field. But for right now, don't press it yet. When you get to the last field of the record below, just leave the cursor there for the time being.

```
FIRST_NAME    Randolf
LAST_NAME     Robbins
COMPANY       Ralph Nicholby Inc.
WORK_PHONE    415-555-1212
HOME_PHONE    415-555-1111
STREET        374 Tipplemeyer Ave.
CITY          Cornmont
STATE         CA
ZIP           94709
NOTES         memo
```

Your screen now looks like Figure 5.2.

How to Fix Typos

There are several special keyboard commands used for correcting mistakes as you type and for moving the cursor around within a record. These commands are called *editing keys.* Table 5.1 summarizes the keys. Many of the editing effects can be acheived in more than one way, using the alternative letter-key forms, which are also listed in the table. Try experimenting with the editing keys just to get used to them.

If you are a WordStar or Sidekick user, you may notice that many of the letter key forms are identical to those you are already familiar with.

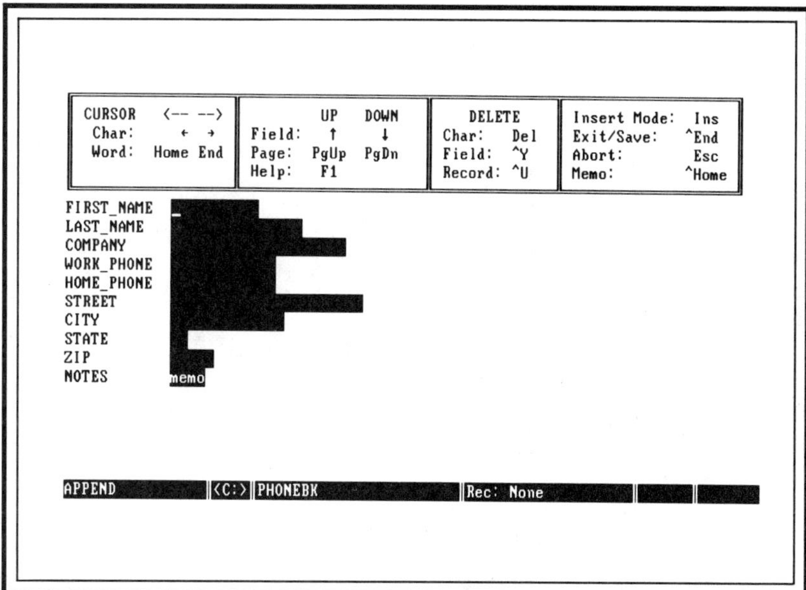

Figure 5.1: A new blank data record

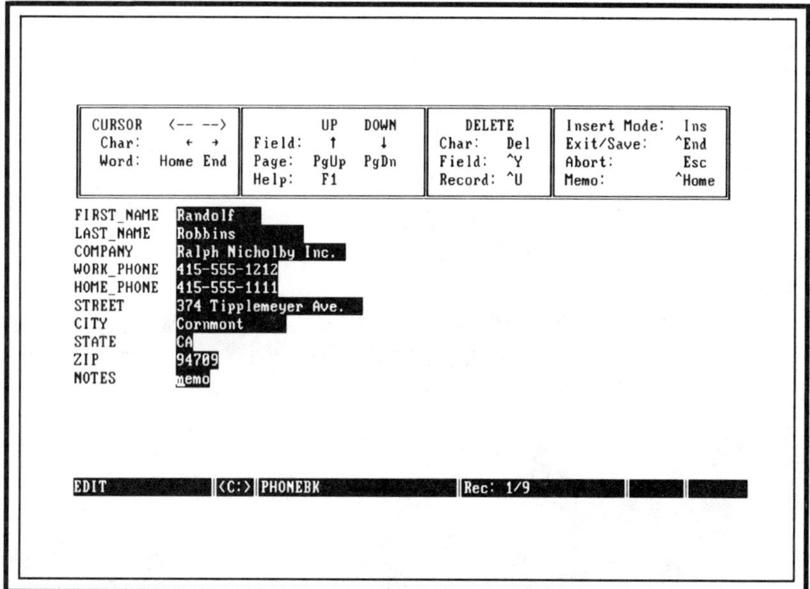

Figure 5.2: Your first data record

Main Key	***Letter Key***	***Result***
↵		Moves cursor to next field
↓	^X	Moves cursor to next field (same as ↵)
↑	^E	Moves cursor to previous field
→	^D	Moves cursor one space forward
←	^S	Moves cursor one space back
Home	^A	Moves to the beginning of a word
End	^F	Moves to the end of a word
^Y		Deletes from the cursor to end of field
Del	^G	Deletes character at cursor position
Backspace		Deletes the character to the left of cursor
Ins	^V	Turns the Insert mode on/off

Table 5.1: Editing commands for data entry

They were chosen so that touch typists could make editing changes without taking their hands away from the "home row" of the keyboard. Notice also that the letter keys for moving the cursor up, down, left, right, right a word, and left a word are arranged in a sensible diamond pattern (see Figure 5.3). This makes it easy to remember which way you are moving, though using these keys requires pressing the Ctrl key with the little finger of your left hand.

Four keys whose locations you may not be familiar with are Home, End, Ins, and Del. These are found near the numeric keypad, as shown in Figure 5.4.

The Insert mode

Press Ins (or ^V) and notice that the letters *Ins* appear in the Status Line, in the second section from the right, indicating you are now in the

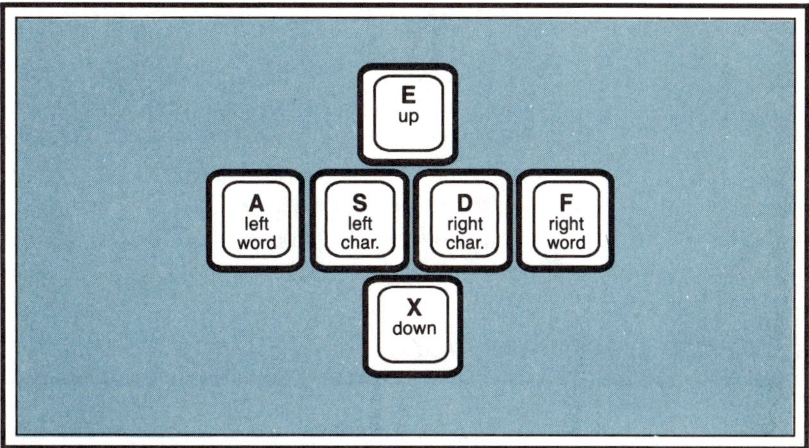

Figure 5.3: The letter keys for cursor movement

Insert mode. While you are in the Insert mode, characters you type are inserted into existing text, causing existing characters to be pushed right to make room.

Press Ins (or ^V) again, and the Ins message goes off, telling you that the Insert mode is off. Typing in a field which already has data in it will now overwrite that data with the new letters or numbers as you type.

Figure 5.4: The Home, End, Ins, and Del keys

Making the Help boxes disappear

Now press the F1 function key. Notice that the Help boxes disappear. This could be useful later on when you have memorized the commands listed in the boxes, especially if you were working with a database that had many fields and you wanted to display the maximum amount of data on the screen at one time. For now, let's keep the boxes visible. Press F1 again. The boxes reappear.

How to Complete Our Sample Database

Move your cursor to the last field in the record now. This is the Memo type field. Rather than dealing with the details of storing memos now, let's move on to add the rest of the people to our sample database. Later on we'll add some real memos.

1. Press ↵. A new blank record appears. Enter the following names and addresses into the database, one after another, using upper-case where shown. When you are finished, wait at the bottom of the last record. Here is the list:

   Hank
   Davies
   Bass-O-Matic
   909-549-3787
   909-398-2563
   333 33rd St.
   West Goshen
   SD
   43312
   memo

   Adriator
   Wegwo
   Rug Flox, Inc.
   321-889-3674
   321-883-9821
   158 Snorewell Blvd.
   Sleepyhollow
   CA
   02587
   memo

Aretha
Phillipson
Soulariums-R-Us
908-776-5298
908-337-8194
999 Motor City Ave.
Detroit
MI
39482
memo

Randy
Batterydown
Voltaics Inc.
809-675-4532
809-777-3300
495 Anode St.
Carbondale
IL
30129
memo

Nimrod
Neverburger
Bab's Fish N Chips
822-991-2861
822-675-4500
77 Easy Street
Khozad
CA
89751
memo

Marcel
Phillip
Feline Frenzy
310-563-0987
310-265-7560
456 Fresno St.
Paris
TX
55493
memo

Valery
Kuletzski
Literary Allusions
529-221-9480
529-559-7300
451 Farenheit Ct.
Oakland
CA
95420
memo

MARIAN
DAVIES
CITY OPERA CO.
211-334-9876
211-441-6111
344 MARKET ST
NEW YORK
NY
10021
memo

Type the last record all uppercase, as shown. This is a deliberate data-entry error that we'll use for illustration later on.

2. With the cursor sitting on the Memo field of the last record, press ↵. Another blank record appears. Press ↵ again. This terminates the appending process and returns you to the Assistant. The PHONEBK database is now filled in with nine records.

How to Make Backups of Your Data

Don't underestimate the value of making backup copies of your databases. Both floppy and hard disks are delicate storage media, and it's not uncommon for a data file to be damaged in one way or another. The best protection against such an unhappy development is to make backup copies of your important files on a regular basis. So, to get into the habit of making backup copies, we'll backup the work we have done so far.

Remember, we are dealing with more than one PHONEBK file now: the main database file, PHONEBK.DBF, and the file that stores the Memo information, PHONEBK.DBT. So in our commands we will use

*PHONEBK.**. This will copy all files with the first name of PHONEBK, regardless of their extension. Here is what to do.

On a hard-disk system, get to the DOS A> prompt, insert a blank, formatted disk in drive A, and (assuming you've been using the DBASE directory on drive C for your data) type

COPY C:\DBASE\PHONEBK.* A: ↵

On a floppy-disk system, leave your data disk in drive B, insert a blank, formatted disk in drive A, and type

COPY B:PHONEBK.* A: ↵

As we proceed, we'll be creating files with a variety of names and extensions. If you need help in using the COPY command to back them up, consult your DOS manual.

Go ahead and make your backups now, label the disks, then store them in a safe place. From now on, it will be up to you to make your own backups. In general, how frequently you decide to backup should be determined by considering the value of your databases. Since most backups will take only a few minutes, it's usually penny-wise to do it and pound-foolish not to.

After you're done, bring up dBASE again so you're ready for the exercises in Chapter 6.

6 Retrieving the Data

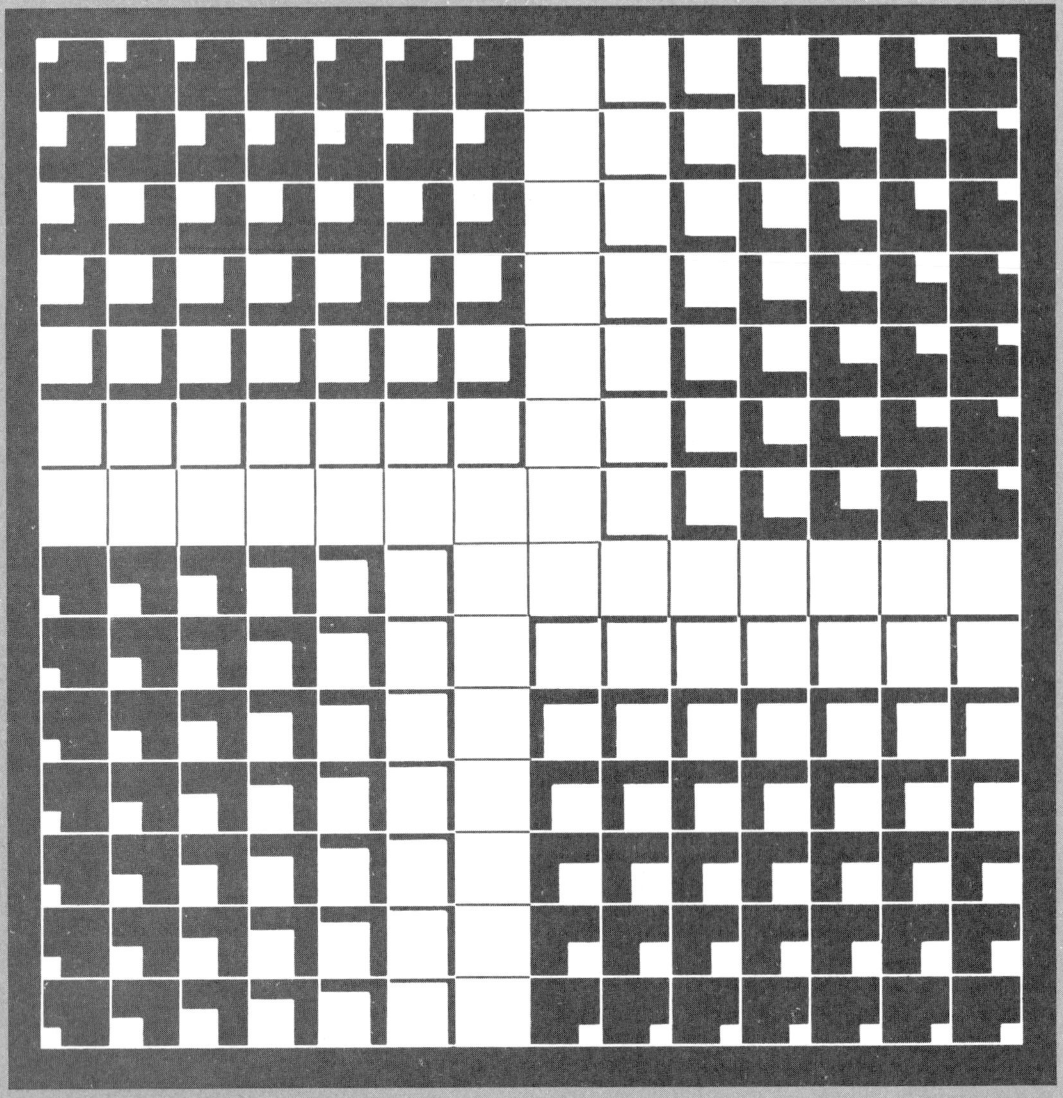

FEATURING:

**viewing the data;
selecting fields;
conditional lists**

Now that you have a number of records in the PHONEBK database, you can begin to experiment with the many useful ways in which dBASE III PLUS allows you to retrieve and manipulate the data you have stored. After all, what good is a database if it doesn't provide quick, easy access to the information you have typed in?

You can get information out of your database in two ways. You can ask dBASE to show you everything in the database, or you can request only data which meets specific conditions. In either case, the process is called *querying the database.* The first case could be called an *unconditional* query, whereas the latter is referred to as *conditional* querying.

Note: Beginning with this section, we will start to abbreviate our terminology somewhat, just to make the exercises easier to follow. Since you now know how to make menu and submenu selections, we can start to use a sort of shorthand method for telling you how to do the examples.

Here's how it works. Instead of explicitly spelling out how to select each menu, each option, and suboption in every example, I'll just put the names of all the selections into a single abbreviated command line, and tell you to "select" that series of names. For example here's how I would tell you to open the PHONEBK database:

Select *Setup/Database file/C:/PHONEBK*

Within the line, a slash mark (/) separates each selection you make along the way. Most of the time, the first word in the list is an Assistant menu name, such as Set Up or Create. The subsequent words are submenu options which, as you already know, are selected by highlighting them and pressing ↵. Don't forget that from now on, it's up to you to remember to press the ↵ key for finalizing every selection.

How to List All the Records

The simplest technique for looking at all the information in your database is to use the *List* option from the Retrieve menu.

1. Select *Retrieve/List.*
2. A new box appears, and the screen looks like Figure 6.1.
3. *Execute the command* is highlighted. Simply press ↵.
4. The Assistant asks if you want to send the listing to the printer. Type N. The screen should now look like Figure 6.2.

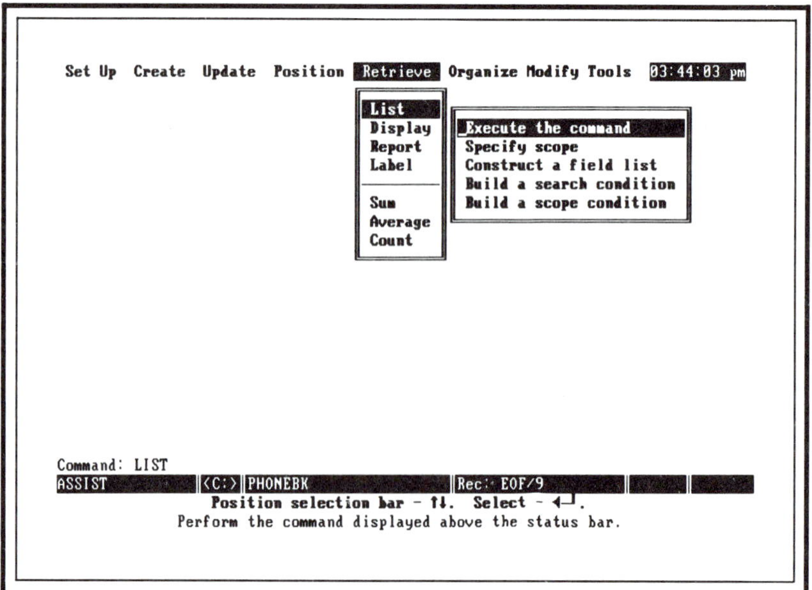

Figure 6.1: The *List* option submenu

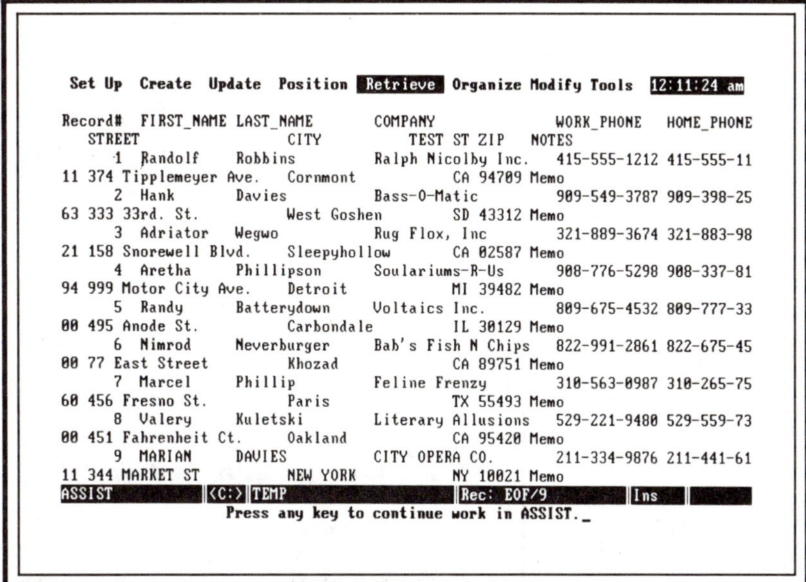

Figure 6.2: All the PHONEBK data

The data on your screen should look familiar to you, although not very orderly. The screen looks a bit jumbled because each record is too long to fit onto a single line, so the records wrap around to the next line. The headings wrap around in a similar fashion.

Luckily, the *List* option, (as well as many other dBASE III PLUS commands) can be used in a selective (conditional) manner, allowing you to tailor your listing to specific needs, rather than listing everything willy-nilly. Let's try limiting the list so we can see something a little more coherent on the screen.

Listing only certain fields

1. Say we still want to see all the records, but only the first name, last name, and company name for each record. This can be easily done. First, press any key to return to the Retrieve menu.
2. The Retrieve menu reappears. Select *List/Construct a field list.*
3. Two new boxes appear, and your screen looks like Figure 6.3.

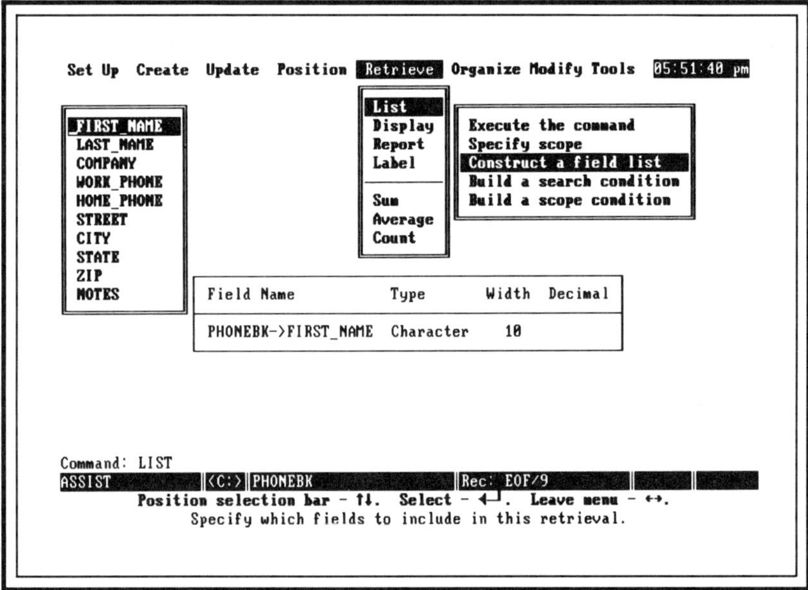

Figure 6.3: Specifying a field list

The box to the left lists the names of all the fields in the database. The box in the middle is simply there to remind you of the size and type of the highlighted field. To select a field or series of fields for inclusion in a listing, just highlight them and press ↵ for each one you want. For now, use the following fields.

4. Select FIRST_NAME, LAST_NAME, and COMPANY. As you do this, keep an eye on the line just above the Status Line, where the word Command appears. Notice that a command is being written automatically for you by the Assistant step-by-step as you select each field. More about this later.

5. Press → or ← to leave the field names box. This jumps you back to the *List* option box.

6. Now select *Execute the command.* Press *N* for the printer question (unless your printer is hooked up and you want to print this listing). In a few seconds, your screen should look like Figure 6.4.

7. Press any key to get back to the *List* submenu. Now, construct another field list, this time with the same fields only select them in

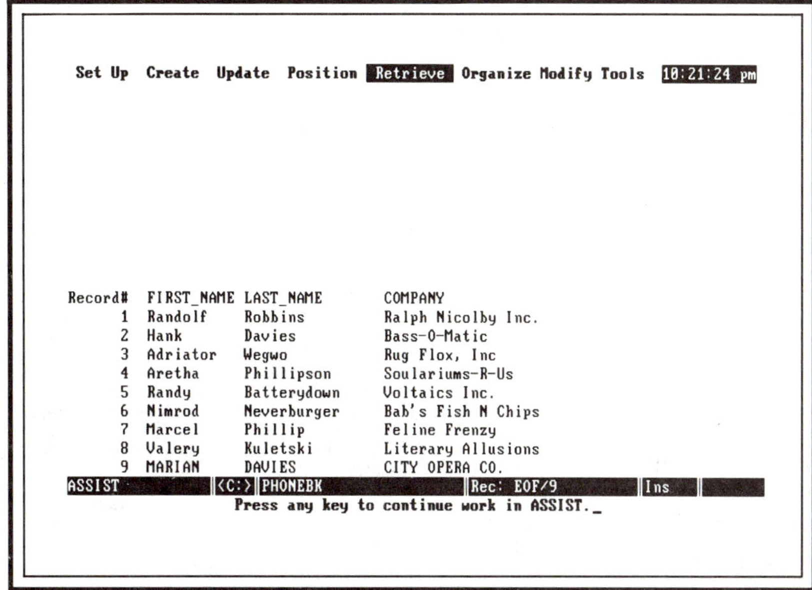

Set Up Create Update Position Retrieve Organize Modify Tools 10:21:24 pm
Record# FIRST_NAME LAST_NAME COMPANY
1 Randolf Robbins Ralph Nicolby Inc.
2 Hank Davies Bass-O-Matic
3 Adriator Wegwo Rug Flox, Inc
4 Aretha Phillipson Soulariums-R-Us
5 Randy Batterydown Voltaics Inc.
6 Nimrod Neverburger Bab's Fish N Chips
7 Marcel Phillip Feline Frenzy
8 Valery Kuletski Literary Allusions
9 MARIAN DAVIES CITY OPERA CO.
ASSIST <C:> PHONEBK Rec: EOF/9 Ins
Press any key to continue work in ASSIST._

Figure 6.4: PHONEBK listing of first name, last name, and company

the reverse order: COMPANY, LAST_NAME, FIRST_NAME. Once again, keep an eye on the Command line to see the actual command that is executed when you select *Execute the command.* The results appear in Figure 6.5.

You see? It's fairly easy to start getting results. You might want to try experimenting with varying arrangements of listings now on your own. Try choosing different fields and putting them in a variety of orders in your listings.

How to List Only Certain Records

Specifying by record number

Notice in the listing that, in addition to the data, a number appears just to the left of the record. This is called the *record number* and is used by

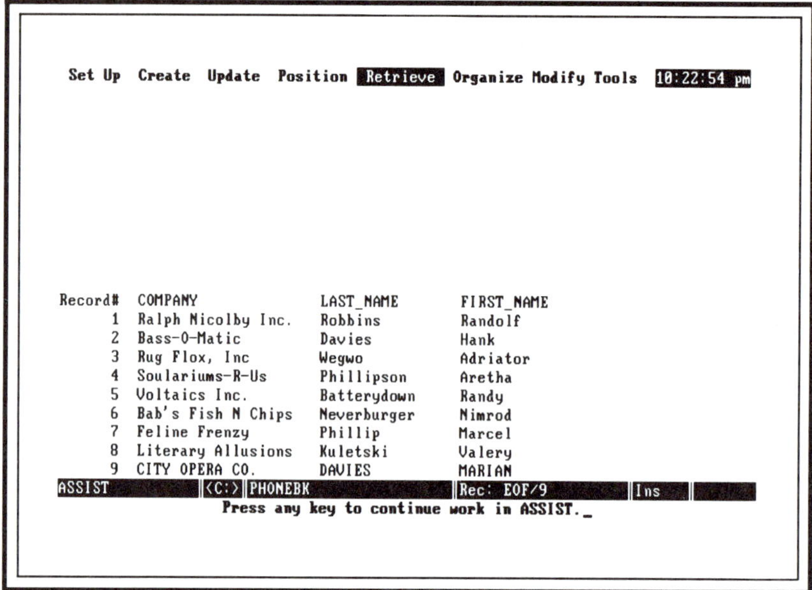

Figure 6.5: The same fields in reverse order

dBASE III PLUS to keep track of your data in an orderly manner. Whenever you add a record to your database, it is automatically assigned a unique record number.

You may have also noticed an unexplained number in the Status Line at the bottom of the screen, both during the listings you just did and also when you were adding new names and addresses as part of the last chapter's exercises. The number on the Status Line (in the fourth section from the left) has the task of displaying the number of the record you are currently working on.

It's important to realize that in the same way that your eyes must focus on one line of text at a time when you read it, dBASE is similarly limited to thinking about just one database record at any given time. The record that dBASE is aware of, or currently positioned on, is kept track of by a record *pointer.* The message on the Status Line, such as

Rec: 1/9

indicates that the pointer is on record number 1 out of a total of 9. (Our database has only nine records in it.) Since our commands so far have listed all the records, the pointer has been left at the end of the file. So your Status Line should say EOF/9. *EOF* means End Of File. (The end of the file is an imaginary record just past the last real record.)

You will often want to retrieve specific records through the manipulation of, or reference to, their record numbers. The most basic way you refer to a particular numbered record is by moving the pointer to that record. You can do this by using the *Position menu.* At first, moving the pointer will seem a bit academic, but the exercises will soon make it clear how the pointer is used.

1. Select *Position/Goto Record.* A box appears, as in Figure 6.6.
2. Select *Top,* and keep an eye on the pointer number on the Status Line. It should have changed from EOF/9 to 1/9.
3. Select *Goto Record* again, but this time choose *Bottom* from the submenu. The pointer number changes to 9/9.
4. The third selection from the submenu is *Record.* This lets you position the pointer on a record you specify by giving its number.

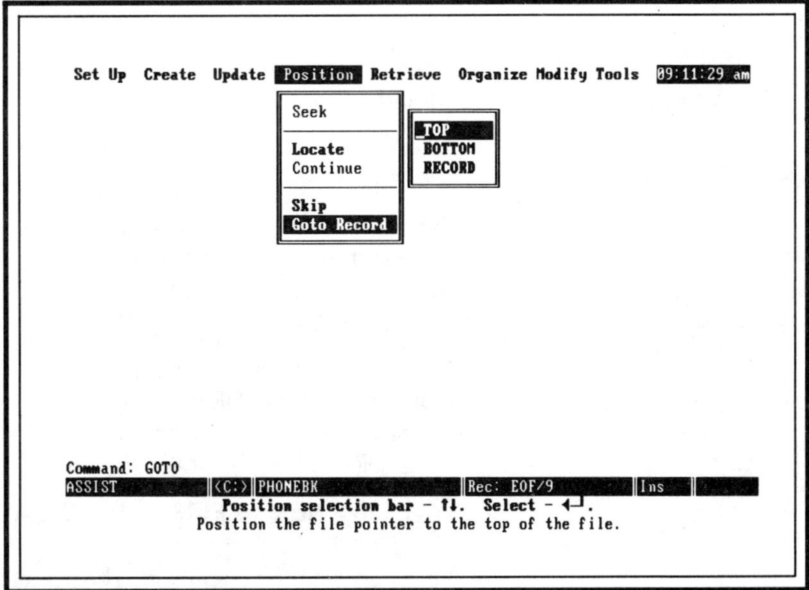

Figure 6.6: Positioning the pointer

Looking back at Figure 6.4, say we wanted to move the pointer to Randy Batterydown's record (record 5). Select *Record* from the *Goto Record* submenu. A box appears, asking for a record number. Type 5 ↵. The pointer number changes to 5/9.

5. Finally select *Position/Skip*. This feature lets you move forward or backwards in the database by a specified number of records. Say you wanted to move the pointer down to Marcel Phillip's record (record 7). When prompted for a "numeric value," enter 2. To move back to record 5, select *Skip* again, and enter –2. Negative numbers move the pointer backwards.

Using record numbers to specify the scope of a listing

Of course moving the pointer around isn't very useful unless it helps you retrieve the information you want. You may have noticed the second option in the *Retrieve/List* submenu, *Specify Scope*. Specifying the scope simply means choosing the number of records you want to list, and from which starting point. For example, suppose we want to list five records, starting with record 1.

1. Select *Position/Goto Record/Top* to get to record 1. The Status Line should show 1/9.
2. Select *Retrieve/List/Specify scope*. A box appears asking you for the scope.
3. Select *Next*. You are asked for a numeric value—in other words, you want to see the next how many records? Since we want to see five, type the number 5, but do not press ↵. Your screen should look like Figure 6.7.
4. Now press ↵. The *Construct a field list* option is highlighted. Select it and then choose FIRST_NAME, LAST_NAME, and COMPANY for the fields to be listed. (Don't forget to press ← or → when you're done selecting fields). Notice the command line. It says

   LIST NEXT 5 FIRST_NAME, LAST_NAME, COMPANY

5. Select *Execute the command.* The screen looks like Figure 6.8.

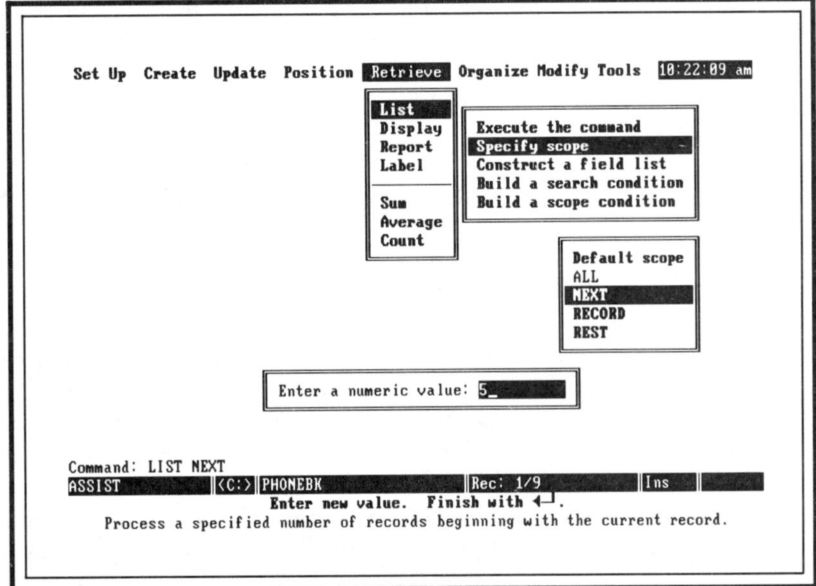

Figure 6.7: Requesting the first five records

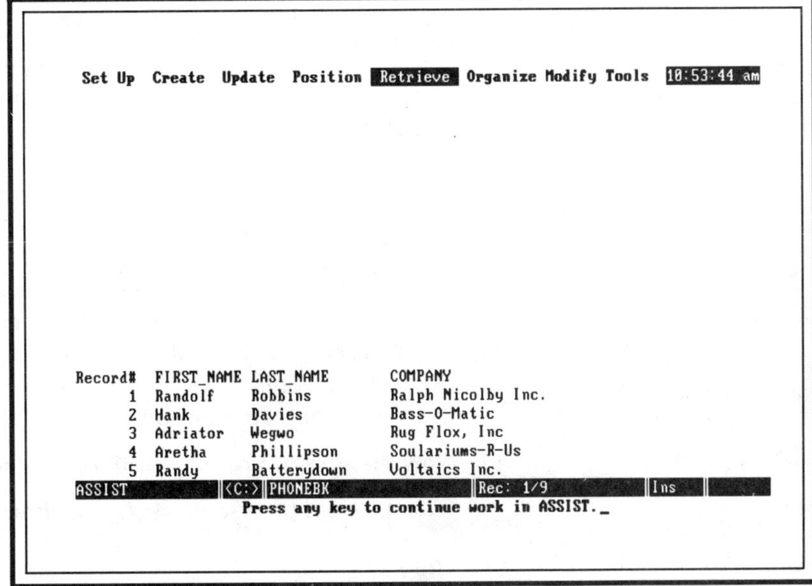

Figure 6.8: Listing three fields of the first five records

As you can see, various conditions can be combined in one query. In this case, you combined the field list condition (three fields) with the record scope condition (Next 5). Other more complex conditions are possible too.

Listing records that meet a specified condition

Up until now, it looks as though you paid several hundred dollars for a program that only gives back lists in pretty much the form you entered them, which is something you could do by saving a piece of paper. True, we've been selective about which fields get displayed and the number of records included, but what if you wanted to list only people who live in California, or who work for a certain company, or who have a certain name? Say we wanted to find an address for Aretha Phillipson. In other words, you may want to impose more useful conditions upon the listing. This is achieved using the last two selections in the *Retrieve/List* submenu: *Build a search condition* and *Build a scope condition*. Let's take a couple of examples.

1. Let's start by asking for only the first names, last names, and state of people who live in California. Start by selecting *Retrieve/List/Construct a field list*. Select FIRST_NAME, LAST_NAME, and STATE.
2. Next, select *Build a search condition*. The fields list appears again. The Assistant wants to know which field(s) the search condition will be based on. We're interested in the STATE field, since we want to select only people in California. So select STATE.
3. Another box appears! Your screen now looks like Figure 6.9.
4. The new box lists a set of *operators*. The operators, though most often used for numerical comparisons can also be used for comparing letters of the alphabet. In this case, our search for California residents translates to "list all the people whose STATE = CA", so use the = *Equal To* selection.
5. Now the Assistant pops up with one more box,

   Enter a character string (without quotes):

   The Assistant is now asking what a record's STATE field will have to

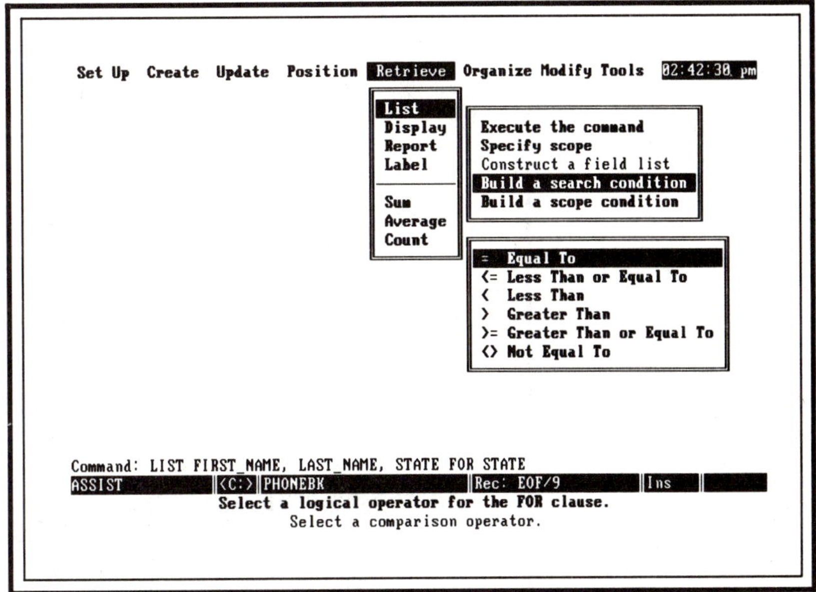

Figure 6.9: The Operators box

be equal to in order to qualify the record for listing. That's easy. Just enter (in uppercase)

CA

6. Another box pops up, allowing you to stipulate additional conditions. But since we don't want to, select *No more conditions* from this box.

7. The Command Line now lists the completed command as the Assistant has constructed it.

LIST FIRST_NAME, LAST_NAME, STATE FOR STATE = 'CA'

8. Select *Execute the command* from the submenu. The command is executed by dBASE and the listing appears as in Figure 6.10.

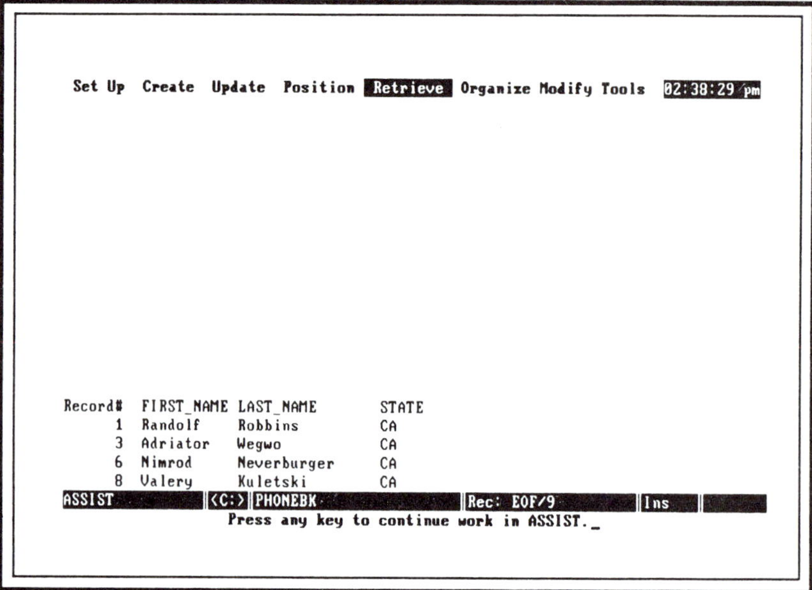

Figure 6.10: The California residents

Exact and inexact searching

Good. You should be getting pretty fast at using the menus and boxes by now, so let's try a search that's a little trickier. Say we're interested in looking up one person to find an address. For example, how would you find Marcel Phillip's address? Try it yourself, and then compare your solution with mine.

1. Select *Retrieve/List/Construct a field list.* Choose first name, last name, street, city, and state.
2. Select *Build a search condition,* and choose LAST_NAME from the fields list. Select *Equal To* from the operator list. For the *Equal To* condition, enter *Phillip* (note the uppercase P).
3. Select *No more conditions,* then execute the command. You get the following listing:

```
4 Aretha Phillipson 999 Motor City Ave. Detroit MI
7 Marcel Phillip    456 Fresno St.      Paris   TX
```

Well, this is interesting. Why did two names show up? Simply because computers, not being very smart, take your commands very literally. As far as dBASE is concerned, you asked to see all records with "Phillip" as the first seven letters in the LAST_NAME field, so "Phillipson" naturally qualifies. This is called an *inexact match.* Sometimes inexact matches are useful, for example if you wanted to list all the people whose last names begin with a certain letter. You could type in just that letter as the *Equal To* search condition on the last name field.

Exact matching, on the other hand, is what we really wanted in order to single out Marcel Phillip's record. You can tell dBASE that all matching should be exact. You have to get out of the Assistant mode to do this.

1. Press Esc until you get back to any of the main Assistant menus.
2. Press Esc again. The DOT prompt appears.
3. Type

   Set ↵

4. A list appears, called the *Set menu.* Highlight *Exact.*
5. Press ↵. An ON message appears to the right.
6. Press Esc.
7. Type

   ASSIST ↵

   This gets you back into the Assistant, from where you can try the search for Marcel again. This time it should work exactly.

Until you reset the Exact setting OFF again, dBASE will interpret all your conditions exactly. ("Phillip" will not list "Phillipson".) Unless noted otherwise, however, the rest of this book assumes that Exact is set to the OFF position. If you do alter it, don't forget to reset it to OFF, using the seven steps listed above.

Uppercase and lowercase are not the same

One final distinction. Regardless of whether Exact is set ON or OFF, dBASE does not consider uppercase and lowercase letters to be the same in search conditions. An *A* is not the same as an *a*. Thus, a search for "phillipson" will not find "Phillipson". Try this example:

1. Select *Retrieve/List/Construct a field list.*
2. Select FIRST_NAME and LAST_NAME.
3. *Build a search condition* using LAST_NAME.
4. Select = as the operator.
5. Enter Davies as the *Equal To* condition.
6. Select *No more conditions.*
7. Execute the command.
8. The result should be

   Hank Davies

Notice that MARIAN DAVIES did not get listed. So the result of our deliberate data-entry error in Chapter 5 is that this name is missed in a perfectly normal search for everyone named Davies. There are ways around this problem that will be discussed in the next chapter. But in general it is important to remember the distinction between uppercase and lowercase. Be consistent about how you enter data into the database so that searching is more reliable later on. If you have no success listing a record that you know is in your database, don't give up. Try changing the case and executing the command again.

The Display and Locate commands

There is another dBASE III PLUS option, *Display,* which is similar to *List,* but adds two new features. Unlike *List* which, with a longer database, will often "scroll" data off the top of your screen before you can look at it, *Display* lists only a screenful of records at a time, asking you to press a key to view the next screenful. With our database, scrolling wasn't a problem, since we had only nine records. But with a larger database, *Display* will often be more useful than *List,* unless the output is to be sent to the printer.

The other distinctive feature of the *Display* option is that it can be used to show only the *current* record (the one on which the pointer is currently located). Thus the various pointer-movement commands and the *Display* option work well together. Try the following example.

1. Select *Position/Goto record/Record/3.* The pointer number in the Status Line changes to 3/9.
2. Select *Retrieve/Display/Execute the command.* Record 3 is displayed.

You could have constructed a field list of course, to make the listing easier to read, and you could have used a search condition. These work just the way they do with the *List* option.

Another option that works well with *Display* is called *Locate. Locate* works just like *List* and *Display* in terms of building search conditions. The only difference is that *Locate* doesn't display a record when it finds one meeting the search condition. Instead, it simply reports the record number and sets the pointer to that number. Try this to see.

1. Select *Position/Locate/Build a search condition.*
2. Select FIRST_NAME as the field to search on.
3. Select = from the operator box.
4. Enter *Valery* as the search string.
5. Select *No more conditions.*
6. Execute the command.

The result shows up just above the Status Line.

Record = 8

This means that a record whose first name field was "Valery" was found and its record number was 8. The pointer is now set on this record (as indicated in the Status Line after you press a key). You can now use *Retrieve/Display/Execute the command* or *Retrieve/Display/Construct a field list/Execute the command* to see the data.

Experimenting on your own

Pulling information out of a database in various ways is really where the fun, and utility, of dBASE begins. As you can surmise from the material covered in this chapter, the sky's the limit when it comes to the number of combinations you can dream up. Try experimenting on your own, based on what you now know. The worst that can happen is a beep and some message at the bottom of the screen suggesting what you did wrong!

In the next chapter, we'll cover some advanced search techniques and tips.

7 More Search Techniques

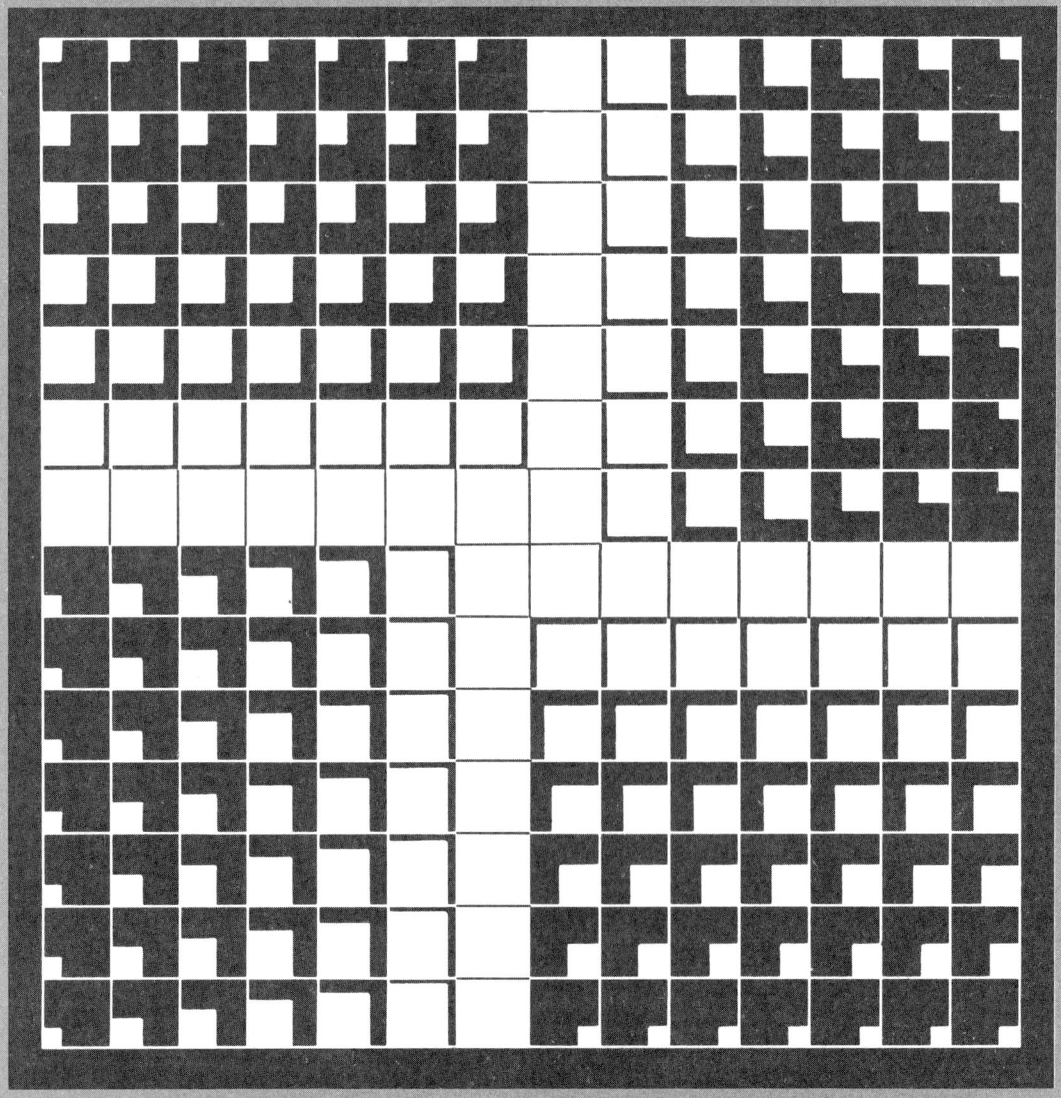

FEATURING:

combined search conditions; the Dot prompt; Character strings

Last chapter we explored some of the most common approaches to retrieving information from a typical database. This chapter we'll try a few more sophisticated techniques.

How to Combine Search Criteria

Up until now, we've searched out records based on only one criterion at a time, such as a last name or a state. But dBASE III PLUS is actually capable of much more complex searches than that. Without much difficulty, you can combine criteria in the search conditions to achieve really powerful data extractions.

Say you want to see all the records of people who live within a certain zip code range—between 30129 and 60000. This requires combining two criteria. For a record to qualify, its zip code must be both greater than 30129 *and* less than 60000. Recall from the *Operator* box that the following operators are available for our use:

=	Equal To
<=	Less Than or Equal To
<	Less Than
>	Greater Than
>=	Greater Than or Equal To
<>	Not Equal To

These are called *comparison* operators, since their job is to compare things (such as the field data) and respond according to the results of the comparison. So far, the only operator we've used is *Equal To*. The *Equal To* operator is particularly useful when you are looking for a particular string of characters, such as a name. You will probably use the *Equal To* operator more than any other. But in this case we need to use both the *Greater Than* and the *Less Than* operators in a combined search condition, since we're interested in determining a whole range rather than an exact match. Here's how to do it.

Using .AND.

1. Select *Retrieve/List/Construct a field list.*
2. Select FIRST_NAME, LAST_NAME, STREET and ZIP as the fields to list.
3. Select *Build a search condition.*
4. Select ZIP as the field.
5. Select > *Greater Than* as the comparison operator.
6. Type in 30129. (Your computer will beep because the box fills up.)
7. Select *Combine with .AND.*
8. Select ZIP again.
9. Select < *Less Than* as the comparison operator.
10. Type in 60000. (Beep again.)
11. Select *No more conditions.*
12. Selecting *Execute the command* gives you

Record#	FIRST_NAME	LAST_NAME	STREET	ZIP
2	Hank	Davies	333 33rd. St.	43312
4	Aretha	Phillipson	999 Motor City Ave.	39482
7	Marcel	Phillip	456 Fresno St.	55493

See how the combined search criteria worked? The *Combine with .AND.* option tells dBASE that a record's zip must be higher than 30129 *and* lower than 60000. You may have noticed that there is a *Combine with*

.OR. option too. This is similar, though a little more inclusive in its requirements. Instead of both requirements having to be true for a record to be listed, only one has to. For example, we might want to list people who live in Illinois *or* Texas. One way would be to run two lists, one for each state, using the *Equal To* operator. But .OR. will do it faster.

Using .OR.

1. Select *Retrieve/List/Construct a field list.*
2. Select FIRST_NAME, LAST_NAME, and STATE.
3. Select *Build a search condition.*
4. Select STATE as the field.
5. Select = *Equal to* as the operator.
6. Type in IL (in caps).
7. Select *Combine with .OR.*
8. Select STATE.
9. Select = *Equal to.*
10. Type in TX (in caps).
11. Select *No more conditions.*
12. The command line should say

```
LIST FIRST_NAME, LAST_NAME, STATE FOR STATE = 'IL' .OR. STATE = 'TX'
```

13. Execute the command and see

```
Record# FIRST_NAME LAST_NAME   STATE
      5 Randy      Batterydown IL
      7 Marcel     Phillip     TX
```

.AND. and .OR., dubbed the *logical operators,* are a real blessing, especially when you are working with a large database. For example, say our database gets very large, and we want to look up a Sally Jones. Chances are good that there would be more than one Sally and more than one Jones. Using the .AND. operator solves the problem. Simply look for a first name of Sally .AND. a last name of Jones.

How to Enter Commands from the Dot Prompt

You've probably wondered why you have been urged to keep an eye on the Command Line as you work through the menus with the Assistant. Actually, it was to bring to your attention the fact that the Assistant, based on your sequence of choices, builds up commands, step-by-step, which are then executed by dBASE. The Assistant simply makes database processes easier by translating the English-like menu choices you make into the more cryptic language of dBASE commands.

Despite its cleverness, the Assistant can sometimes be more trouble than it is worth. To more experienced users, turning off the Assistant and typing in a simple command line is easier than making one choice after another from all those boxes. Besides, there are some things the Assistant just can't do for you. You will have to decide for yourself how you want to do your work. So just to give you the flavor of working with commands, let's take a try at entering some commands directly, without the Assistant. Then I'll show you two really useful commands that can't be entered from the Assistant at all.

Getting out of Assist mode

Notice that the left end of the Status Line says

Assist

This means you are in Assist mode.

1. Press Esc once or twice, until the menu names disappear and the Status Line says

   Command Line

   The cursor is now at the bottom of the screen, blinking next to a little dot, called the *Dot Prompt*. This means dBASE III PLUS is waiting for you to type in commands.

2. Type in

   LIST ↵

   Look familiar?

3. Now try

LIST FIRST_NAME, LAST_NAME, STREET ↵

and see

Record#	FIRST_NAME	LAST_NAME	STREET
1	Randolf	Robbins	374 Tipplemeyer Ave.
2	Hank	Davies	333 33rd. St.
3	Adriator	Wegwo	158 Snorewell Blvd.
4	Aretha	Phillipson	999 Motor City Ave.
5	Randy	Batterydown	495 Anode St.
6	Nimrod	Neverburger	77 East Street
7	Marcel	Phillip	456 Fresno St.
8	Valery	Kuletski	451 Fahrenheit Ct.
9	MARIAN	DAVIES	344 MARKET ST

If you got something like this instead,

```
Syntax error.
                                    ?
LIST FIRST_NAME, LAST_NAME STREET
```

then you probably typed the command in wrong. This is dBASE's not-so-nice way of informing you that you've given it a command it can't figure out (these computers really aren't very smart). Perhaps you forgot a comma (that is the error shown above), or typed in a field name incorrectly (getting an underline requires you press the Shift key). If you got the Syntax error message, simply press Esc and type in the command again. Here you can see another advantage of the Assistant. It eliminates a lot of typing, and, as a result, typographical errors! There is one saving grace to the Dot prompt, however. You can recall a command you typed by pressing ^E. Then you can edit the line without retyping the whole thing by using these letter-key commands:

- ^D moves forward one letter
- ^F moves forward one word
- ^S moves back one letter
- ^A moves back one word
- ^Y erase to end of line

This makes fixing your mistakes, or even repeating a command several times, rather easy. Actually dBASE remembers the last 20 commands it executed, so that you can easily recall them. It even remembers commands the Assistant constructed for you. This way you can let the Assistant create a command, then try editing it on your own from the Dot prompt. You can move backward or forward through the list of commands using ^E to go back or ^X to move forward. When you get to either end of the list, you'll hear a beep. To see the complete list of 20 commands at any given time, simply type

DISPLAY HISTORY ↵

Incidentally, you may use either uppercase or lowercase in commands. I've shown the commands in the command lines in uppercase to make them stand out.

4. To clear the screen, type

   CLEAR ↵

5. Now let's try the same command the Assistant constructed to make a listing of people living in either Illinois or Texas.

LIST FIRST_NAME, LAST_NAME, STATE FOR STATE = 'IL' .OR. STATE = 'TX' ↵

Same result as with the Assistant, right? Good. So now you get the general picture. Keep an eye on the Command Line when using the Assistant, and you will learn how to concoct the Dot prompt versions of the commands. Then try them out yourself. Now for some tricks which you might not otherwise guess just from using the Assistant.

How to Convert from Lowercase to Uppercase

In Chapter 6 we did a listing for LAST_NAME = Davies. As you may recall, Marian Davies did not appear in the listing because her last name was entered as *DAVIES,* not *Davies.* From the Dot prompt, there is a way around this. There are in dBASE III PLUS a number of helpful tools called *functions,* one of which will overlook the difference between lowercase and uppercase letters, but it can only be used from the Dot prompt. Here's how it works.

1. To see both Davies, we can tell dBASE to check the uppercase equivalent of the LAST_NAME field for 'DAVIES'. Simply enter

```
LIST FIRST_NAME, LAST_NAME FOR UPPER(LAST_NAME) = 'DAVIES'
```

What this does is go through all the records, look at the last name of each person, convert it to uppercase (only temporarily) and check to see if it equals "DAVIES". You should now see both records.

```
Record#  FIRST_NAME  LAST_NAME
      2  Hank        Davies
      9  MARIAN      DAVIES
```

How to Find Embedded Strings

Until now all the searches we've done were on the first and only word found in a field. What if you want to check for a word in the middle of a field, such as part of a street address or a company name? Such a word is called an *embedded string* because it's probably surrounded by other words or characters (called "character strings" in database lingo), and is not necessarily the first word in the field. The **$** sign is used to find an embedded word, and is called the *substring search function.*

Say we wanted to list all residents of Snorewell Blvd. who might be on our list.

1. Type in

```
LIST FIRST_NAME, LAST_NAME, STREET FOR 'Snorewell' $STREET ↵
```

Translated, this command means "Display the first name, last name, and street address fields of any record whose street address has the word 'Snorewell' embedded in it. The result is:

```
Record#  FIRST_NAME  LAST_NAME  STREET
      3  Adriator    Wegwo      158 Snorewell Blvd.
```

Of course you can use the combination operators to combine substring searches along with other command elements as well. A typical command might be

LIST FOR LAST_NAME = 'Neverburger' .AND. 'Fahrenheit' $STREET

which will display the entire record if the last name is Neverburger and the street address includes 'Fahrenheit'. Another example might be

LIST LAST_NAME, STREET FOR 'FRESNO' $(UPPER(STREET))

A trick? Well, sort of. This one combines the uppercase function and the substring search function in one command. Notice how the parentheses are used. The translation might be: "Display the last name and street of any record whose street address, once converted to uppercase, has the word 'FRESNO' embedded in it."

How to Take It from Here

Good. You've learned the basics of using the Dot prompt as well as several useful functions—uppercase, substring, two logical operators (.AND. and .OR.) and two comparison operators (*Less Than* and *Greater Than*). If you didn't catch it all first time around, don't worry. Some of this is just icing on the cake, and you may not have need for these tricks too often.

Just to get you thinking about some ways you might want to put together the tools you now have available, I will leave you with a number of commands and their English equivalents, with only brief explanations of each one. These are for further thought and study; you might want to skip them now and go over them another time. Also, bear in mind that you can produce any of these commands wih the help of the Assistant, instead of typing them in directly. (The only exceptions are those that use the uppercase and substring functions.)

Examples

Here's the list:

GOTO TOP

Positions the pointer on the first record.

? RECNO( )

Asks dBASE what record the pointer is on. Use this after any of the pointer-movement commands to find the number of the record that the pointer landed on. (The pointer number is also shown on the Status Line, as explained in Chapter 8.)

GOTO BOTTOM

Positions the pointer on the last record.

GO TOP

Short for GOTO TOP.

GO BOTT

Short for GOTO BOTTOM.

SKIP −5

Moves the pointer back five records.

DISPLAY

Shows all fields in the record the pointer is on (the current record).

DISPLAY ALL

Shows all fields in all records, a screenful at a time.

LIST

Shows all fields in all records, without stopping at each screenful.

DISPLAY FIRST_NAME, LAST_NAME

Shows first and last name fields in current record.

SKIP

Moves pointer ahead one record.

DISPLAY RECORD 5 FIRST_NAME, LAST_NAME, STREET

Goes to a record number 5 and shows the named fields.

DISP RECO 3 FIRST_NAME, LAST_NAME, COMPANY

Shorthand version, similar to last command. Note that only first four letters of any command are actually necessary.

```
DISP NEXT 5 LAST_NAME, FIRST_NAME, ZIP
```

Shows first name, last name, and zip code for the next five records.

```
DISPLAY FIRST_NAME, LAST_NAME FOR FIRST_NAME = 'ADRIATOR'
```

Shows first and last name if first name is ADRIATOR in uppercase letters.

```
DISPLAY FIRST_NAME, LAST_NAME FOR FIRST_NAME = 'adriator'
```

Shows same thing as above if the name is in all lowercase letters.

```
DISPLAY FIRST_NAME, LAST_NAME FOR FIRST_NAME = 'Adriator'
```

Shows same thing again for proper capitalization. This is the one that should work.

```
DISPLAY FIRST_NAME, LAST_NAME FOR FIRST_NAME = 'Ad'
```

Would display for any records whose first name starts with the letters *Ad*.

```
SET EXACT ON
```

Prevents the above technique from working properly (see explanation in text).

```
DISPLAY FIRST_NAME, LAST_NAME, WORK_PHONE FOR LAST_NAME = 'P'
```

Illustrates that with Exact ON, 'P' will not list Phillip or Phillipson.

```
SET EXACT OFF
```

Turns exact matching OFF again.

```
LOCATE FOR FIRST_NAME = 'Marcel'
```

Positions the pointer on the record whose first name is Marcel.

```
DISP FIRST_NAME
```

After previous command, should display "Marcel."

```
LOCATE FOR UPPER(LAST_NAME) = 'DAVIES'
```

Positions pointer on record whose last name, converted to uppercase, is DAVIES.

CONTINUE

Beginning at the current pointer position, looks for the next record that meets the last Locate condition, and stops there.

LIST FIRST_NAME, LAST_NAME
FOR FIRST_NAME = 'Nimrod' .OR. LAST_NAME = 'Wegwo'

(*Note:* We had to break some lines for the book page. You can enter the commands all on one line.) Starts at the top of the file, and lists first and last names for any records that have a first name of Nimrod or a last name of Wegwo.

LIST FIRST_NAME, LAST_NAME, STATE
FOR (FIRST_NAME = 'Nimrod' .OR. LAST_NAME = 'Wegwo') .AND. (STATE = 'TX')

Starts at the top of the file and lists first name, last name and state for any record that meets *both* of two conditions:

1. Has either
   - a. first name of Nimrod
   - b. or a last name of Wegwo
2. *and* has a state of Texas.

8 Rearranging the Records for Faster Access

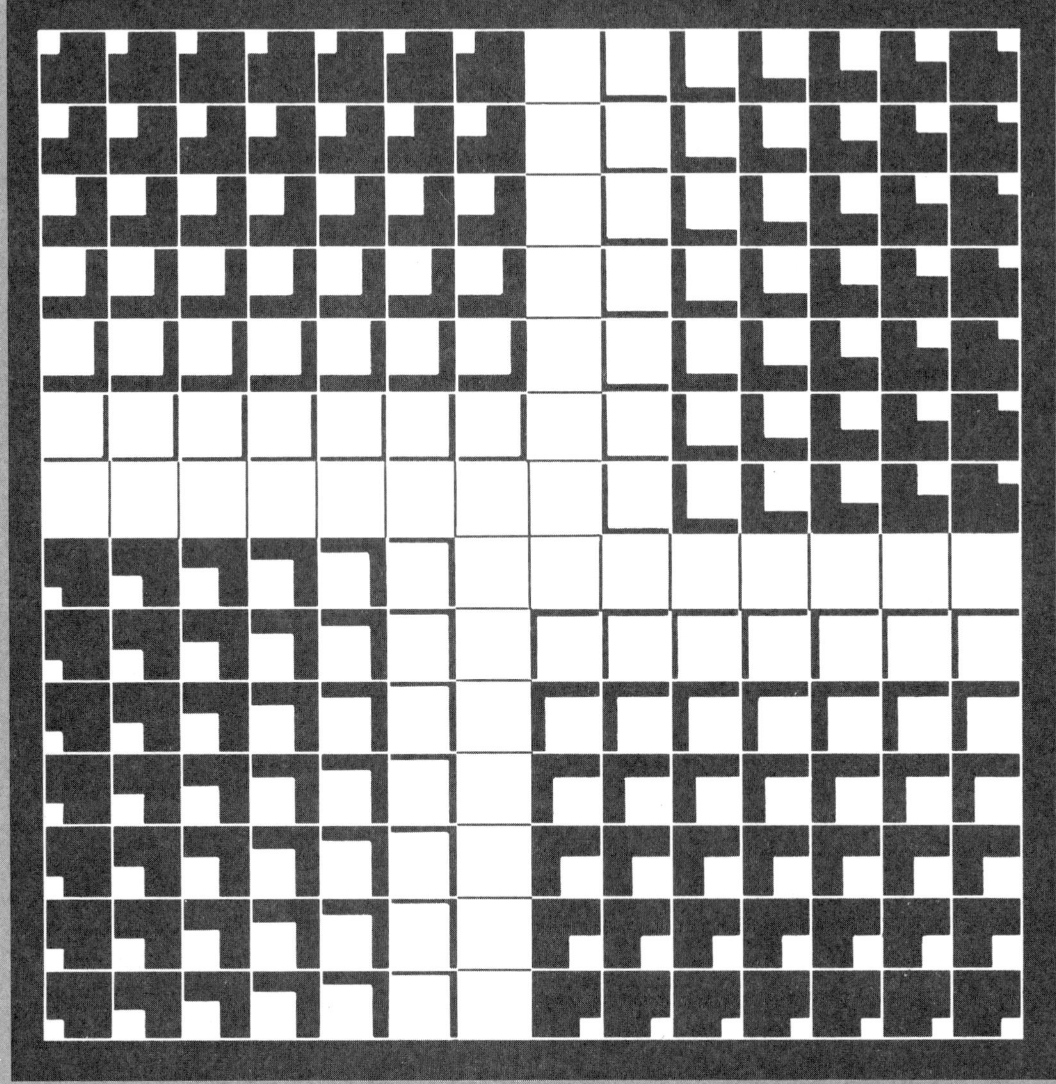

sorting records;
indexing records;
quick searches

The order of the records in most databases, even our short phone book one, is often rather haphazard. For example, you didn't enter the phone book records in alphabetical order or even in zip code order. And when you listed your data, it simply came out on the screen in the order in which you had entered it.

Record#	FIRST_NAME	LAST_NAME	STREET	ZIP
1	Randolf	Robbins	374 Tipplemeyer Ave.	94709
2	Hank	Davies	333 33rd. St.	43312
3	Adriator	Wegwo	158 Snorewell Blvd.	02587
4	Aretha	Phillipson	999 Motor City Ave.	39482
5	Randy	Batterydown	495 Anode St.	30129
6	Nimrod	Neverburger	77 Easy Street	89751
7	Marcel	Phillip	456 Fresno St.	55493
8	Valery	Kuletski	451 Fahrenheit Ct.	95420
9	MARIAN	DAVIES	344 MARKET ST	10021

Typically, records are added to databases as they become available, and thus are stored in a more or less random order. However, there are times when it is useful to rearrange an entire database into an order that is useful for a specific purpose. The telephone book you receive from the phone company is a good example. Once they have added all the new data for a year, the phone company prints out a list in alphabetical order according to name, and that is the list you see in your phone book. That way, you can easily look someone up, even without using dBASE III PLUS! In dBASE, there are two means for achieving this kind of reordering: *Sorting* and *Indexing*. Let's experiment with Sorting first.

How to Sort Your Database

The previous chapters have used a telephone book database for examples. But for this chapter, let's create a new database that will contain a list of items to take along on a camping trip.

1. Select *Create/Database* to create the new database. Name the file CAMPLIST, and use the structure shown in Figure 8.1. Notice that WEIGHT and COST are Numeric type fields (our first ones) and that the COST field will have two decimal places.

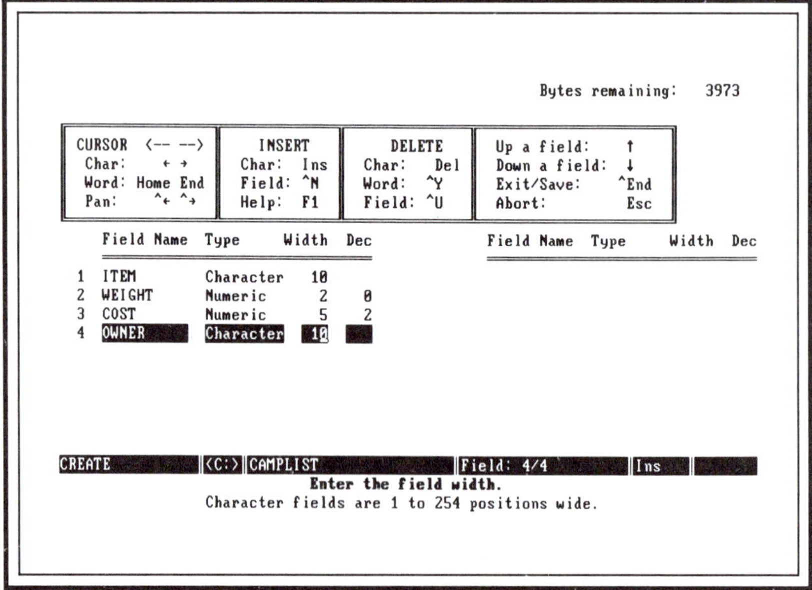

Figure 8.1: The CAMPLIST database structure

2. When asked if you want to add records, type Y and enter the following data records:

Record#	ITEM	WEIGHT	COST	OWNER
1	Back pack	10	65.00	Rich
2	Stove	25	85.00	Rich
3	Tent	12	62.33	Lisa B.
4	Food	30	45.27	Group
5	Rain gear	7	12.95	Renee
6	Flashlight	2	7.50	Jean
7	Hammock	5	15.00	John

You may have noticed that it took some extra care to enter the cost of the flashlight at 7.50 instead of 75.00. With the other costs, this wasn't a problem since they were all ten dollars or over. With them, once you typed in the first two digits, dBASE shipped the cursor past the decimal point, assuming any further digits were for cents. But for the flashlight, it was up to you to press the decimal point yourself. If you are doing lots of data entry with decimal places, you can avoid this type of problem by always entering the decimal point yourself. If dBASE has already skipped past it, your computer will merely beep when you enter the decimal point. If it hasn't skipped past it, your entering the decimal point manually will ensure it proper position.

Now that we have some data in the file, let's do a sort. Suppose we'd like to organize the file so that it lists the items in order of weight.

1. Select *Organize/Sort.*
2. A field list appears, because the Assistant wants to know which field, or fields, you want to sort by. In other words, which field's data should determine the new order of the records. Since we want the listing arranged by the weight of the items, rather than the owner or the cost, highlight WEIGHT. Your screen should look like Figure 8.2.
3. Press ↵ to select WEIGHT, and then press → to leave the field list.
4. Now the Assistant asks a couple of questions about where you want the newly arranged file stored. You see, sorting doesn't actually rearrange the records in the original CAMPLIST database. Instead, it makes a new copy of the database, with the records in the requested order. So, the Assistant needs to know where you

want to store the new database when the sorting is done. First, a drive designator appears, with the default drive letter (A, B, or C) highlighted. Select the letter of your data disk (B for floppy-disk systems and C for hard-disk).

5. Now it asks for the name of the destination file. Type in

   CAMP2 ↵

   as shown in Figure 8.3. dBASE now sorts the file, and a message appears above the Status Line.

   100% Sorted   7 Records sorted

6. To see the list in sorted order, you have to open the new file. Press any key to get back to the Assistant, then open the new file via the *Set Up/Database file* option. Select the correct drive designator for your system and then *CAMP2.* Type N to the index question.

7. Select *Retrieve/List/Execute the command* to see the listing:

Record#	ITEM	WEIGHT	COST	OWNER
1	Flashlight	2	7.50	Jean
2	Hammock	5	15.00	John
3	Rain gear	7	12.95	Renee
4	Back pack	10	65.00	Rich
5	Tent	12	62.33	Lisa B.
6	Stove	25	85.00	Rich
7	Food	30	45.27	Group

Obviously, dBASE has reordered the records by weight, as requested. Incidentally, in database lingo, the field you have sorted on is called the *key* or *key field.*

Ascending vs descending order

dBASE assumes you want to use an ascending order in your sorts, which is why the larger weights appear at the end of the new list. But what if you want the heavier weights first? Specifying a *descending* order is also possible, though only from the Dot prompt. Let's try it:

1. Make sure the drive designator on the status line indicates the correct data drive for your system. If not, use *Tools/Set drive* to change it.

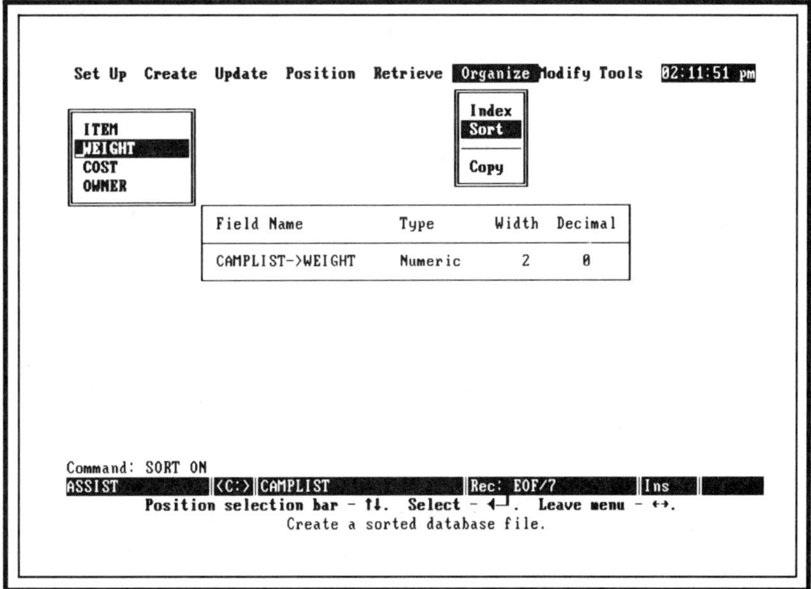

Figure 8.2: Selecting the WEIGHT field to sort by

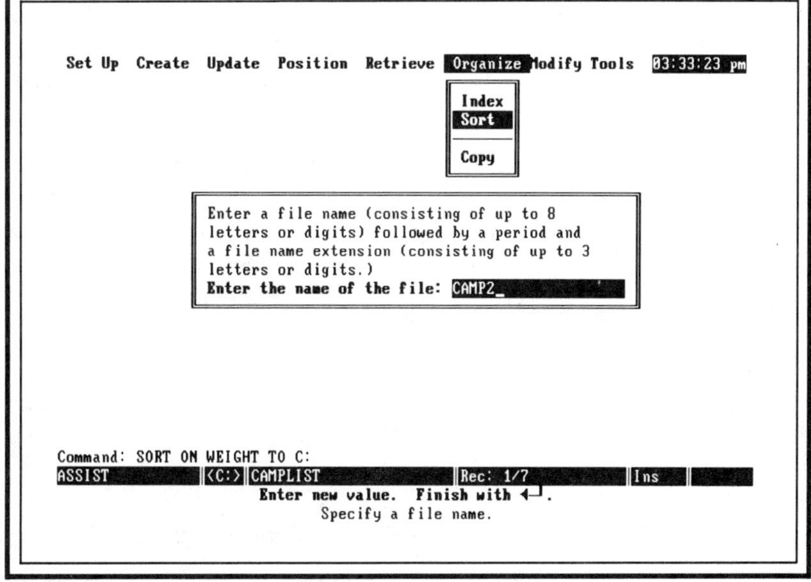

Figure 8.3: Entering the name of the sorted file

2. Get to the dot prompt by pressing ESC a few times. Then, from the Dot prompt, type

   SORT ON WEIGHT TO CAMP3 DESCENDING ↵

   This tells dBASE to

   - Sort, using the WEIGHT field as the key.
   - Call the new file CAMP3.
   - Do the sort in a descending order.

3. Now look at the list by opening the file. From the Dot prompt, type

   USE CAMP3 ↵
   LIST ↵

   dBASE responds with

Record#	ITEM	WEIGHT	COST	OWNER
1	Food	30	45.27	Group
2	Stove	25	85.00	Rich
3	Tent	12	62.33	Lisa B.
4	Back pack	10	65.00	Rich
5	Rain gear	7	12.95	Renee
6	Hammock	5	15.00	John
7	Flashlight	2	7.50	Jean

Sorting on a character field

dBASE will also allow you to sort on a character field in either ascending or descending alphabetical order. For example, try this from the Dot prompt (since we're already there):

1. Type

   SORT ON ITEM TO CAMP4 ↵
   USE CAMP4 ↵
   LIST ↵

   dBASE lists the following:

Record#	ITEM	WEIGHT	COST	OWNER
1	Back pack	10	65.00	Rich
2	Flashlight	2	7.50	Jean

```
3 Food         30 45.27 Group
4 Hammock       5 15.00 John
5 Rain gear     7 12.95 Renee
6 Stove        25 85.00 Rich
7 Tent         12 62.33 Lisa B.
```

Notice that the items are listed in alphabetical order.

Multilevel sorting

Another useful feature of the *Sort* command is the ability to create databases which are sorted on more than one field. This is referred to as a *multilevel* sort; a good example would be our phone book. Say you sorted according to last name, but within each last name wanted first names alphabetized (e.g. Suzy Raymond listed before Tina Raymond). To achieve this, you sort on the least significant field first (first name) and then the most significant field (last name). Using our camplist, say that for each owner of an item, we want the items themselves alphabetized too. This would be a multilevel sort using OWNER as the most significant key, and ITEM as least significant key. Since the rule is to sort on the least significant key first, we're half way there because we just did a sort on ITEM to CAMP4, which is already open. So now all we have to do is sort on *OWNER.*

1. Type in

   ```
   SORT ON OWNER TO CAMP5 ↵
   USE CAMP5 ↵
   LIST ↵
   ```

   dBASE responds:

   ```
   Record# ITEM       WEIGHT  COST OWNER
         1 Food           30 45.27 Group
         2 Flashlight      2  7.50 Jean
         3 Hammock         5 15.00 John
         4 Tent           12 62.33 Lisa B.
         5 Rain gear       7 12.95 Renee
         6 Back pack      10 65.00 Rich
         7 Stove          25 85.00 Rich
   ```

2. Only Rich's records are relevant here since only he owns more than one item. Notice that his back pack is listed before his stove, since alphabetically, B comes before S.

As you can see, it's easy to create quite a number of differently organized databases from one master list, using either the Assistant or the Dot prompt. However useful sorting is, this technique has its problems too. One is that every time you add new records to a sorted database, it must be re-sorted if you want its order to be maintained. That might be OK except that sorting large databases takes quite a bit of time, sometimes several hours. Another problem is that dBASE makes an entire copy of the sorted file on your disk when it does a sort. For a large file, this can be a serious problem, limiting you to data files that are no larger than half of your available disk space. Additionally, if you want your sorted database to have the name it originally had (in our case CAMPLIST), you'd have to erase CAMPLIST and then rename the sorted file of your choice to CAMPLIST. Finally, every time you re-sort, all the records in a file will be assigned new record numbers according to their new order. This makes locating a given record by its number unlikely. For these reasons, experienced dBASE users rely on sorting only occassionally.

How to Index Your Database

Luckily, another option, *Index,* solves all these problems and then some. *Index* is a very powerful option and is often the basis for sophisticated database systems. In contrast to *Sort, Index* does not copy your entire database. Instead, it creates a new file that contains "pointers" to records in your database. This "pointer file" works similarly to the card catalogues in a library. Instead of searching through all the books in a library, you look through card indexes (author, title, and subject) to point you to the actual book you want. Since the catalogues are kept in alphabetical order, this is usually a quick and simple process.

dBASE III PLUS indexes work the same way, only faster, thanks to your computer, and indexes consume less disk space than sorted files do. In addition, dBASE can automatically keep the indexes up-to-date whenever you make changes to your master database, without the hassle of re-sorting, erasing, and renaming files. Best of all, indexed databases allow you to use another command, *Seek* which is very much like *Locate,* but is significantly faster (more about that later).

Now for the details of indexing. For starters, let's create an index.

1. Get back into Assist mode.
2. Open the CAMPLIST database.

3. Select *Organize/Index.*

4. Now you see this message:

   The index key can be any character, numeric, or date expression involving one or more fields in the database file. It is usually a single field.
   Enter an index key expression:

   Don't worry if the message is a bit confusing. It basically means to type in the name of the field you want to index on (the *index key,* just like the sort key). Let's use WEIGHT again, just as we did for the sort. Type in

   WEIGHT ↵

5. Select the disk drive, and you see this:

   Enter a file name (consisting of up to 8 letters or digits) followed by a period and a file name extension (consisting of up to 3 letters or digits.)
   Enter the name of the file:

6. Simply enter *WEIGHT.* dBASE will add an extension to the name, .NDX. Thus, this index will be stored on disk as WEIGHT.NDX.)

7. In a few seconds the CAMPFILE database is indexed. Just for fun, let's use the Assistant to see whether there really is a new index file on the disk. Select *Tools/Directory,* and then select the drive. Then highlight *.ndx Index Files.* Your screen should look like Figure 8.4.

   Press ↵ and you should see:

   WEIGHT.NDX

   1024 bytes in 1 files.

8. Now to verify the results of the indexing process, select *Retrieve/List/Execute the command.* You should see

Record#	ITEM	WEIGHT	COST	OWNER
6	Flashlight	2	7.50	Jean
7	Hammock	5	15.00	John
5	Rain gear	7	12.95	Renee
1	Back pack	10	65.00	Rich

3	Tent	12	62.33	Lisa B.
2	Stove	25	85.00	Rich
4	Food	30	45.27	Group

Hmmm. This is interesting. As you can see, the record numbers are out of order even though the records do appear in order of increasing weight. Why is this? Remember the library example—the books remain in the same order on the shelves. Only the catalogue varies. Your records have not been rearranged, only the index pointers have. It's just that the new index file takes over displaying the data in the order you wanted it.

You can create as many indexes as you want, incidentally, and switch them on or off for the purposes of retrieving data in a variety of orders. To see this, we'll first create another index, this time on COST.

1. Select *Organize/Index.*
2. For the index key type in

   COST ↵

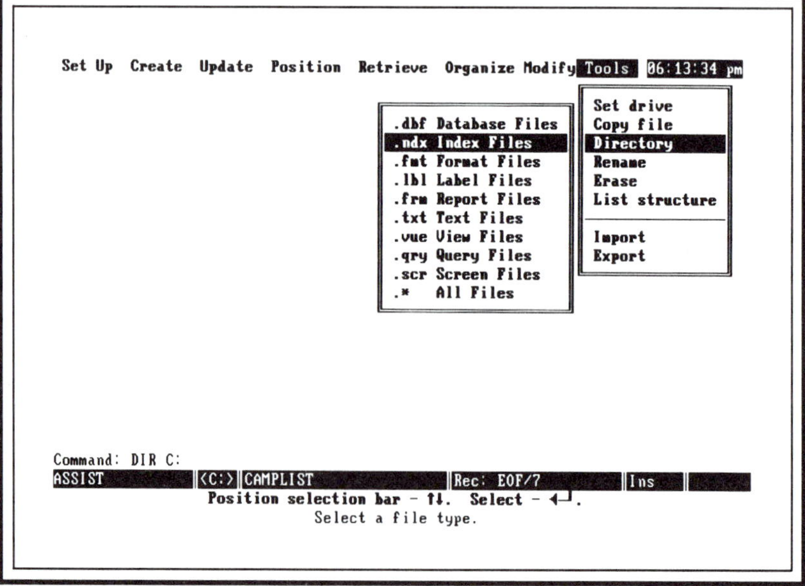

Figure 8.4: Using the Tools menu to check for index files

3. Select the drive designator
4. For the file name, also type in

   COST ↵

5. Now list the data (using *Retrieve/List/Execute*). You should see:

Record#	ITEM	WEIGHT	COST	OWNER
6	Flashlight	2	7.50	Jean
5	Rain gear	7	12.95	Renee
7	Hammock	5	15.00	John
4	Food	30	45.27	Group
3	Tent	12	62.33	Lisa B.
1	Back pack	10	65.00	Rich
2	Stove	25	85.00	Rich

Notice that as soon as you create a new index, your data file takes on the order of that index. Obviously the Cost index is now in charge, and the Weight index is not, since the weights are out of order. What if you want to see the Weights in order again? To do this, you have to open the appropriate index. This is done from the Set Up menu (or it can be done from the Dot prompt, as can the indexing itself).

Activating an index from the Assistant

As an example, let's reactivate our existing Weight index, by doing the following:

1. Select *Setup/Database file.*
2. Select the drive and CAMPLIST.
3. Answer Y to "Is the file indexed?"
4. A list of the indexes on that drive appears. Most likely there are only two, unless you've made some others.
5. Select WEIGHT.NDX and press ↵. You see a screen like Figure 8.5. Notice the word "Master" shows up next to the index you selected. This only has significance when using more than one index at a time, a topic that will be covered later.
6. Press → (*not* ↵) to exit the index selection box. That's all there is to it. Try doing a listing, and you'll see that the Weight index is, in fact, active.

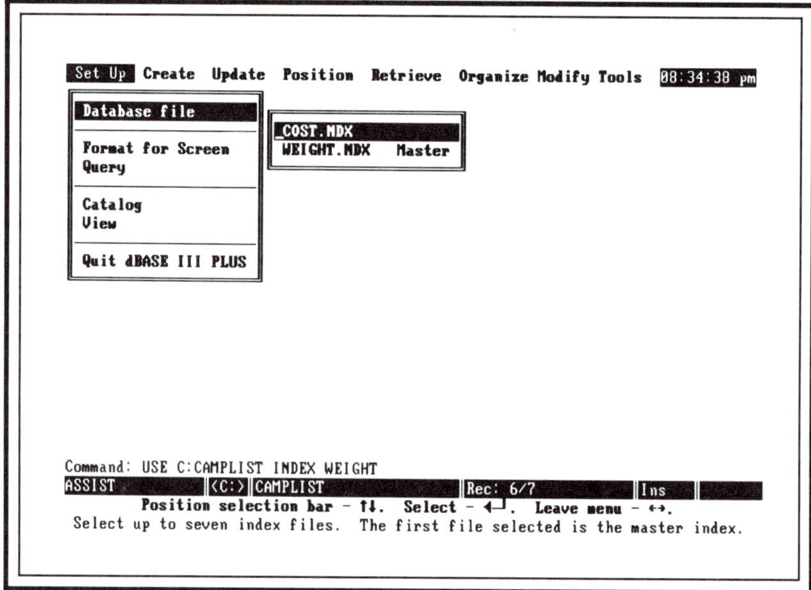

Figure 8.5: Activating an index

Activating an index from the Dot prompt

Activating indexes from the Dot prompt is actually a fair bit easier than using the Assistant.

1. Get to the Dot prompt
2. Type

   SET INDEX TO COST ↵

   Pretty easy, assuming you know the name of the index in advance. If you don't remember the index name and would like to see a list, just type

   DIR *.NDX ↵

   and the names of the the available indexes will appear.

Multilevel indexing

Just as with sorting, you can create a single index based on several fields. As a parallel to the sorting example, assume we want to create an index that will list records in order according to owner, and in case an owner has more than one item, we want those items to appear in alphabetical order as well.

1. From the Assistant, select *Organize/Index*.
2. Type in

   OWNER + ITEM ↵

3. Select the drive, and for the file name type in

   TEST ↵

4. To activate the new index, select *Set Up/Database file/CAMPLIST.*
5. Answer Y to the index question.
6. Select TEST as the index. Press →.
7. Select *Retrieve/List/Execute.* You should see this:

Record#	ITEM	WEIGHT	COST	OWNER
4	Food	30	45.27	Group
6	Flashlight	2	7.50	Jean
7	Hammock	5	15.00	John
3	Tent	12	62.33	Lisa B.
5	Rain gear	7	12.95	Renee
1	Back pack	10	65.00	Rich
2	Stove	25	85.00	Rich

Notice that the owner names are in order, and that Rich's items are listed alphabetically.

Seeing which index is active

A fringe benefit of selecting indexes from the Dot prompt is that you can check out which index is currently active—something you can't find out from the Assistant. To do this, get to the Dot prompt and

1. Type

   DISPLAY STATUS

   This appears:

   Currently Selected Database:
   Select area: 1, Database in Use: C:CAMPLIST.dbf Alias: CAMPLIST
   Master index file: C:TEST.NDX Key: OWNER + ITEM

   File search path:
   Default disk drive: C:
   Print destination: PRN:
   Margin = 0
   Current work area = 1

   Press any key to continue...

   You can ignore all but the first three lines of this. The second line tells you that the database in use is CAMPLIST. The third line reports that TEST.NDX is the current Master index file (more about Master index files below).

2. Press any key to see the rest of what the Display Status command shows you. Most of it really isn't important, though you might take note of what the function keys are set to do. For instance pressing F3 will show a List of the currently open database.

How to Find Data the Fast Way—with Seek

Now for the fun part. The main reason for indexing is so you can use the *Seek* option. Using *Seek,* you can locate a desired record in extremely short order, whereas listing out an entire database (especially if it is large) or using the Locate command can take ages. The only thing to remember is that *Seek* must be used with the field the index was created on.

Say we wanted to find out what that receipt for $7.50 on our camping trip was for. First, make sure the Cost index is activated. Then,

1. From the Assistant, select *Position/Seek.*

2. A box appears, asking you to enter an expression.

3. Type in

   7.50 ↵

   It will appear as though nothing happens after this. But actually, dBASE went looking for the record whose Cost field had 7.50 in it.

4. To see what it found, select *Retrieve/Display/Execute the command.* dBASE responds with

```
Record# ITEM        WEIGHT COST OWNER
      6 Flashlight       2 7.50 Jean
```

If you try to *Seek* an item that is not in the database, dBASE will let you know about it by saying

No find.

just above the Status Line, immediately after you execute the *Seek* command. This is the only way to know that dBASE didn't find the record you were looking for. Also, if you try selecting *Seek* without having an index open, the Assistant will not let you. You simply cannot highlight Seek from the Retrieve menu. If you try doing a *Seek* from the Dot prompt with no index open, dBASE will respond:

Database is not indexed.

If you see this message, make sure you have created an index and that it is active.

One more note about Seeking. In the last example, we were using a numerical field upon which to *Seek*. This allowed you to simply type in a number as the expression. However, when using a character field, this won't work.

1. Create a new index based on the OWNER field and call it OWNER. Now activate the index.

2. Select *Position/Seek,* and type in

   Rich ↵

   dBASE responds with a beep and this message:

   Variable not found

That's really "user friendly," for you, isn't it? Well, you'll simply have to remember on your own that this means "Hey, you forgot to use quote marks around the word you entered."

3. Press any key, and try the *Seek* again, this time using using single quotes. Enter

   'Rich' ↵

   This time you shouldn't get a beep.

4. Select *Retrieve/Display/Execute the command* to see what dBASE found.

```
Record#  ITEM          WEIGHT  COST   OWNER
      1  Back pack         10  65.00  Rich
```

A few more notes on indexing

There are a few other things you should know about indexing. To begin with, it is allowable to have more than one index open at a time. As mentioned above, the first index you activate is called the *Master index.* If you go ahead and select additional indexes, they will be numbered 2, 3, 4, and so on (these are called *secondary indexes*). You may have as many as seven indexes active at one time, but the thing to remember is that the Seek option works only on the Master index field. So, for example, if you select Weight as the Master and Owner as the number 2 index, don't expect to be able to *Seek* Rich, since he is an owner, not a weight!

But if you can't use the secondary indexes, why activate them? Good question. Actually, the answer is simple. If you have several indexes for a database, you will naturally want dBASE III PLUS to keep them up-to-date as you add, delete, and edit your records. This eliminates the need for continual re-sorting or reindexing whenever you want to look something up. But dBASE can only keep the indexes current if they are active when changes are being made to the main database. Otherwise your indexes will not agree with your main database and you will have to reindex frequently. (The details of editing records will be covered in the next chapter.)

Next point. To select more than one index from the Dot prompt, separate the index names with commas. For example:

SET INDEX TO ITEM, OWNER, WEIGHT, COST ↵

In this case, ITEM is the Master index.

One more point. Though this only applies to larger databases, it's good to remember that, in general the more indexes you have open, the slower things get, especially when appending (adding) records to your database. This is because dBASE has to update all the active indexes for each added record. Don't use any more indexes than you have to, unless your database is going to remain small.

9 Keeping Your Databases Up-to-Date

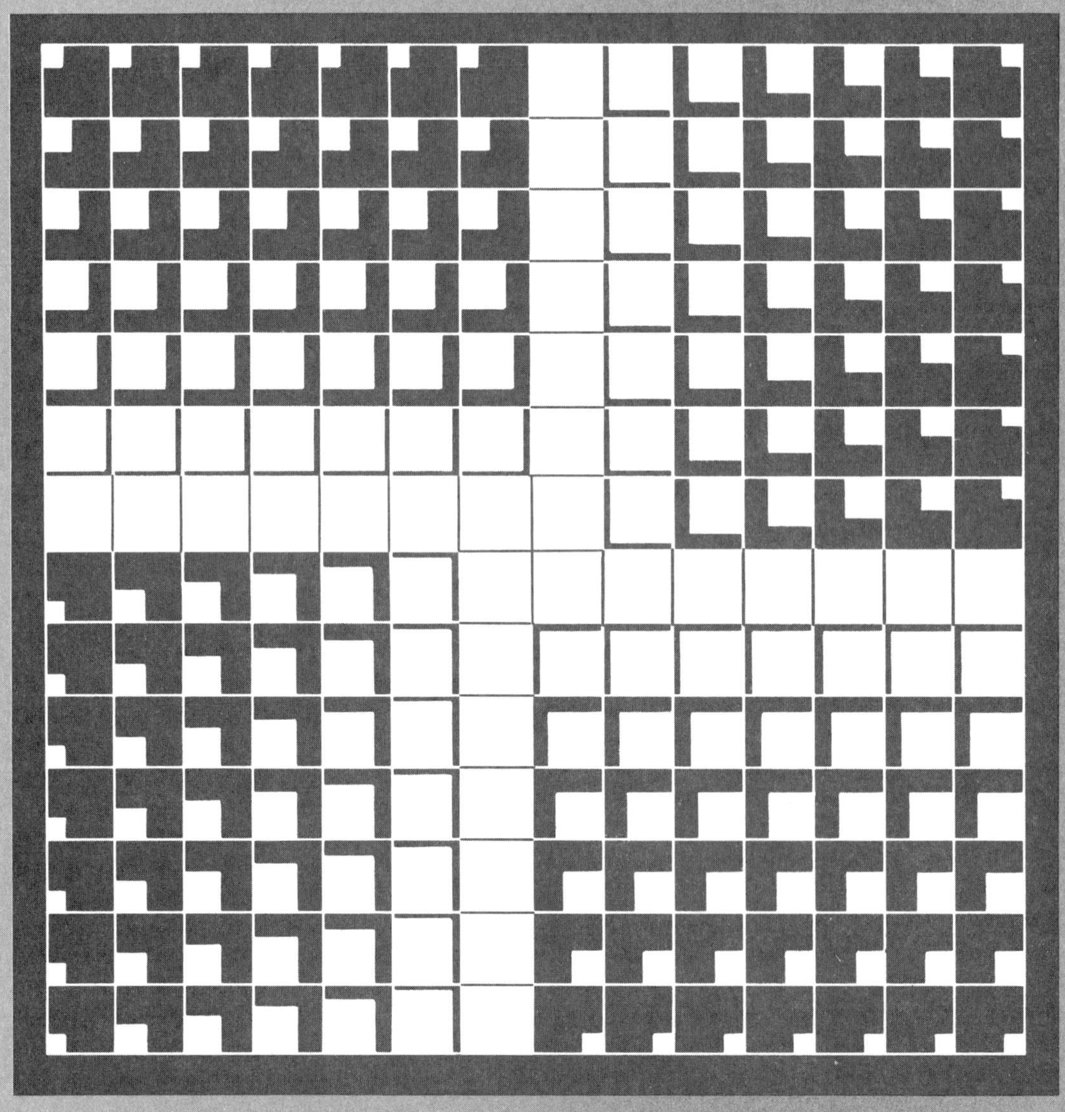

Edit mode; Browse mode; deleting, undeleting, and packing

There will probably come a time when you'll want to alter some of the data records in your databases. As an example, consider once again your phone book file. People have a habit of moving around, acquiring new addresses, phone numbers, and jobs.

In anticipation of the ever-changing nature of most databases, dBASE III PLUS allows you to edit your data records easily, using several commands that will be covered in this chapter.

We'll be using the PHONEBK database for this section, so please open the file again. And while you're at it, try putting your newly learned indexing skills to use too. Let's create three indexes—one for first name, one for last name, and one for company—and then activate them. I'm sure you are comfortable with doing all this from the Assistant, but since some of you may want to do it from the Dot prompt, I'll list the commands for both. From the Assistant:

1. Select *Setup/Database file/PHONEBK.*
2. Answer N to the index question.
3. Select *Organize/Index.*
4. Type in FIRST_NAME ↵.
5. Select the appropriate drive.
6. Type in FIRST for the file name, and press ↵.

7. Press any key to get back to the Assistant.
8. Select *Organize/Index* again.
9. Type in LAST_NAME ↵.
10. Select the drive.
11. Type in LAST for the file name and press ↵.
12. Press any key to return to the Assistant.
13. Select *Organize/Index* again.
14. Type in COMPANY ↵.
15. Select the drive.
16. Type in COMP as the file name and press ↵.
17. Press any key to return to the Assistant. Activate the indexes now by selecting *Setup/Database file*. Choose the drive and PHONEBK.
18. Answer Y to the index question.
19. From the list of indexes, choose

    FIRST
    LAST
    COMP

    in that order. Press ← or → to activate the indexes.

These are the commands from the Dot prompt:

```
USE PHONEBK ↵
INDEX ON FIRST_NAME TO FIRST ↵
INDEX ON LAST_NAME TO LAST ↵
INDEX ON COMPANY TO COMP ↵
SET INDEX TO FIRST, LAST, COMP ↵
```

What you have done is to set the Master index to First, and the secondary indexes to Last and Comp. In other words, our database will now appear to be ordered alphabetically by first name and, in addition, any changes made to the records in the database will be made to all three indexes. Now we can get down to some editing, with the knowledge that any changed data will be reflected in the three indexes.

How to Modify Data with Edit

The most straightforward technique for changing a record's data is called *Edit*. *Edit* appears on the Assistant Screen as an option on the Update menu, shown in Figure 9.1.

Edit works very much the same way as *Append* does. That is, you see one record at a time on the screen, and you can move the cursor around and make your changes. The only trick is that dBASE first needs to know which record you want to modify. Let's try editing some records in the PHONEBK database.

1. Get into the Assistant if you are at the Dot prompt.
2. Select *Update/Edit*.
3. Your screen should look like Figure 9.2. Notice that the pointer number on the Status Line indicates we're on record three. Why three rather than one? Because we are using the first name index as the Master index. The first name for record 3 being Adriator,

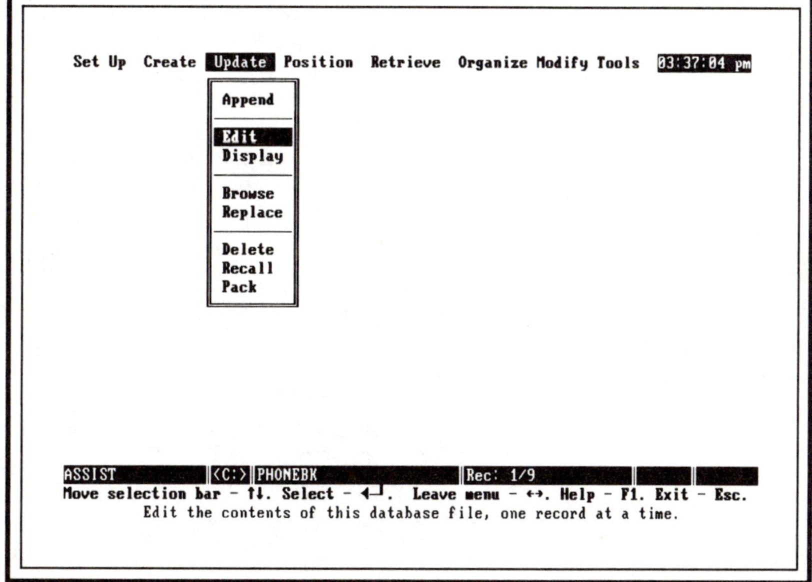

Figure 9.1: The *Edit* option

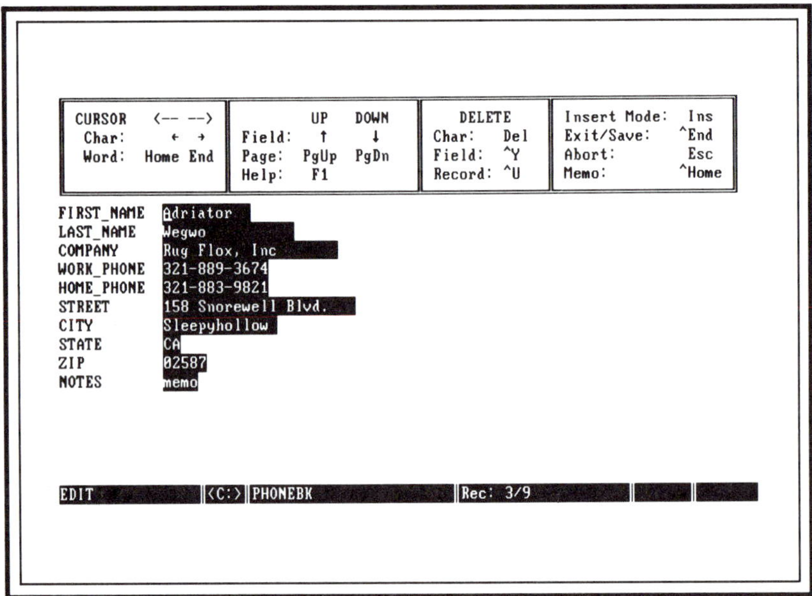

Figure 9.2: The *Edit* screen

puts record 3 at the top of the heap, alphabetically. Also notice the Status Line says *Edit* on the far left end. This means you are in the Edit mode.

4. This screen should look very familiar. It is identical to the Append screen. In fact, the editing commands that you can use here are the same as those you are already familiar with. There is one difference though. You can move up and down between your data file's records by pressing the *PgUp* (page up) and *PgDn* (page down) keys (above and below the → key). Try pressing PgDn once to see what happpens. You should see

   Aretha
   Phillipson
   Soulariums-R-Us
   908-776-5298
   908-337-8194
   999 Motor City Ave.
   Detroit
   MI
   39482
   memo

5. Now press PgUp to get back to Adriator Wegwo's record.

6. Say you've just received a letter from the famous writer, Randolf Robbins, announcing that he will be working under a new pen name: Wackford Squeers. You'll want to change his name in your database, but you have to call up his record first. You can get there in any of three ways.

   - You can press the PgDn key until you find him, but that's a bother, particularly if you are working with a large database.
   - If you know his record number, you can get there directly, using *Position/Goto record* from the Assistant. But the chances are you wouldn't know it.
   - The best way to find the record for editing is to use *Seek,* especially since our database is already indexed.

7. Press Esc to get out of Edit mode. This brings you back to the Assistant. Now select *Position/Seek.* Type in 'Randolf' ↵. (Don't forget the quotes.)

8. Press any key to return to the Assistant. Since you didn't get a message saying "No find," you can be assured that Randolf's record was found and the pointer is located on it.

9. Edit the record by selecting *Update/Edit.* Randolf's record appears. Just selecting *Edit* means to dBASE to go into the Edit mode, starting with the record the pointer is currently positioned on.

10. Now alter the name fields. Position the cursor on the FIRST_NAME field and type ^Y to erase the current contents. Type in *Wackford.*

11. Press ↵ once to move to the LAST_NAME field. Press ^Y again, and enter *Squeers.* The record now looks like this:

    Wackford
    Squeers
    Ralph Nicolby Inc.
    415-555-1212
    415-555-1111
    374 Tipplemeyer Ave.
    Cornmont
    CA
    94709
    memo

12. Now, let's make a note about why the name was changed, for future reference. Use the ↵ or ↓ key to move to the NOTES Memo field.

13. Press ^Home. The Memo screen appears, as shown in Figure 9.3. This screen is like a blank notepad where you can type in notes about the record you are on. The editing codes are listed at the top of the screen, and most of the alternate keys you are already familiar with work too. As usual, F1 toggles the editing box on and off. You can type as many as 5,000 characters (letters and spaces) into a memo. dBASE III PLUS stores all the memos for the database in a separate file with the same first name as the database file and the extension of .DBT. Thus, our Memo fields will be stored in a file called PHONEBK.DBT.

    Incidentally, You can list the Memo field contents along with other fields by constructing a field list that includes the Memo field. For example, selecting *Retreive/List/Construct a field list/FIRST_NAME/LAST_NAME/NOTES* would do the trick. However, you cannot do searches based on words in the Memo field to find or retrieve a record in the database.

14. For now type in some notes and press ^End or ^W to save them.

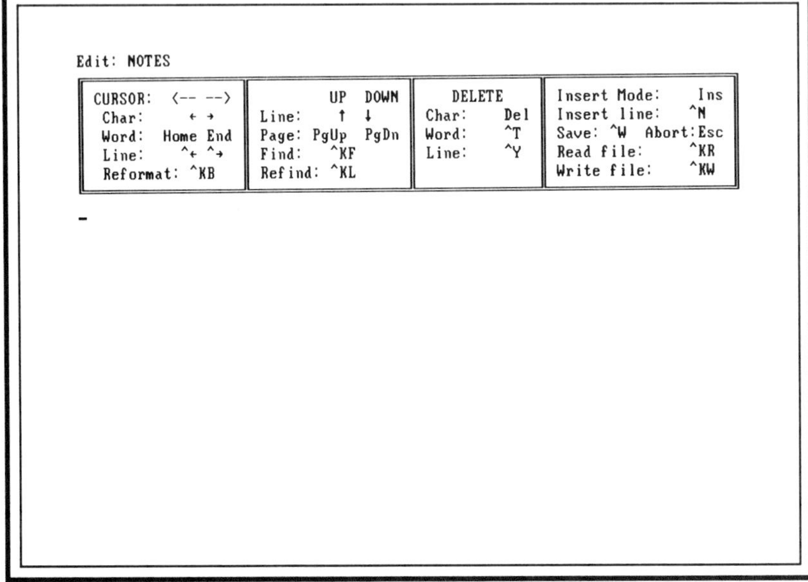

Figure 9.3: The Memo screen

15. This brings you back to Wackford's record. Press ^End or ^W again, to save the entire record as it now stands, with the new name and the notes added. An easy way to remember how to save your changes is this: ^W *writes* the changes. ^Q *quits* (or abandons) the changes.

As an alternative to using Seek as we just did, if you know the number of a record you'd like to edit, for instance record 3, you can select *Position/Goto record/RECORD/3* and then select *Update/Edit*. Or, from the Dot prompt you can simply type:

EDIT 3 ↵

How to Modify Data with Browse

There is another dBASE III PLUS option that can make updating your database a bit easier, particularly if you plan on editing more than a few records. *Browse* lets you scan through your database as though you were reading a newspaper with a magnifying glass. Visually, this command lays out a table of rows and columns on your screen as though your database were on grid paper. Then, using keyboard commands, you can "pan" up and down through your records, as well as right and left through your fields, editing as you go. You can even add or delete records in this mode.

Browse will display as many records as will fit on the screen, with one record per line. The fields that don't fit on the screen don't wrap around to the next line; they simply extend beyond the edge of the screen. To bring a field into view, you pan right or left until you reach it. The column of record numbers that you see in listings does not appear with *Browse*.

With all that in mind, try *Browsing* through your PHONEBK.

1. First, let's get the pointer on record 1 so that Browse will start from the top of the database. Select *Position/Goto record/TOP*. Or, from the Dot prompt type

   GOTO TOP ↵

2. Now get into Browse mode. Select *Update/Browse*. Or, from the Dot prompt type

   BROWSE ↵

   Your screen changes to the one in Figure 9.4.

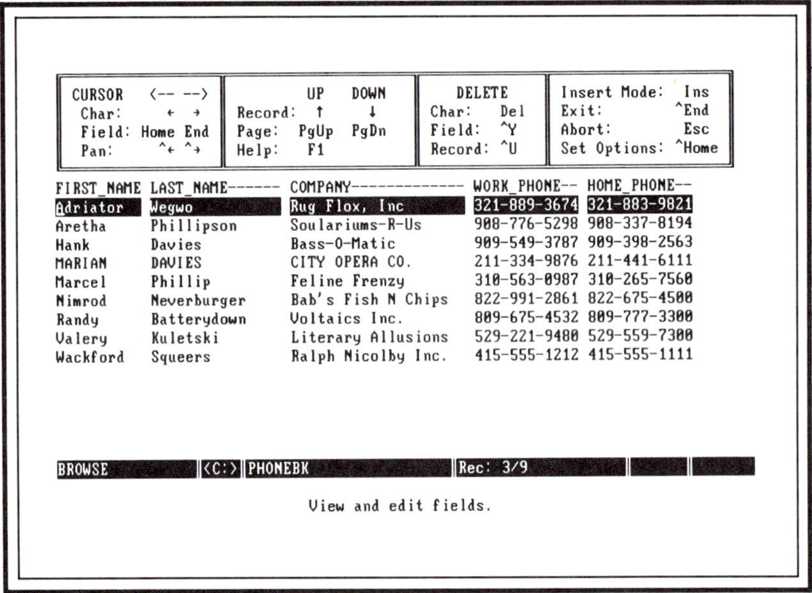

Figure 9.4: The *Browse* screen

Moving and editing in Browse mode

You can use the keyboard commands summarized in Table 9.1 to move around on screen and edit data while in the Browse mode.

1. Using the the arrow keys or ^E and ^X, move up and down a few records just to get the feel of it.

2. We can't see all the fields of a PHONEBK record at one time. The street, city, state, zip code, and notes fields are off beyond the right edge of the screen. Press ^→ several times to pan the window all the way right, until the NOTES field appears. For the NOTES field you see only the placeholder word "memo." You cannot see or edit the Memo field in Browse mode. Now, move back again with ^← until the FIRST_NAME field appears at the left of the screen again.

3. Move to the last record, Wackford's. Note that it has moved to its new alphabetical position without any reindexing, because the indexes were active when we updated the record. Now try

Main Key	*Letter Key*	*Action*
Home	^A	Left one field
End	^F	Right one field
←	^S	Left one letter
→	^D	Right one letter
↑	^E	Save record and back up one record
↓	^X	Save record and move down to next record
	^R	Save record and move up one screenful
^→	^B	Pan the screen to the right
^←	^Z	Pan the screen to the left
Del	^G	Delete character at cursor position
	^Y	Delete to end of a field from cursor
	^U	Mark entire record for later deletion
^End	^W	Save changes in current record made in Browse
Esc	^Q	Exit current record without saving changes made in Browse

Table 9.1: Editing keys for Browse mode

moving down just one more record. A message appears on the message line.

Add new records? (Y/N)

4. Type Y and notice that new, blank fields appear. Actually this is a different way of appending a record. Changed your mind? Just press ↵ or ↑ and the new record disappears (assuming you've not typed in anything other than spaces). For right now, don't add another record; just remember that it can be done this way.

5. Press F1 and notice that the editing key menu goes off. Press F1 again and it reappears.

6. Now press F10. Six menu selections appear at the top of the screen. These are Browse options that make it easier to move around and see particular fields. Here's what each one does:

   Bottom Moves cursor to the last record (bottom) of the database.

   Top Moves the cursor to the first record (top) of the database.

   Lock Lets you specify a number of fields, starting from the leftmost field, which will stay stationary on the screen, even when you are panning left or right to view or edit other fields.

   Record no Gets you to any record number quickly.

   Freeze Lets you specify one particular field to edit. All other fields are displayed, but cannot be altered.

   Find Assuming your file is indexed and an index is active, lets you type in a name (or whatever), and lands you on the record.

   The *Top* and *Bottom* selections are straightforward. You just highlight and press ↵. With *Record no.*, you supply the number when prompted. Don't forget to press F10 to get the *Browse* menu back each each time.

Locking fields in Browse mode

Now let's try locking a couple of fields so that they don't disappear when we're panning rightward. Since we don't really need to see the phone numbers, we can lock FIRST_NAME, LAST_NAME, and COMPANY and then pan right to get the address on the screen.

1. Make sure the FIRST_NAME field is in on the screen, and the cursor is on FIRST_NAME.

2. Press F10 and select *Lock*.

3. When asked for the number of columns to lock, type

   3 ↵

4. This should lock the first three fields on the left.

5. Now, press ^→ five times. Your screen should look like Figure 9.5.

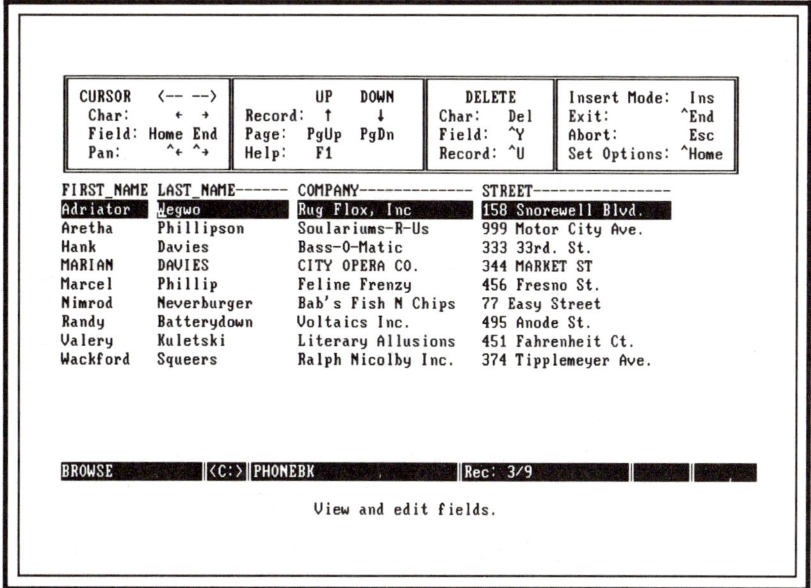

Figure 9.5: Panning rightward with three fields locked

6. Now let's say we only want to modify the zip codes because some of them were erroneous. Press ^→ once again. Now several more fields appear, including the zip code, which we will *Freeze.*

7. Press F10 and select *Freeze.* When asked for the field name, type ZIP ↵. Now only the ZIP field is highlighted and editable. This makes editing a single field really easy. Try using the arrow keys to move up and down between records.

8. Since we don't actually want to make any changes to the zip codes, press F10, select *Freeze* again, and just press ↵ when asked for the field name. This *unfreezes* the frozen zip code field, returning you to normal Browse mode.

9. Finally, let's try using *Find.* Remember the Master index, which we activated some time ago, is still *First,* based on the FIRST_NAME field. Press F10, and select *Find.* When dBASE says

   Enter search string:

   type in

   Sally ↵

Notice that the message at the bottom of the screen says

*** * Not Found * ***

since we don't have a Sally in our database. The window at the top waits for you to try another name. This time type

Nimrod ↵

and the cursor jumps to record 6 for editing.

A few more points about Browse mode

A few notes about Browse mode are in order. A field will not appear on the screen unless all of it can fit on. You may have to keep panning several times to get some larger fields displayed. Also, the ^Q (Esc) and ^W (^End) commands apply only to the record you are currently on. Once you move off of a record (other than with ^Q or Esc), it is saved as you left it. In other words, if you mess up a bunch of records and then type ^Q thinking that none of your changes will be saved, you are in for a surprise. Only the last record will be spared.

Finally, there is a way to get *Browse* to display only a specific list of fields. Say we really wanted to see only last names, streets, and cities during a browse. You have to do this from the Dot prompt, but here is the formula:

```
GOTO TOP ↵
BROWSE FIELDS LAST_NAME, STREET, CITY ↵
```

The screen should look like the one in Figure 9.6.

How to Delete Unwanted Records

Keeping your database clean and uncluttered is central to optimizing the efficiency of dBASE III PLUS. Duplicate, incomplete, erroneous, and outdated records can slow down many dBASE processes. They can also lead to other types of data contamination and potentially embarrassing situations like invoices and phone calls made to the wrong people, etc. So, it is good practice to purge your database of unwanted records regularly.

How is this done? You may have noticed that the list of control codes for use with *Browse* includes the *Delete* option (^U). Pressing ^U when

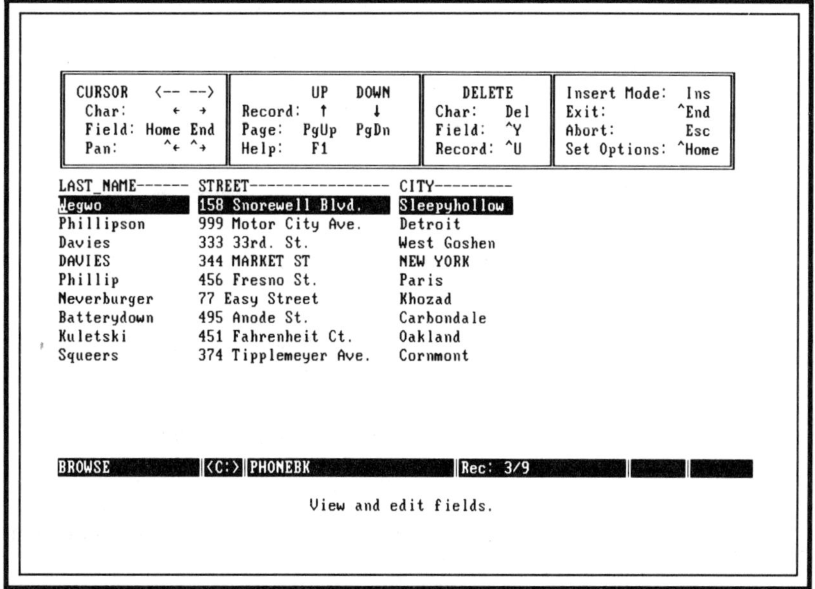

Figure 9.6: Browsing only specified fields

you are either Editing or Browsing marks the current record for *later* deletion. If you have tried this, you probably noticed that a *Del* message appears on the Status Line. Pressing ^U a second time removes the message. All that the *Delete* option really does is insert an asterisk between the record number and the first field, which you can see if you *List* the data. It doesn't actually erase the record from the database. This prevents accidental castastrophes. (Another step, *Pack* is required before dBASE III PLUS will eliminate the record for good. More about this later.)

Say we wanted to delete Nimrod Neverburger from our database. There are a number of ways to do this.

1. Move the record pointer to Nimrod's record by using the *Locate* or *Edit* options from the Assistant (or in any other way). Then select *Update/Delete.* As long as the record pointer is on the right record, selecting *Delete* will do the job.

2. From the Dot prompt type

   SEEK "Nimrod" ↵
   DELETE ↵

DBASE responds with

1 record deleted

unless the record has already been deleted, in which case dBASE says:

No records deleted

3. While editing or browsing a record, pressing ^U deletes the record. The *Del* sign shows up on the Status Line.
4. Say we wanted to delete a whole series of records—all people from California. Try the following:

   - Select *Update/Delete/Build a search condition.*
   - Choose STATE as the field.
   - Select *Equal To* = as the comparison operator.
   - Type in CA.
   - Then select *No more conditions* and *Execute the command.*

   Or, from the Dot prompt:

   DELETE FOR STATE = 'CA' ↵

Who's already deleted?

Having tried those commands, you've marked several records for deletion. Just to find out who's marked, type (from the Dot prompt)

DISPLAY FOR DELETED( ) ↵

or, for a less cluttered screen

DISPLAY FIRST_NAME, LAST_NAME FOR DELETED( ) ↵

dBASE responds with

Record#	FIRST_NAME	LAST_NAME
3	*Adriator	Wegwo
6	*Nimrod	Neverburger

```
8   *Valery     Kuletski
1   *Wackford   Squeers
```

Oops! Or undeleting records

Now, what if you decide that you actually want to hang on to those marked records after all? No problem. You can "undelete" them with the *Recall* option. It works exactly like *Delete* except in reverse. You can select it either from the Assistant or from the Dot prompt. To save all your marked records, just type from the Dot prompt

RECALL ALL ↵

You can, of course, recall only specific records as well, using the same approach outlined above for *Delete*. You can also recall records from the Assistant. Just select *Update/Recall,* and select the sub-option you want. In this case, to recall all records, you'd simply choose *Execute the Command.*

Packing your database

The process of actually deleting marked records is called *Packing*. Let's try it.

1. Get back to the Assistant.
2. Select *Update/Pack*.
3. In a few seconds the screen should say

```
      9 records copied
Rebuilding index—C:first.ndx
   100% indexed          9 Records indexed
Rebuilding index—C:last.ndx
   100% indexed          9 Records indexed
Rebuilding index—C:comp.ndx
   100% indexed          9 Records indexed
```

What happened? Well, the database was packed, and since packing could rearrange things in the main database, dBASE goes ahead and updates any open indexes at the same time (good thing we had our indexes open!).

Since you had already *Recalled* all marked records, the *Pack* should not have eliminated any records from your database, so you are still left with nine records.

Incidentally, there are no other options available with the *Pack* command, but that doesn't mean it isn't powerful. One false move and your deleted records will vanish irretrievably. Once you *Pack* your database, there is no way to recall your *Deleted* records. They are erased, and the remaining records are moved up to fill in the gaps. Thus, your old record numbers will also change.

A good technique for determining whether your database needs to be marked and packed for house cleaning is to print it out on paper and examine it. You can do this with the *List* option from the Assistant, specifying, when asked, that output should go to the printer.

Once the database prints out, mark all the records which need modification or deletion, then return to the computer and make the changes.

10

Creating Professional-Looking Reports

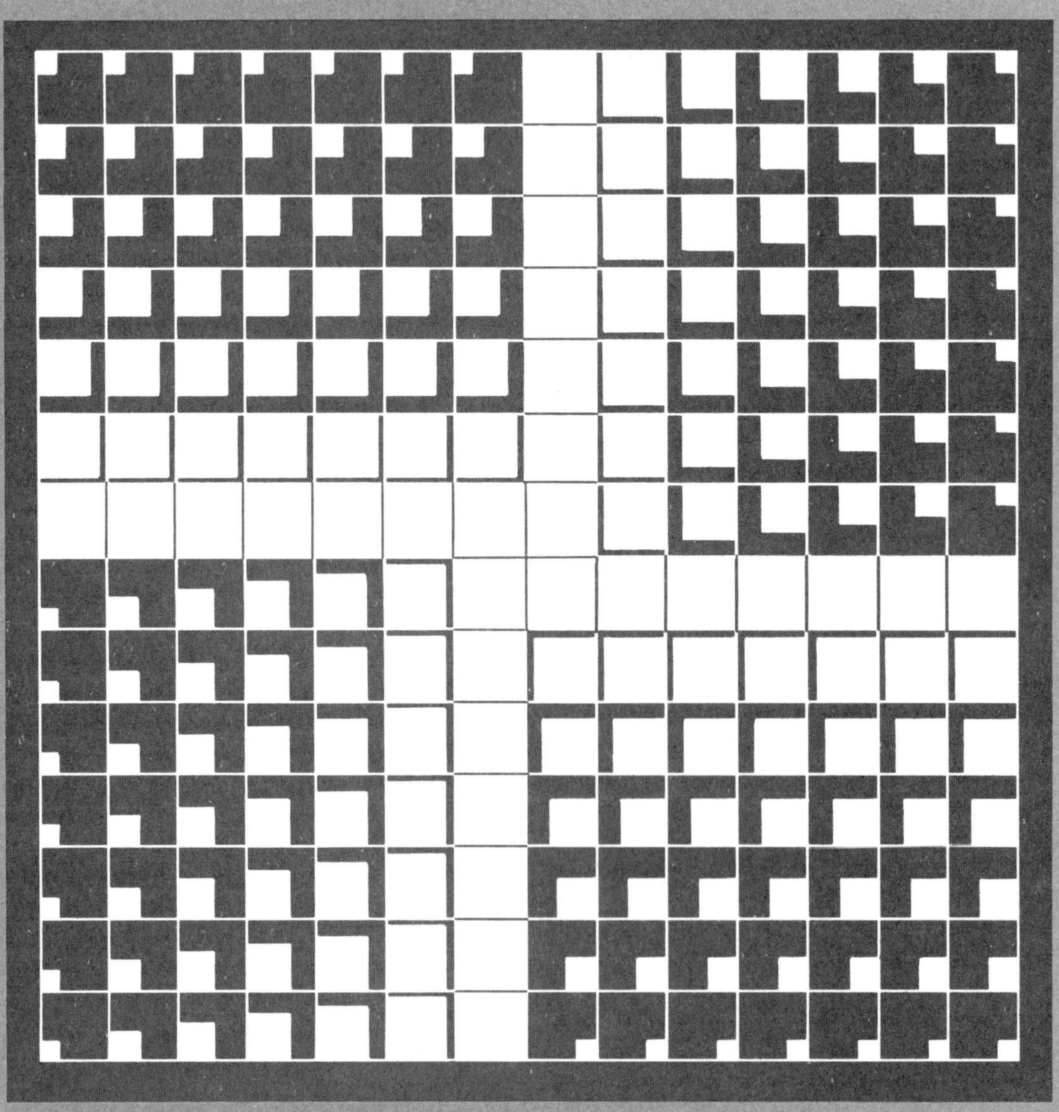

report formats;
calculations;
subtotals; summaries

Congratulations! Assuming you've followed along thus far without serious incident, you should now have the basic techniques for creating and maintaining databases under your belt.

Now you can take the next step: creating a report from data you have entered. Not that we haven't created some simple reports already, using the List and Display commands with selected fields and so forth. You may even have tried sending those listings to your printer by typing Y at the question about printing. Similarly, from the Dot prompt printing could have been turned on by adding the words TO PRINT after the rest of the command, as in

```
LIST FIRST_NAME, LAST_NAME FOR STATE = 'CA' TO PRINT
```

However, there will be occasions when you'll want to create listings that look more official, with column headings using real English (not just strange field names), a title at the top, and so on. This kind of listing is is called a *Report,* and is one of the primary reasons for the existence of database management systems such as dBASE III PLUS.

Luckily, dBASE III PLUS has what's called a built-in *report generator* that can, within only a few minutes, create fairly sophisticated printouts (either on screen or on paper) based on information in a database. Even though this feature is not advanced enough for creating highly complex reports (you'll need to do some dBASE III PLUS programming for that), it will often do the trick nicely for everyday reports such as a general ledger, a list of sales figures for the year, mailing labels, or an inventory list.

With dBASE III PLUS, reports can be prepared right from the keyboard, in response to prompts. Additionally, once the prompts are answered, dBASE saves your answers for future use. This way, the report can be run instantly next time, without your having to answer the prompt questions again.

Before experimenting with the *Report* option, you will need some new material to work with. Although we could use the CAMPLIST or PHONEBK database to demonstrate the *Report* option, a slightly more complex database, typical of a business environment, would be better.

1. Create a new database, called STEREO. It will be an inventory list from a stereo shop that you just inherited—Uncle Bob's Hi-Fi Anachronisms. Use the following structure:

	Field Name	Type	Width	Dec
1	CATEGORY	Character	10	
2	BRAND	Character	10	
3	MODEL	Character	6	
4	QUANTITY	Numeric	2	0
5	WHOLESALE	Numeric	6	2
6	RETAIL	Numeric	6	2

2. Now fill STEREO in with the data shown below.

Record#	CATEGORY	BRAND	MODEL	QUANTITY	WHOLESALE	RETAIL
1	RECEIVER	NIZO	T-33	5	225.49	350.49
2	RECEIVER	NIZO	T-35	4	312.00	425.25
3	RECEIVER	ACME	R25-MT	13	19.99	49.99
4	RECEIVER	NADIR	2-CHP	50	12.95	29.99
5	SPEAKERS	RAZCO	L-55	30	199.00	249.00
6	SPEAKERS	TALBEST	BG-20	6	250.00	350.88
7	TAPE DECK	ROLLEM	CAS-3	10	125.65	212.99
8	TAPE DECK	FLOWUTTER	WBL-5	5	149.33	250.77
9	TURNTABLE	XIRTAM	25-L	5	99.99	149.99
10	TURNTABLE	RALURIC	RND-1	3	595.00	850.00

After you've entered all the data, list it or use *Browse* to check it for accuracy.

How to Name and Title the Report

Now, say you'd like to create a report that lists all the products and calculates your total investment in inventory (total wholesale cost) for the quantities you have on hand of each item, and for all the items put together. Let's also calculate your percentage gross margin for each item, so you can see the anticipated gross margins associated with your various inventory investments. Since your computer is basically a powerful calculator, the figures should be a cinch. Here's how to create the report.

1. From the Assistant, select *Create/Report.* Or from the Dot prompt, type

   CREATE REPORT ↵

2. Select the appropriate drive designator.

3. The next thing asked is what the file name of your report will be. As with other file names, you may use up to eight letters, a period and an extension (the three letters after the period). If you do not use an extension, dBASE will add *.FRM* to the file name. Since this report file is to be used with the STEREO database, let's call it STEREO. (dBASE III PLUS will be able to differentiate between these two STEREO files because the main database file name has a .DBF extension.) So, type in

   STEREO ↵

4. You are now presented with the Report screen shown in Figure 10.1. Notice that there are five menu choices across the top of the screen, only the first of which, *Options,* is currently active. Take a quick look at each of the other menus before we continue. When you select *Columns,* notice that a blank report form appears on the bottom of the screen. The purpose of this will become clear shortly.

5. Now, here's the gist of how to make a report and what each menu choice is for, just so you have an overview of what we're going to be doing.

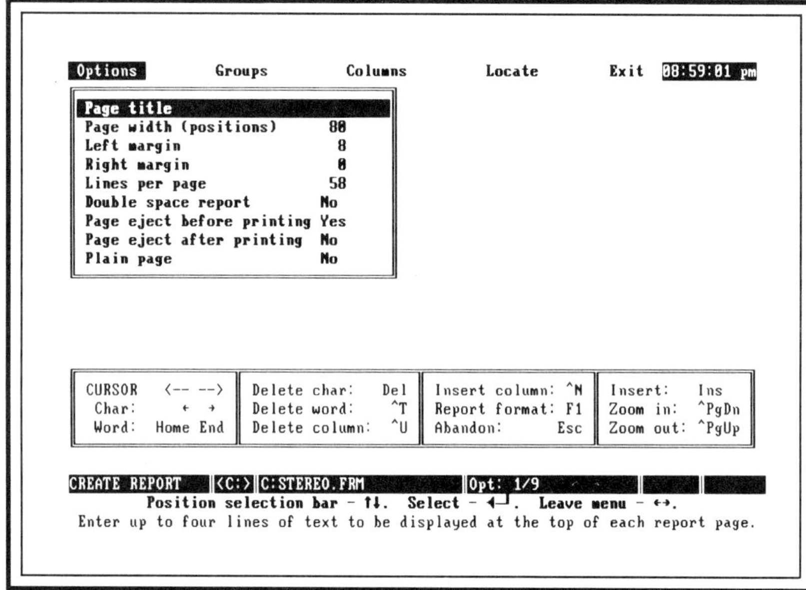

Figure 10.1: The Report screen

- First you set up your basic options such as what title should appear on the report, whether the report should be double spaced, and so on.
- Next, if you want, you can decide how your data should be grouped in the report for subtotals. dBASE can figure out subtotals on any numerical field. For example, you might want to know the total wholesale cost just for receivers. You could also group all products from the same manufacturer together, and so forth.
- Then you select what data will appear in each column of the report, assign a column title, and indicate whether the column, if it's numerical, should be totaled at the bottom.
- Finally, you save the report file and run it.

6. So, getting back to our report, select *Options/Page title.* A box appears for you to type in the page title which will appear at the

top of each page of your report (though in this case we'll only have one page). Type in

Uncle Bob's Hi-Fi Inventory ↵

and press ^End to get out of the title box. Notice that only the first few words of the title fit in the *Options* box. That's OK. If you select *Page title* again, you will see that it's all there. All the default settings in the *Options* box look acceptable for now, so let's move on. The functions of all the options for each menu are listed in Appendix B. Except for those discussed in this chapter, you will find the dBASE III PLUS default values serve well for almost all purposes.

How to Set Up the Columns

We'll set up some subtotal groupings later on, so we can skip past the *Groups* menu for now.

To set up the columns in the report, select *Columns.* At this stage, you tell dBASE the sizes and contents of the columns that are to appear in your report. As for size, you may make a column as wide or as narrow as you wish. If the data in the field being displayed is too long to fit on one line, it will be wrapped around to the next line automatically. This may be acceptable for character fields, but not for numbers, obviously. Extra width will also allow for space between the columns in the report. With experimentation you will find the right column sizes to separate columns or bring them closer together in a way that appeals to you. Here's how to define the column sizes and contents.

1. *Contents* should be highlighted. Now press ↵. An arrow appears on the highlighted line, waiting for you to indicate what data you want listed in the first column of your report.
2. At this point you have two options. You can either type in a field name, or press F10 to see a field list and pick fields from it. For clarity, press F10. This way you can see how long each field is, which will help you in formatting the report. Your screen now looks like Figure 10.2.
3. Select BRAND. The fields box disappears.

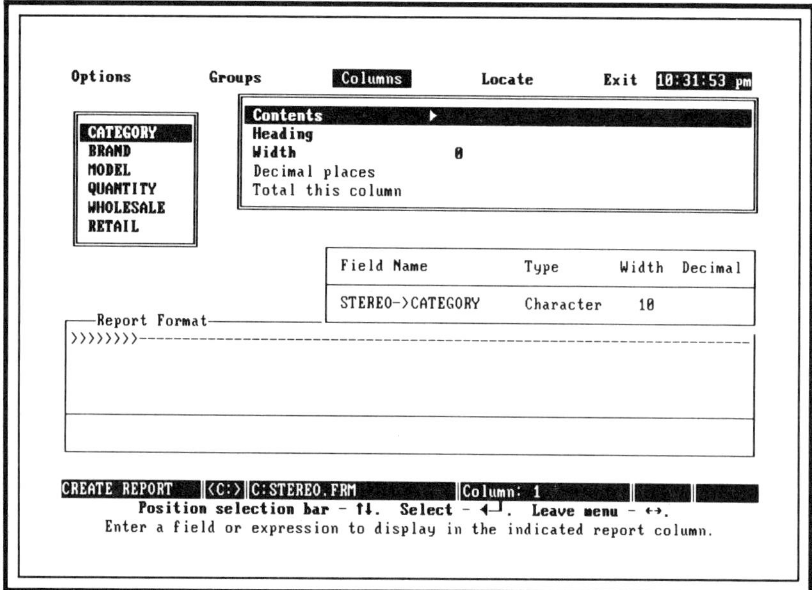

Figure 10.2: Defining the first column in the report

4. Since we want this column to contain only the contents of the BRANDS field, just press ↵ to complete the column contents definition. It is possible to construct more elaborate column contents by stuffing the data from several fields into one column or doing a calculation based on them. We will cover this in a bit.

5. Highlight *Heading* and press ↵. The arrow appears, and a box appears for you to type the heading into. Type in Brand for the column heading and then press ^End to save this heading. The heading box disappears, and your heading shows up on the highlighted line.

6. The column width and any decimal places are assumed by dBASE to be the size of the field or the size of the column heading, whichever is larger. In this case the field size is larger, so the column width is listed as 10. (You could type over the width, if you wished.) The last line in the column box pertains to totals. We will not be asking dBASE to Total up all the brand names, of course, so this finishes the first column's definition, as shown in Figure 10.3. The blank report form at the bottom of the screen now shows the

```
Options          Groups          Columns          Locate          Exit  10:33:19 pm

                        Contents                  BRAND
                        Heading                   Brand
                        Width                      10
                        Decimal places
                        Total this column

┌─Report Format──────────────────────────────────────────────────────────
│>>>>>>>>Brand         -----------------------------------------------------
│
│
├────────────────────────────────────────────────────────────────────────
│       XXXXXXXXXX
└────────────────────────────────────────────────────────────────────────
CREATE REPORT   <C:> C:STEREO.FRM                Column: 1
   Position selection bar - ↑↓.  Select - ←┘.  Prev/Next column - PgUp/PgDn.
     Enter up to four lines of text to display above the indicated column.
```

Figure 10.3: The first column defined

column heading "Brand" and the location and size (indicated by X's) of the column.

7. Press PgDn to begin defining the rest of the columns. Notice the Status Line inicates we are working on column 2. Define the remaining columns as you did the first one, but use the following information. And remember, you have to highlight each selection and press ↵ before dBASE III PLUS will accept your information, and you have to press ↵ again after entering each line of information. Also don't forget to press ^End to save each heading and to use the PgDn key to move ahead to the next column each time. (Keep your eye on the bottom two lines for help.)

Column 2	
Contents	CATEGORY
Heading	Category
Width	10
Decimal places	
Total this column	

Column 3	
Contents	MODEL
Heading	Model
Width	6
Decimal places	
Total this column	

Column 4	
Contents	QUANTITY
Heading	Quan.
Width	5
Decimal places	0
Total this column	Y

Note: For all numeric fields, dBASE assumes you want totals. But since we don't want totals for Wholesale and Retail, you'll have to turn *off* the totals for these columns. After entering the contents and heading, just highlight *Total this column* and press ↵ to set total to *NO*.

Column 5	
Contents	WHOLESALE
Heading	My Cost
Width	7
Decimal places	2
Total this column	No

Column 6	
Contents	RETAIL
Heading	Retail
Width	6
Decimal places	2
Total this column	No

Column 7	
Contents	QUANTITY*WHOLESALE
Heading	Invested
Width	9
Decimal places	2
Total this column	Y

Don't let that last one throw you. Usually, a column will contain data from one of your database fields. But it may also contain a value which is calculated by the computer from other numbers. Notice that column 7 in this report will contain the product of QUANTITY times WHOLESALE (the * symbol tells dBASE to multiply), which should reveal the amount of investment you have in each type of item. And since you are requesting a total for this column, the report will provide you with the total current investment for all the items in inventory.

8. Before saving the report form, let's add one more column. As mentioned earlier, this one is for displaying the percentage gross margin for each item (i.e. the markup as a percentage of the retail price). We can tell dBASE to calculate this figure with the following equation:

   ((Retail – Wholesale) / Retail) * 100

   So for column 8, use the following definition:

Contents	((Retail – Wholesale)/Retail)*100
Heading	Margin
Width	7
Decimal places	2
Total this column	No

9. After you hit the ↵ key to change the Y to a No on the last line of column 8, type the letter E. This selects the Exit menu. Now, to save your work onto the disk, you must select *Save*. This saves your report format and returns you to the Assistant or Dot prompt from which you can run the report.

How to View or Print the Report

1. To actually see the fruits of all this work, do one of the following:

   - From the Assistant, select *Retrieve/Report*. Select the drive and our report form, STEREO.FRM. Execute the command, and type N to the printer question (unless you have a printer attached and ready to go).
   - From the Dot prompt, type

   REPORT FORM STEREO ↵

or if you have a printer connected and want a paper printout

REPORT FORM STEREO TO PRINT ↵

2. In any case, here's what your report should show you:

Page No. 1
07/22/86

Uncle Bob's Hi-Fi Inventory

Brand	Category	Model	Quan.	My Cost	Retail	Invested	Margin
NIZO	RECEIVER	T-33	5	225.49	350.49	1127.45	35.66
NIZO	RECEIVER	T-35	4	312.00	425.25	1248.00	26.63
ACME	RECEIVER	R25-MT	13	19.99	49.99	259.87	60.01
NADIR	RECEIVER	2-CHP	50	12.95	29.99	647.50	56.82
RAZCO	SPEAKERS	L-55	30	199.00	249.00	5970.00	20.08
TALBEST	SPEAKERS	BG-20	6	250.00	350.88	1500.00	28.75
ROLLEM	TAPE DECK	CAS-3	10	125.65	212.99	1256.50	41.01
FLOWUTTER	TAPE DECK	WBL-5	5	149.33	250.77	746.65	40.45
XIRTAM	TURNTABLE	25-L	5	99.99	149.99	499.95	33.34
RALURIC	TURNTABLE	RND-1	3	595.00	850.00	1785.00	30.00
*** Total ***							
			131			15040.92	

This might seem like a big hassle for generating such a simple report. But remember, our database is not very extensive. If it were larger, this could be a real time-saver. Besides, next time you want this report, based on updated figures, all you have to do is select it.

Furthermore, this is just a sample of what you can get a report to do. You just have to ask the questions that interest you and create a report that answers them. Let's modify this report to answer a few more questions, this time electing to show subtotals. When selecting subtotals, it's important to understand that you're not selecting the field whose contents will be added up to arrive at the subtotal. You are indicating which records will be grouped together for the various subtotal calculations. You do that by telling dBASE which field to look at in order to round up records that have something in common. For example, say you want to see a subtotal of the inventory investment for each category of stereo equipment. In other words, the total invested for Receivers, Speakers,

Tape Decks, and Turntables, listed separately. So conceptually, here is how we want dBASE to group the records for subtotalling:

Brand	Category	Model	Quan.	My Cost	Retail	Invested	Margin
NIZO	RECEIVER	T-33	5	225.49	350.49	1127.45	35.66
NIZO	RECEIVER	T-35	4	312.00	425.25	1248.00	26.63
ACME	RECEIVER	R25-MT	13	19.99	49.99	259.87	60.01
NADIR	RECEIVER	2-CHP	50	12.95	29.99	647.50	56.82
RAZCO	SPEAKERS	L-55	30	199.00	249.00	5970.00	20.08
TALBEST	SPEAKERS	BG-20	6	250.00	350.88	1500.00	28.75
ROLLEM	TAPE DECK	CAS-3	10	125.65	212.99	1256.50	41.01
FLOWUTTER	TAPE DECK	WBL-5	5	149.33	250.77	746.65	40.45
XIRTAM	TURNTABLE	25-L	5	99.99	149.99	499.95	33.34
RALURIC	TURNTABLE	RND-1	3	595.00	850.00	1785.00	30.00

Obviously, the field we want to group on is CATEGORY. This is how you'd modify your report to calculate and display the subtotals:

1. From the Assistant, select *Modify/Report.*
2. Select the drive letter and the report name, STEREO.FRM.
3. When the Report screen comes up, select *Groups/Group on expression.*
4. The arrow appears, waiting for your input. Now you have to type in the name of the field on which the records will be grouped. In this case it's CATEGORY, since we want a subtotal for each different category. Type in

   CATEGORY ↵

5. Press the ↓ once to move down to *Group heading* and press ↵. Enter

   Figures for all ↵

6. Finally, let's do a little something to make the headings stand out a little more in this report. Let's modify the headings by putting a row

of equal signs (=) under them. Just select *Columns/Heading* for each column. The box with the heading appears. Press ↓ to move down to the second line of the heading, where you can enter the equal signs. Then press ^End to save that change. Do this for each column (via the PgDn key, remember?). This will have an underline effect on the headings.

7. Now save the report, and run it as before but make sure to turn your printer on and say Y to the printer question. If you don't have a printer, say N and watch closely as the report scrolls up your screen. This report is too long to fit on one screen.

```
Page No. 1
07/22/86
                     Uncle Bob's Hi-Fi Inventory

Brand       Category    Model   Quan. My Cost  Retail Invested Margin

** Figures for all RECEIVER
NIZO        RECEIVER    T-33        5  225.49  350.49  1127.45  35.66
NIZO        RECEIVER    T-35        4  312.00  425.25  1248.00  26.63
ACME        RECEIVER    R25-MT     13   19.99   49.99   259.87  60.01
NADIR       RECEIVER    2-CHP      50   12.95   29.99   647.50  56.82
** Subtotal **
                                   72                  3282.82

** Figures for all SPEAKERS
RAZCO       SPEAKERS    L-55       30  199.00  249.00  5970.00  20.08
TALBEST     SPEAKERS    BG-20       6  250.00  350.88  1500.00  28.75
** Subtotal **
                                   36                  7470.00

** Figures for all TAPE DECK
ROLLEM      TAPE DECK   CAS-3      10  125.65  212.99  1256.50  41.01
FLOWUTTER   TAPE DECK   WBL-5       5  149.33  250.77   746.65  40.45
** Subtotal **
                                   15                  2003.15

** Figures for all TURNTABLE
XIRTAM      TURNTABLE   25-L        5   99.99  149.99   499.95  33.34
RALURIC     TURNTABLE   RND-1       3  595.00  850.00  1785.00  30.00
** Subtotal **
                                    8                  2284.95
*** Total ***
                                  131                 15040.92
```

Other options for reports

The number of permutations on a possible report theme are virtually endless, of course. There are a few basic ones you could consider, however.

- You probably noticed that under *Groups* you could select *Summary report only.* If you set this option to YES, the details of each category would have been eliminated, with only the subtotals remaining. Here is how our report looks in the summary mode:

```
PAGE NO. 00001
                              Uncle Bob's Hi-Fi Inventory

Brand   Category   Model   Quan   Invested
=====   ========   =====   ====   ========

* Figures for all RECEIVER
** SUBTOTAL **
                            72     3282.82

* Figures for all SPEAKERS
** SUBTOTAL **
                            36     7470.00

* Figures for all TAPE DECK
** SUBTOTAL **
                            15     2003.15

* Figures for all TURNTABLE
** SUBTOTAL **
                             8     2284.95

** TOTAL **
                           131    15040.92
```

- The option, *Page eject after group* applies only to printing out your report on paper. With this option, you can print a separate page for each category (i.e. each subtotal).
- We didn't experiment with the *Locate* option from the Report menus. It simply lets you quickly get to a specific column to make modifications once you've defined it. This prevents having to use the PgDn or PgUp keys repetitively while in the the Column menu.
- You can put indexing and sorting to use with reports too. They will influence the order in which records are listed in the report. For example, you might want records to appear in alphabetical order

according to the brand name. Simply index on BRAND, activate your new index, and run the report.

- When you want to include subtotals in a report, be sure the file is either indexed or sorted on the field you are grouping on. (Our STEREO database was already sorted on Category, you might have noticed.) If you don't index or sort it, your subtotals will be a mess.
- If you want to make several different reports, all of which are similar, you can use the *Tools/Copy file* option or the DOS COPY command to make several copies of your original report form under a different name for each additional report. For example, in our case, the report name appears as STEREO.FRM in the directory. You'd then copy this file to STEREO1, then to STEREO2, then to STEREO3 (dBASE will put in the .FRM extension). Then use *Modify/Report* to alter each copy as you like. This avoids the repetitious task of typing in the field names, sizes and headings for each variant report.
- Finally, don't overlook using the *Build a search condition* option when running a report from the Assistant. For example, say you only wanted to see totals for Turntables, or for products from ACME. This option works with reports the same way you've already used it with List or Display. Just build the condition by selecting from the field list and using the comparison operators. From the Dot prompt, a typical command would be

  REPORT FORM STEREO FOR BRAND = 'ACME' ↵

As you can see, the Report generator is pretty powerful. With knowledge of only a few commands—Create, Append, and Report you can do really useful database work. And since you can create many report forms for each database, any number of applications can be run based on the same collection of information, eliminating duplication of effort.

11

Printing Mailing Labels

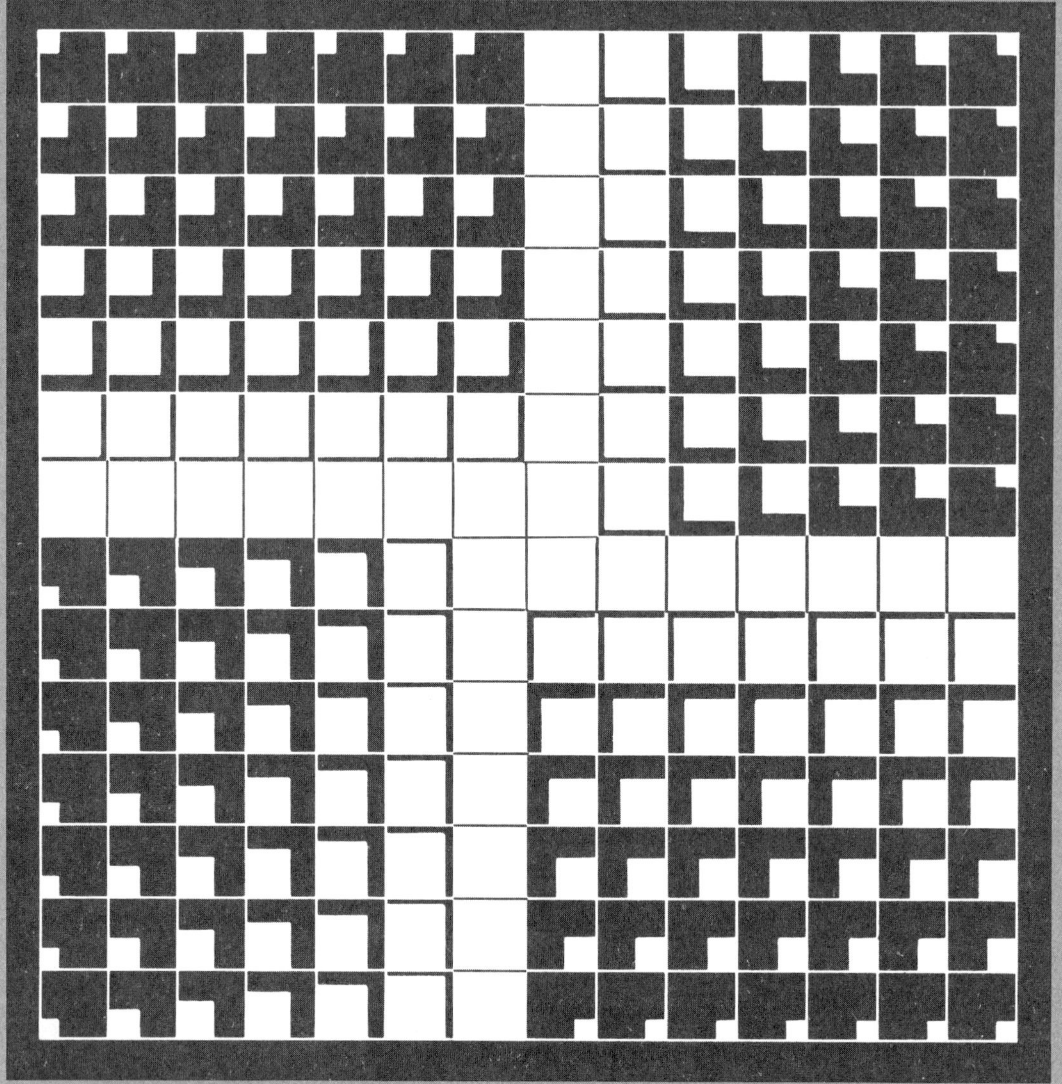

FEATURING:

standard labels;
custom formats;
printing out

A common use for a database is to create mailing labels for bulk mailings, one of the classic computerized time savers. dBASE III PLUS provides a built-in *label generator* that makes it easy to print addresses neatly onto various sizes of commercially available pressure-sensitive mailing labels. As many as four labels across the page can be printed, for use with wide label stock. Of course, for label printing of any magnitude, you'll need a printer with a *tractor* (sprockets) that can feed the labels accurately, since spacing and alignment are critical.

How to Prepare the Label Data

The first step is to open the database you plan to use for the labels and index it according to zip code, since that's how the U.S. Post Office requires bulk mailings to be sorted.

1. Open the PHONEBK database with no indexes.
2. Index it on ZIP. Call the index file ZIP.
3. Select *Create/Label.*
4. Select the drive, and call the label file MAILING.
5. Your screen now looks like Figure 11.1.

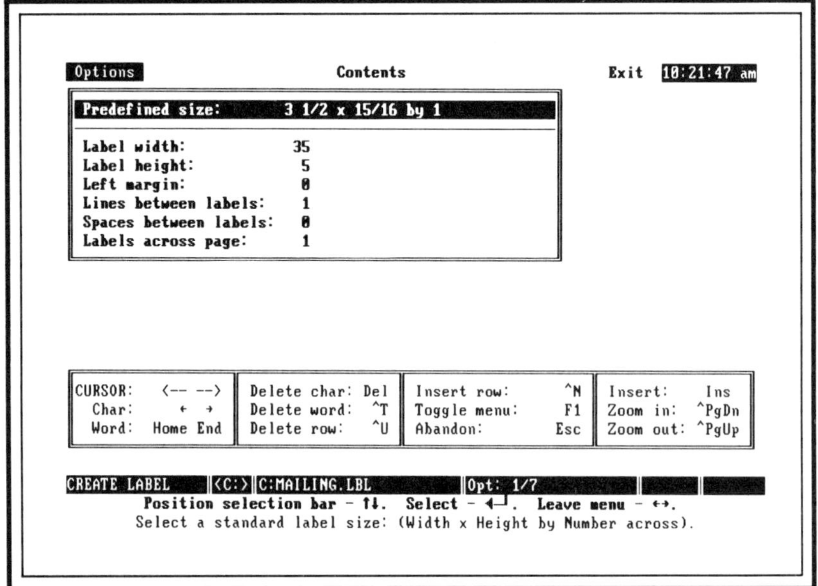

Figure 11.1: The *Label* Screen

As you can see, there are only two main menu selections you have to deal with here—*Options* and *Contents*. *Options* lets you select from five different predefined label formats. If none of these suit your needs, you can modify the label specifications. The six modifications you can make are explained in Table 11.1. However, for most popular label types, the five predefined sizes should suffice, and we will use one of them.

1. Highlight the top line of the *Options* menu, and press ←┘ several times. Notice that the Predefined size changes with each press.
2. For this example, we'll use 3 1/2 × 15/16 by 2 (the "by 2" means two labels across the page). Make sure this setting is selected.
3. Press → to exit the *Options* menu. The *Contents* menu appears. This is where we select which database fields we want printed on the labels.
4. Fill in lines 1 through 3 as they appear in Figure 11.2. Remember to press ←┘ after each entry, and use the ↓ to advance to the next line, otherwise your screen will start blinking when you try to type.

Option	***Meaning***
Label width	Number of characters across any one line of the label. Maximum is 120.
Label Height	Number of lines on one label, from 1 to 16.
Left margin	Number of spaces from the left edge of the backing paper to the first printed letter, from 0 to 250.
Lines between labels	Vertical distance, in blank lines, between two labels, from 0 to 16.
Spaces between labels	Number of spaces, horizontally, between two labels, from 0 to 120.
Labels across page	Number of labels across the page to be printed, from 1 to 15.

Table 11.1: Label options

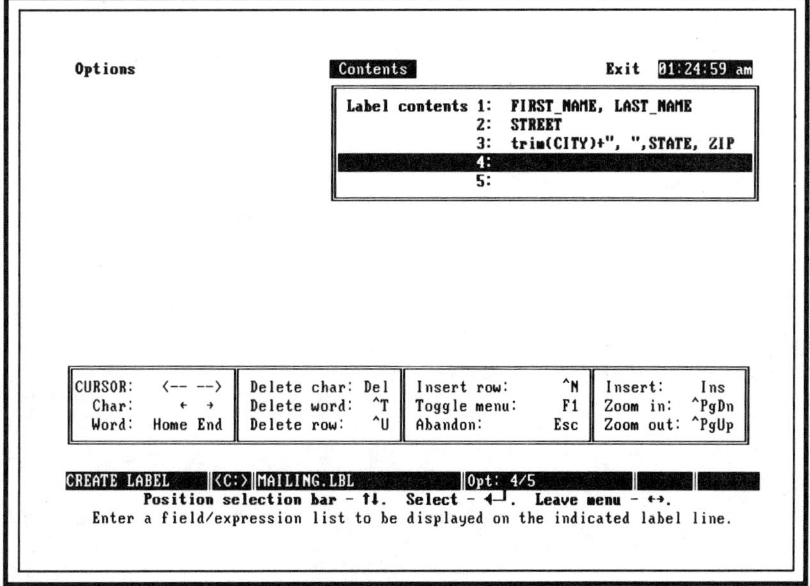

Figure 11.2: Filling in the mailing-label contents

Now for an explanation of what you just entered. Since we want the FIRST_NAME and LAST_NAME fields to be printed on the first line of each label, both of those field names go on line 1. The comma will not appear on the labels; it is necessary for separating the two field names.

On the next line, we want the street address to appear, thus the STREET field name.

Line 3 is the tricky one. We want CITY, STATE, and ZIP all to appear on this line. Here's the problem. Since we want the state to appear just a few spaces after the city, we have to cut out any extra spaces in the CITY field before printing the label. Otherwise the city and state line might look like

```
Paris             , TX 55493
```

instead of

```
Paris, TX 55493
```

The section of line 3 that reads

```
Trim(CITY) + ", "
```

strips off any extra spaces in the CITY field not used up by the city's name. It then adds (+) a comma and one space to separate the city and the state. The last part of the line tacks the zip code on the end.

One more rule. Notice that all the "elements" (field names, and quote mark pairs) are separated by commas. The commas are absolutely required. If you skip one, or put it in the wrong place, dBASE will give you an error message when you try to print the labels.

Syntax error in contents expression

How to Print the Labels

To save your work and print the labels out:

1. Press the ↵ key until the arrow disappears.
2. Select *Exit/save.*
3. Select *Retrieve/Label.*

4. Choose the drive and the label file name (MAILING.LBL).
5. Notice the Command Line for future reference, in case you want to run mailing labels from the Dot prompt.
6. Select *Execute the command,* but notice that you could stipulate search criteria at this stage, such as only people in a certain zip code range.
7. Prepare your printer. It's best to do a trial run on regular paper in case things aren't aligned right the first time. Then compare the print-out to the labels you have. If things are wrong, you can always press the Esc key to stop the printing.
8. Answer Y to the printer question if you intend to print. The labels should begin rolling out.

```
Adriator Wegwo              MARIAN DAVIES
158 Snorewell Blvd.         344 MARKET ST
Sleepyhollow, CA 02587      NEW YORK, NY 10021

Randy Batterydown           Aretha Phillipson
495 Anode St.               999 Motor City Ave.
Carbondale, IL 30129        Detroit, MI 39482

Hank Davies                 Marcel Phillip
333 33rd. St.               456 Fresno St.
West Goshen, SD 43312       Paris, TX 55493

Nimrod Neverburger          Wackford Squeers
77 Easy Street              374 Tipplemeyer Ave.
Khozad, CA 89751            Cornmont, CA 94709

Valery Kuletski
451 Fahrenheit Ct.
Oakland, CA 95420
```

Modifying a label format

Just as with our report forms, you can modify a label file quite easily. Just select *Modify/Label* and pick the right file. It's not uncommon for labels to give you some problems first time around, and it may take several tries until they come out right. Just keep modifying and trying again. Also, don't overlook the possibility that switches on your printer are not set properly, especially if you are getting blank lines between every printed line or if the labels are coming out too wide. In the first instance, it may be that the printer's "local line feed" switch is set ON. Try turning it OFF. If you are having the latter problem, your printer may be set for too few characters per inch (e.g. 10 instead of 12), forcing the printing to be too wide. Reset to 12 and try again.

12
Working with Numbers

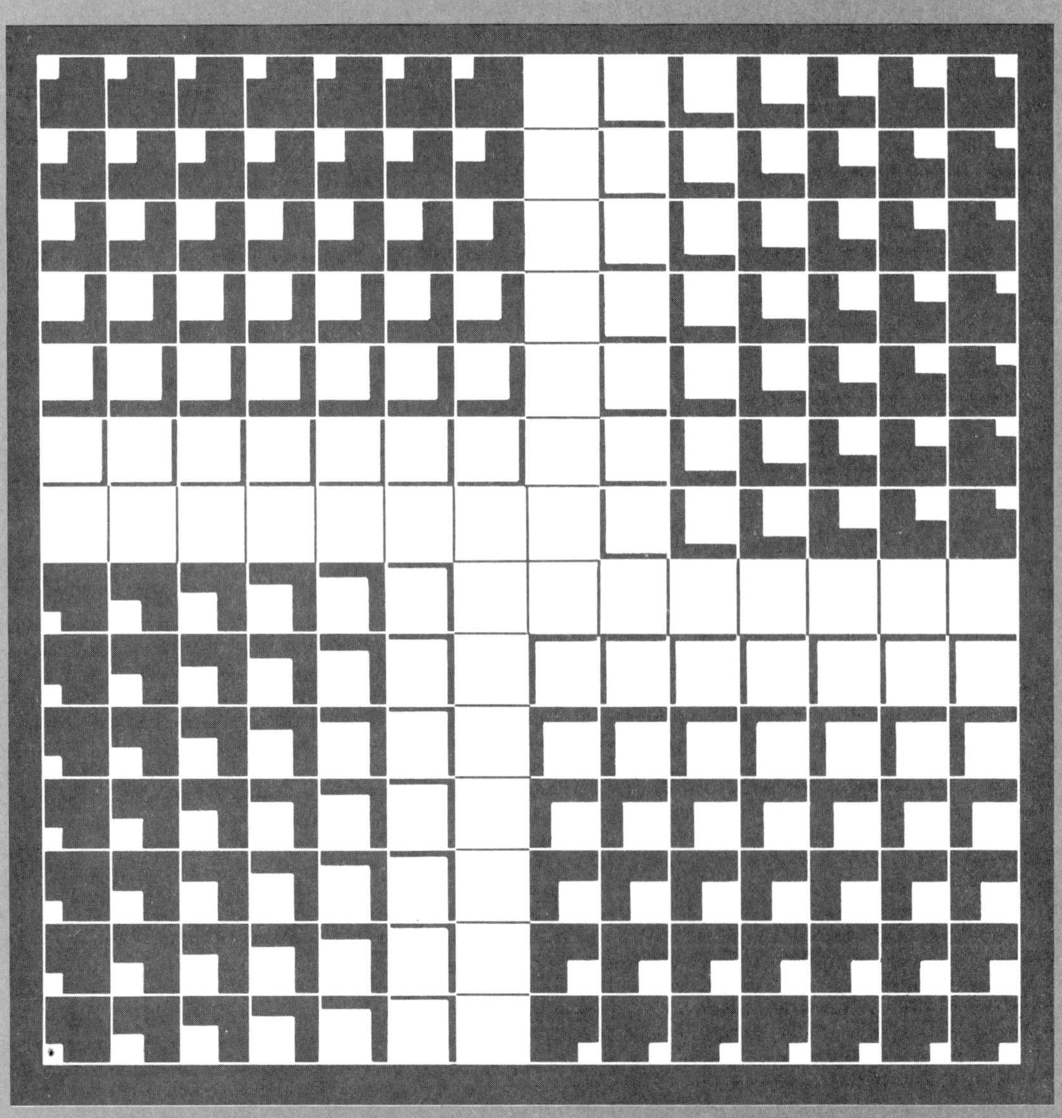

field arithmetic;
comparisons; sums;
averages; counts;
Replacing data

We've already dealt with numerical fields to some extent in previous chapters, using the CAMPLIST and STEREO databases. In this chapter, we'll cover some more techniques for managing numerical fields to your best advantage.

dBASE III PLUS allows you to ask some pretty sophisticated questions about the information in your database. Some of this capability was made evident when the List and Display commands were covered in Chapter 7. But in addition to what you've gleaned already, there are a few other commands pertaining to numbers and numerical fields which can be useful. So now let's consider asking dBASE to do a little more work for us. For instance, consider our CAMPLIST database for a moment. Even though it holds only a modicum of data, you still might want to know the following:

- Without running a Report, what do all the costs add up to?
- What is the total weight of all the items?
- Which of the items cost more than $20.00?
- Which items weigh less than 20 pounds, cost more than $12.50, and are owned by Renee?

These are examples of queries (requests for specific data) that dBASE can easily resolve for you with just a slight bit of work on your part. But in order to go any further in this direction, we'll have to take a closer look at some of the built-in features of dBASE III PLUS.

How to Use Operators

One set of features that can help out is called the *operators.* They are called operators because they operate on information in your database, producing a result. The operators that have relevence to numerical data manipulation are the Arithmetic and Comparitive operators.

Arithmetic operators

For many people, arithmetic operations are the more familiar of these two. Saying that dBASE has arithmetic operators is really a fancy way of saying it has a built in four-function calculator with tons of memory for storing its input and answers. You can add, subtract, multiply, or divide, just as if you were using a calculator, or you can ask dBASE questions about your databases using these operators.

Let's give the calculator mode a try. (The / means "divided by," the * means "multiplied by," and the parentheses are used for grouping numbers together before dividing or multiplying. Also, the question marks in the following commands mean "What is the value of?").

1. Get to the Dot prompt, since you can't do this from the Assistant.
2. Type in each line that starts with a question mark. The following line in each case is dBASE's answer.

```
 ? 3+5 ↵
8

 ? 5/2.5 ↵
2.00

 ? (3+2)+(14-10) ↵
9

 ? (3+2)+(14-10)-((12.56+3.5)*(126.23/25)) ↵
-72.0902
```

Were you surprised by how quickly your computer (and dBASE) arrived at that last result? Good evidence of the fact that computers are twiddling their thumbs most of the time. You can tell by the result of that last calculation, should you care to analyze it, that the numbers stored in the innermost parentheses are processed first. Using parentheses is often necessary for obtaining proper results.

Now, instead of just using meaningless numbers for our calculations, let's use data in the CAMPLIST database. To experiment with the following commands, open your CAMPLIST file with no indexes, and list the data.

```
Record#  ITEM        WEIGHT   COST  OWNER
      1  Back pack       10  65.00  Rich
      2  Stove           25  85.00  Rich
      3  Tent            12  62.33  Lisa B.
      4  Food            30  45.27  Group
      5  Rain gear        7  12.95  Renee
      6  Flashlight       2   7.50  Jean
      7  Hammock          5  15.00  John
GOTO 4 ↵
DISPLAY ↵
Record#  ITEM        WEIGHT   COST  OWNER
      4  Food            30  45.27  Group
 ? COST+WEIGHT ↵
75.27
 ? COST-WEIGHT ↵
15.27
 ? COST/WEIGHT ↵
1.51
```

Well, adding cost and weight together doesn't make much sense, but as long as both fields are numerical in type, dBASE lets you do it. Dividing cost by weight, however, gives you the price per pound that the group paid for food—something a tad more practical. Anyway, you get the idea.

Notice that the calculation is only performed on the current record which, in this case, was record 4. Repositioning the pointer would give us different results.

Once we get a little more into this you will see that this type of operation can be a real time saver. We'll use the STEREO store inventory database to put the arithmetic operators to a more practical use a little later.

Comparison operators

Recall that comparison operators compare two pieces of data and produce a result. You've used the *Equal To* operator several times already, when looking for names of people in the PHONEBK database. In those cases you were comparing *character strings,* not numbers. A character string is a series of non-numerical information such as letters. But comparitive operators can also be used to compare numbers. "Is X larger than Y?" is an example of a numerical comparison operation. Here's the complete list of comparison operators available in dBASE and their symbols:

Symbol	***Meaning***
=	Equal To
<=	Less Than or Equal To
<	Less Than
>	Greater Than
>=	Greater Than or Equal To
<>	Not Equal To

You may recognize this as the same list that appears in the Comparison box when you build a search condition from the Assistant. You may also recall having used the < and the > operators for selecting a zip code range earlier. But what about <= and >=? These operators work similarly, but allow you to construct a search condition that includes the endpoints of a numerical range. For example, using the STEREO database, say we wanted to see the wholesale price of all products costing $250 or more:

1. Get to the Assistant.
2. Open the STEREO database.
3. Select *Retrieve/List/Execute the command.* You see

Record#	CATEGORY	BRAND	MODEL	QUANTITY	WHOLESALE	RETAIL
1	RECEIVER	NIZO	T-33	5	225.49	350.49
2	RECEIVER	NIZO	T-35	4	312.00	425.25
3	RECEIVER	ACME	R25-MT	13	19.99	49.99
4	RECEIVER	NADIR	2-CHP	50	12.95	29.99
5	SPEAKERS	RAZCO	L-55	30	199.00	249.00
6	SPEAKERS	TALBEST	BG-20	6	250.00	350.88
7	TAPE DECK	ROLLEM	CAS-3	10	125.65	212.99
8	TAPE DECK	FLOWUTTER	WBL-5	5	149.33	250.77
9	TURNTABLE	XIRTAM	25-L	5	99.99	149.99
10	TURNTABLE	RALURIC	RND-1	3	595.00	850.00

4. Select *Retrieve/List/Build a search condition.*
5. Select WHOLESALE from the fields list.

6. Select >= *Greater Than or Equal To.*

7. Type in 250.00.

8. Select *No more conditions,* then *Execute the command.* You will see

Record#	CATEGORY	BRAND	MODEL	QUANTITY	WHOLESALE	RETAIL
2	RECEIVER	NIZO	T-35	4	312.00	425.25
6	SPEAKERS	TALBEST	BG-20	6	250.00	350.88
10	TURNTABLE	RALURIC	RND-1	3	595.00	850.00

Notice that record 6, the Talbest speakers, was listed because the wholesale price is exactly 250.00. The plain *Greater Than* operator would have excluded it.

Now for the <> *Not Equal To* operator. This one might seem a bit strange at first. When would you want to know that an item or value *isn't* equal to something? Imagine you want to contact all of your clients *except* those living in a specific zip code, 89751, since you've already done a mailing to that area:

1. Open the PHONEBK database.

2. Select *Retrieve/List.*

3. Create a field list including FIRST_NAME, LAST_NAME, STREET, and ZIP.

4. Execute the command.

Record#	FIRST_NAME	LAST_NAME	STREET	ZIP
1	Wackford	Squeers	374 Tipplemeyer Ave.	94709
2	Hank	Davies	333 33rd. St.	43312
3	Adriator	Wegwo	158 Snorewell Blvd.	02587
4	Aretha	Phillipson	999 Motor City Ave.	39482
5	Randy	Batterydown	495 Anode St.	30129
6	Nimrod	Neverburger	77 Easy Street	89751
7	Marcel	Phillip	456 Fresno St.	55493
8	Valery	Kuletski	451 Fahrenheit Ct.	95420
9	MARIAN	DAVIES	344 MARKET ST	10021

This shows us all the records, 1 through 9, just for illustration. Note that Nimrod lives in the 89751 zip code area.

5. Now to eliminate the undesirable record from a listing, repeat steps 2 and 3.

6. Select *Build a search condition* and choose ZIP as the field.
7. Select <> as the operator.
8. Type in 89751 ↵.
9. Select *No more conditions.*
10. Execute the command.

Record#	FIRST_NAME	LAST_NAME	STREET	ZIP
1	Wackford	Squeers	374 Tipplemeyer Ave.	94709
2	Hank	Davies	333 33rd. St.	43312
3	Adriator	Wegwo	158 Snorewell Blvd.	02587
4	Aretha	Phillipson	999 Motor City Ave.	39482
5	Randy	Batterydown	495 Anode St.	30129
7	Marcel	Phillip	456 Fresno St.	55493
8	Valery	Kuletski	451 Fahrenheit Ct.	95420
9	MARIAN	DAVIES	344 MARKET ST	10021

Notice that we successfully eliminated Nimrod, record 6, from this listing, because his zip code is 89751.

If you do this from the Dot prompt, remember to use single quotes around the zip code, since the ZIP field is actually a Character field, not a real Numeric field. (For Numeric fields, simply forgo the quotes.)

How to Use Sum

When it comes to numbers, another useful option is *Sum.* This command is similar to the arithmetic operator **+**, which we used earlier, except that it adds information from a number of different records into one total. The + operator only referred to fields in the current record, but sum operates on the whole database. For instance, say we wanted to add up the cost of all the items in the CAMPLIST. Try these examples from the Dot prompt, for practice. Explanations follow.

```
USE CAMPLIST ↵
LIST ↵
```

Record#	ITEM	WEIGHT	COST	OWNER
1	Back pack	10	65.00	Rich
2	Stove	25	85.00	Rich

```
3    Tent          12   62.33   Lisa B.
4    Food          30   45.27   Group
5    Rain gear      7   12.95   Renee
6    Flashlight     2    7.50   Jean
7    Hammock        5   15.00   John
```

```
SUM COST ←┘
  7 records summed
COST
   293.05

SUM WEIGHT ←┘
  7 records summed
WEIGHT
   91

SUM WEIGHT,COST ←┘
  7 records summed
WEIGHT COST
   91 293.05

SUM WEIGHT + COST ←┘
  7 records summed
WEIGHT + COST
   384.05
```

The first command simply summed up the COST column. The second command did the same for the WEIGHT column. In the third example, we executed both commands at once, using a comma to separate the two field names. Finally, the last command—using a + instead of a comma—resulted in one large number which is the sum of all the weights added to the sum of all the costs.

For a more complex example, let's do something a bit more practical, this time with the STEREO inventory database. Suppose you want to see quickly, without running a report, what the total amount of capital investment you have tied up in inventory is. That is, what'd you like to see is the wholesale cost of each item times the quantity of that item on hand, for all items. Then you'd want all those subtotals added for a grand total. Here's how to do it using *Sum*. (We'll clear the screen first, with *Clear.* You may also want to list contents of STEREO before executing these commands.)

```
CLEAR ←┘
USE STEREO ←┘
```

```
SUM QUANTITY * WHOLESALE ↵
 10 records summed
QUANTITY * WHOLESALE
        15040.92
```

The first command is a new one. It simply erases the entire screen. As for the results, it looks like you have over $15,000 tied up. Let's see how much you have tied up in receivers alone:

```
SUM QUANTITY*WHOLESALE FOR CATEGORY = 'RECEIVER' ↵
 4 records summed
QUANTITY * WHOLESALE
        3282.82
```

Most of the above examples could have been done from the Assistant too, with the exclusion of those using the arithmetic operators. *Sum* is the fifth option on the Retrieve menu. To arrive at a sum from that mode, try this. It amounts to using the *Sum* command with no further specifications:

1. Get into Assist mode.
2. Select *Retrieve/Sum.*
3. Execute the command.
4. You see this:

```
 10 records summed
QUANTITY  WHOLESALE  RETAIL
     131    1989.40  2919.35
```

Using the *Sum* option alone instructs dBASE to calculate a sum for each Numeric field in the database. Of course, you could have constructed a field list, built a search condition, and so on from the Assistant, just as you did from the Dot prompt, to get the same results.

How to Calculate Averages

Just below *Sum* in the Retrieve menu is *Average.* As the name implies, *Average* produces the arithmetic mean of one or more fields in the currently open database.

1. Select *Retrieve/Average.*
2. Execute the command.
3. You see:

10 records averaged
QUANTITY WHOLESALE RETAIL
13 198.94 291.94

Since you did not construct a field list, averages were calculated for each Numeric field. Now let's try something more practical. Suppose you're considering carrying a new brand of receiver, but the local sales representative for the line seems to be quoting too high a price for the product. A quick check of your database displays the average price you are currently paying for receivers:

1. Select *Retrieve/Average.*
2. Select *Construct a field list.*
3. Choose WHOLESALE.
4. Select *Build a search condition.*
5. Select CATEGORY from the field list.
6. Select = *Equal To* as the comparison operator.
7. Type in RECEIVER ↵.
8. Select *No more conditions* and execute the command. dBASE responds

4 records averaged
WHOLESALE
142.61

You could also have achieved this from the Dot prompt by typing

AVERAGE WHOLESALE FOR CATEGORY = 'RECEIVER' ↵

How to Make Counts

Occassionally, instead of adding or averaging numbers, you'll just want to know how many records there are in your database that meet a certain requirement. Say you have a mailing list, and are planning to print mailing labels from it. You may need to know the number of labels that will be printed for a specific zip code or range of zip codes, in order to calculate the number of labels to buy and what the postage is going to be. The combinations are almost limitless, but if and when you need to know "How many...?", the answer usually rests with the *Count* option.

Try this, now using the CAMPLIST database:

1. Select *Retrieve/Count.*
2. Execute the command. dBASE responds

   7 records

Since we didn't stipulate any particulars, dBASE just counted the number of records in the database. Now let's do some more complex counts. I'll show them as executed from the Dot prompt, but you can do them from the Assistant if you wish.

```
    COUNT FOR WEIGHT <50 .AND. WEIGHT >20 ↵
2 records

    COUNT FOR COST <13.00 .AND. WEIGHT >30 ↵
No records

    COUNT FOR OWNER = 'Rich' ↵
2 records
```

Another use for *Count* is to report how many records have been marked for deletion. This one can only be done from the Dot prompt. Try this to see:

```
GOTO 3 ↵
DELETE NEXT 2 ↵
   2 records deleted

COUNT FOR DELETED( ) ↵
   2 records
```

Getting back to the label counting idea, the typical format for figuring the number of people in a given zip code area (say, in the 90000s) would be:

```
COUNT FOR ZIP >= 90000 .AND. ZIP <= 99999
```

However, dBASE will issue an error message—"Data type mismatch"—if you had tried this command with our PHONEBK database. This is because the <= and >= operators are attempting to do a numerical comparison on a Character field. If your zip code field is a Character rather than Numeric field, replace the word "ZIP" (assuming that's your zip code field name) with "VAL(ZIP)". This converts the Character field data into a numerical value temporarily while performing the comparisons. Thus the command would be:

```
COUNT FOR VAL(ZIP) >= 90000 .AND. VAL(ZIP) <= 99999
```

How to Use Arithmetic Operators with Replace

One more trick with numbers. You can tell dBASE to fill a given field in each record of a database with the results of a mathematical calculation based on other fields in the same record. An example will illustrate this. Recall that our STEREO database file has these two fields:

QUANTITY WHOLESALE

Now, suppose we wanted to add another field, INVESTED, which displays the capital tied up in inventory for each product. This figure would be derived by multiplying QUANTITY by WHOLESALE. Remember from Chapter 10 that we actually included this calculated figure in a report. However, it wasn't stored in the database file—it only appeared in the report. Now, instead of letting dBASE forget that number, let's pop it into a new field so you can look at it later.

1. Get back to the Assistant.
2. Open the STEREO database. (No indexes.)
3. Select *Modify/Database file.* Add a field at the end to achieve the structure shown:

	Field Name	Type	Width	Dec
1	CATEGORY	Character	10	
2	BRAND	Character	10	
3	MODEL	Character	6	
4	QUANTITY	Numeric	2	0

5	WHOLESALE	Numeric	6	2
6	RETAIL	Numeric	6	2
7	INVESTED	Numeric	7	2

4. Save the new structure.
5. Select *Update/Replace.*
6. Select INVESTED as the field to do the replacement into.
7. Type in

   QUANTITY*WHOLESALE ↵

8. Press → to leave the fields list. (The fields lists appeared again to allow you the option of stipulating an additional field to do a replacement on if you wanted to. But we're only replacing in a single field now.)
9. Now select *Specify scope* from the "execute" box, and choose *ALL,* since we want to do the *Replace* process for all the records in the database.
10. Execute the command. dBASE responds:

    10 records replaced

11. To see the effect, list the file contents.

Record#	CATEGORY	BRAND	MODEL	QUANTITY	WHOLESALE	RETAIL	INVESTED
1	RECEIVER	NIZO	T-33	5	225.49	350.49	1127.50
2	RECEIVER	NIZO	T-35	4	312.00	425.25	1248.00
3	RECEIVER	ACME	R25-MT	13	19.99	49.99	259.87
4	RECEIVER	NADIR	2-CHP	50	12.95	29.99	647.50
5	SPEAKERS	RAZCO	L-55	30	199.00	249.00	5970.00
6	SPEAKERS	TALBEST	BG-20	6	250.00	350.88	1500.00
7	TAPE DECK	ROLLEM	CAS-3	10	125.65	212.99	1256.50
8	TAPE DECK	FLOWUTTER	WBL-5	5	149.33	250.77	746.65
9	TURNTABLE	XIRTAM	25-L	5	99.99	149.99	499.95
10	TURNTABLE	RALURIC	RND-1	3	595.00	850.00	1785.00

12. From the Dot prompt, the command would have been

    REPLACE ALL INVESTED WITH QUANTITY*WHOLESALE ↵

You may have noticed a discrepancy if you compare this line with that generated by the Assistant. The Assistant put the word ALL at the end of the command. It works either way, but it makes more sense where I put it.

Incidentally, should you like to see a listing without the record numbers taking up space on the screen and confusing things, put the word OFF at the end of any *List* or *Display* command. This supresses the record number. For example:

LIST BRAND, MODEL, QUANTITY, INVESTED OFF ↵

BRAND	MODEL	QUANTITY	INVESTED
NIZO	T-33	5	1127.50
NIZO	T-35	4	1248.00
ACME	R25-MT	13	259.87
NADIR	2-CHP	50	647.50
RAZCO	L-55	30	5970.00
TALBEST	BG-20	6	1500.00
ROLLEM	CAS-3	10	1256.50
FLOWUTTER	WBL-5	5	746.65
XIRTAM	25-L	5	499.95
RALURIC	RND-1	3	1785.00

Note: This can only be done from the Dot prompt.

13 Working with Dates

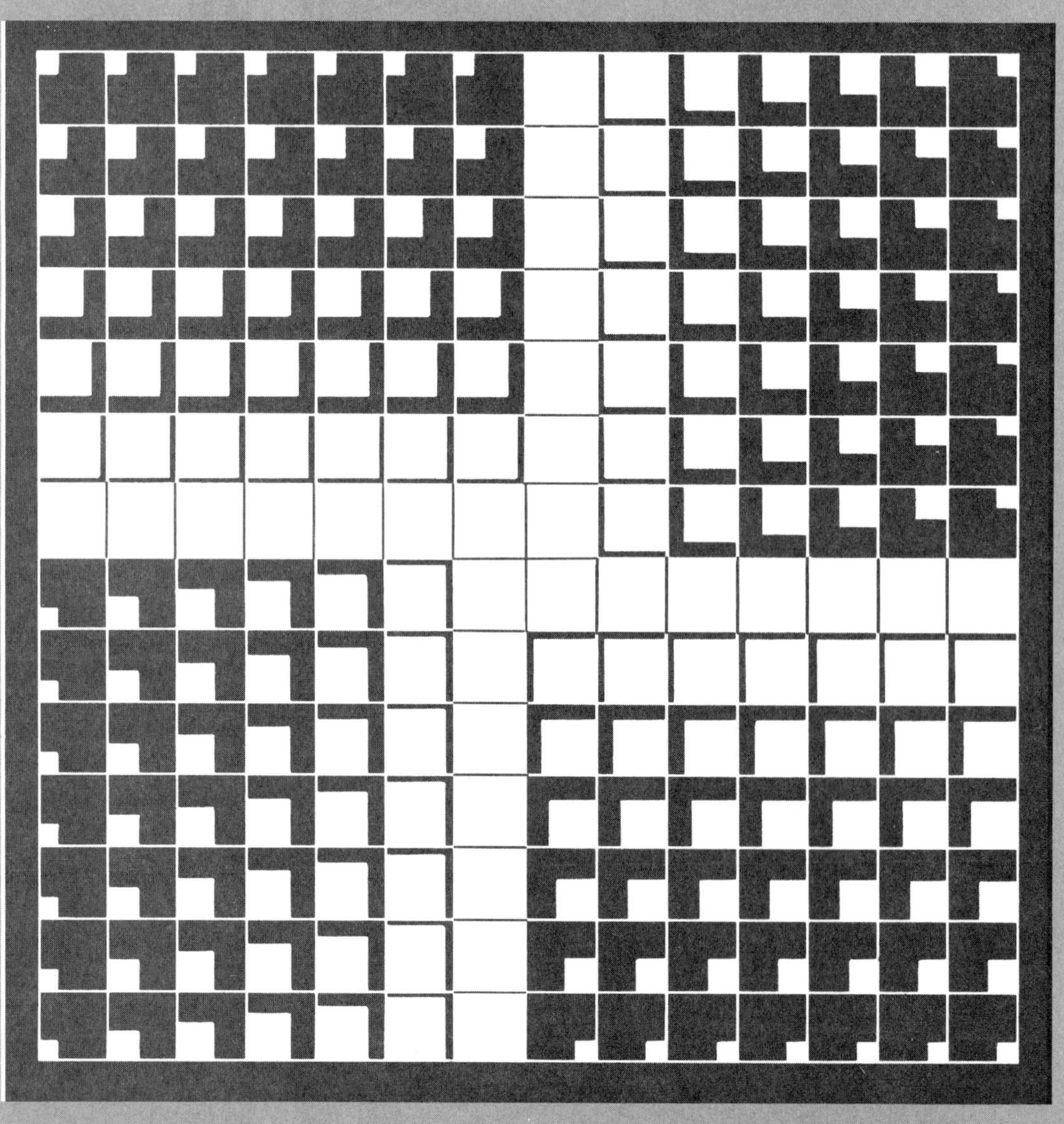

FEATURING:

Date fields; Date conditions, functions, calculations, and ordering

Next to numbers, dates are often the most important type of information in many business databases. Whether you're keeping track of sales, payables and receivables, clients, or project scheduling, you'll often want to store and retrieve information covering a certain period of time. Unfortunately, although dates are fairly easy for us humans to deal with, computers occasionally need a helping hand. That is why dBASE has a specific field type dedicated to dates only. Additionally, dBASE has numerous tools, called *functions,* for manipulating dates. Together, these make it possible to perform a variety of calculations and retrievals based on time periods.

How to Use Date Fields

Date fields are always eight spaces long (two for the / marks). Dates may be as early as 01/01/01 A.D. As it arrives from the publisher in the U.S., dBASE III PLUS is set to accept and display dates in the format mm/dd/yy (month/day/year). This can be changed however, for use in other countries or by people who prefer other arrangements. This must be done from the Dot prompt. Type

SET DATE *country* ↵

where *country* is one of the words in the left column below. The right column shows the effect.

AMERICAN	mm/dd/yy
ANSI	yy.mm.dd
BRITISH	dd/mm/yy
FRENCH	dd/mm/yy
GERMAN	dd.mm.yy
ITALIAN	dd-mm-yy

Normally, the first two digits of the century are left off of dates. Thus, 1986 appears as 86. This can be remedied, for use with other centuries, by issuing the command

```
SET CENTURY ON ↵
```

Typing OFF in place of ON reverses the effect.

Adding a Date field

Before we can experiment with dates, we'll need something to work with. Let's add a Date field to the STEREO database to store the date on which each product was last ordered.

1. Open the STEREO data file.
2. Select *Modify/Database file.*
3. Add an eighth field called LAST_ORDER. Make it a Date field. dBASE fills in the width.
4. Now eliminate field 7, INVESTED, since we don't need that anymore. Position the cursor the word INVESTED and press ^U.
5. Save the modified structure by pressing ^W or ^End followed by ↵. Your structure should now look like this:

	Field Name	Type	Width	Dec
1	CATEGORY	Character	10	
2	BRAND	Character	10	
3	MODEL	Character	6	
4	QUANTITY	Numeric	2	0
5	WHOLESALE	Numeric	6	2
6	RETAIL	Numeric	6	2
7	LAST_ORDER	Date	8	

6. Select *Update/Browse* and move to the first record in the file.

7. Move the cursor over to the LAST_ORDER field, using ^F.

8. Now, just for fun, try typing the date 15/15/86 into the field. What happens?

   Invalid date. (Press SPACE)

   dBASE is smart enough to know there isn't a fifteenth month. Press the space bar, as the message suggests.

9. Now go ahead and enter the rest of the last-order dates to match the listing below. It should be easy, since the cursor just steps down to each subsequent record's Date field after you enter each date. Notice that the cursor jumps over the / marks automatically too.

CATEGORY--	BRAND------	MODEL-	QUANTITY	WHOLESALE	RETAIL	LAST_ORDER
RECEIVER	NIZO	T-33	5	225.49	350.49	01/12/86
RECEIVER	NIZO	T-35	4	312.00	425.25	01/12/86
RECEIVER	ACME	R25-MT	13	19.99	49.99	05/15/86
RECEIVER	NADIR	2-CHP	50	12.95	29.99	03/06/53
SPEAKERS	RAZCO	L-55	30	199.00	249.00	03/01/85
SPEAKERS	TALBEST	BG-20	6	250.00	350.88	07/13/86
TAPE DECK	ROLLEM	CAS-3	10	125.65	212.99	09/01/86
TAPE DECK	FLOWUTTER	WBL-5	5	149.33	250.77	09/15/86
TURNTABLE	XIRTAM	25-L	5	99.99	149.99	02/29/84
TURNTABLE	RALURIC	RND-1	3	595.00	850.00	10/01/86

Using the Date field for conditional searching

OK. Now let's do some listings, based on dates. How about checking to see if there are any items that were ordered in 1985 and haven't been ordered since?

1. Select *Retrieve/List/Build a search condition.*

2. Select LAST_ORDER from the field list. (Incidentally, you can get down to LAST_ORDER by pressing ↑ once, rather than ↓ several times.)

3. Select < *Less Than.*

4. Type in 01/01/86. (You have to enter the / marks here.)

5. Select *Combine with .AND.*

6. Select LAST_ORDER from the fields list again.
7. Select > *Greater Than.*
8. Type in 12/31/84.
9. Select *No more conditions.*
10. Execute the command and see

```
SPEAKERS RAZCO L-55          30       199.00  249.00  03/01/85
```

In a nutshell, what we did here was to say, "Show me all the records whose dates fall between December 31, 1984 and January 1, 1986. This technique could be used to select records for quarterly sales figures, tax preparation, or what have you. This type of search condition, using date fields, is particularly useful when printing reports. As long as you have a date field in your file, you can print out a report for say, first quarter sales of 1986.

How to Use Date Functions from the Dot Prompt

dBASE III PLUS has a few more built-in tools for manipulating dates. These are called *functions.* Table 13.1 is a list of the functions, with an example after each one. You will see how to use them in a moment.

Function	*Effect*
DOW	The day of the week in numbers (Sunday = 1)
CDOW	The day of the week in characters (Friday)
DAY	The day of the month (03)
MONTH	The month in numbers (1-12)
CMONTH	The month in characters (March)
YEAR	The year (1986)
DATE()	The current system date

Table 13.1: Date functions

The value of these functions lies in the fact that they can be used in conjunction with Date fields to create queries. This allows you to specify more complex date search conditions. Try these examples to see. (These functions can be used only from the Dot prompt, so leave the Assistant for now.)

1. Suppose you only wanted to see orders in the STEREO database that were placed on Fridays. You'd apply the DOW (day of the week) function to our Date field, LAST_ORDER, and specify 6 as the day (remember that Sunday is 1) Try it.

   LIST FOR DOW(LAST_ORDER) = 6 ↵

   dBASE responds

Record#	CATEGORY	BRAND	MODEL	QUANTITY	WHOLESALE	RETAIL	LAST_ORDER
4	RECEIVER	NADIR	2-CHP	50	12.95	29.99	03/06/53
5	SPEAKERS	RAZCO	L-55	30	199.00	249.00	03/01/85

   The command formula may seem a little foreign at first, but actually it makes perfect sense. Think of the last command this way: "List a record if the day-of-the-week of the last-order date was equal to the sixth day of the week (Friday)."

2. Let's try the same thing using the name of the day, rather than it's number. We'll use the second function listed in the table: CDOW.

   LIST FOR CDOW(LAST_ORDER) = 'Friday' ↵

   dBASE responds just as before:

Record#	CATEGORY	BRAND	MODEL	QUANTITY	WHOLESALE	RETAIL	LAST_ORDER
4	RECEIVER	NADIR	2-CHP	50	12.95	29.99	03/06/53
5	SPEAKERS	RAZCO	L-55	30	199.00	249.00	03/01/85

3. OK, let's try another one. How about orders placed on the 15th of any month?

   LIST FOR DAY(LAST_ORDER) = 15 ↵

Record#	CATEGORY	BRAND	MODEL	QUANTITY	WHOLESALE	RETAIL	LAST_ORDER
3	RECEIVER	ACME	R25-MT	13	19.99	49.99	05/15/86
8	TAPE DECK	FLOWUTTER	WBL-5	5	149.33	250.77	09/15/86

4. Now, for all orders placed in March of any year:

LIST FOR MONTH(LAST_ORDER) = 3 ↵

Record#	CATEGORY	BRAND	MODEL	QUANTITY	WHOLESALE	RETAIL	LAST_ORDER
4	RECEIVER	NADIR	2-CHP	50	12.95	29.99	03/06/53
5	SPEAKERS	RAZCO	L-55	30	199.00	249.00	03/01/85

Here is the same query, using the name of the month instead of the number:

LIST FOR CMONTH(LAST_ORDER) = 'March' ↵

Record#	CATEGORY	BRAND	MODEL	QUANTITY	WHOLESALE	RETAIL	LAST_ORDER
4	RECEIVER	NADIR	2-CHP	50	12.95	29.99	03/06/53
5	SPEAKERS	RAZCO	L-55	30	199.00	249.00	03/01/85

Note: You must begin the names of days and months with a capital letter. The remaining letters must be in lowercase.

5. Now let's look for items which haven't been ordered since 1985. We already did this from the Assistant, but it required specifying beginning and ending dates and combining them with the .AND. operator and the < and > comparison operators. Here's an easier way.

LIST FOR YEAR(LAST_ORDER) = 1985 ↵

Record#	CATEGORY	BRAND	MODEL	QUANTITY	WHOLESALE	RETAIL	LAST_ORDER
5	SPEAKERS	RAZCO	L-55	30	199.00	249.00	03/01/85

Note: You must type all four digits of the year into the command. ("85" will not suffice.)

6. The last function in Table 13.1 is the *system date* function. The system date is the date that your computer thinks is the current date (today). You may have entered the system date in response to a prompt when you started up, or your computer may have a built-in clock that supplies it. To see the system date, type

? DATE( ) ↵

My computer responded

07/11/86

Your date will, no doubt, be different (unless your system date is wrong or you've been travelling faster than the speed of light recently). In any case, you can use the system date as a comparison against dates stored in your database. Typically this is done to list events which occurred "today," such as listing today's sales from a transaction account. If we wanted to see all the orders we'd placed today, the command would look like this:

LIST FOR LAST_ORDER = DATE() ↵

How to Display the Date of the Last Edit

dBASE keeps track of when changes are made to any database. It does this by embedding a date in a part of the file which you cannot see (called the file *header*). Sometimes it is useful to see this date, particularly if you have two copies of a database and want to know which is the more recent one—before accidentally erasing the wrong one! There are a number of ways to check this.

1. You can get out of dBASE altogether (with *Setup/Quit* or just *Quit* ↵ from the Dot prompt), and use the DOS *DIR* command. For example, assuming your data disk is drive C, the command below will list the names of all your dBASE database files, their sizes (in bytes) and their last updates.

   C> DIR *.DBF ↵

   You'll see something like this:

```
STEREO     DBF    748   7-10-86    7:22p
PHONEBK    DBF   1493   7-09-86    7:53p
CAMPLIST   DBF    358   7-10-86    5:06p
         3 File(s)     38912 bytes free
```

2. Then there are three approaches from within dBASE:

- From the Dot prompt, type

  DISPLAY FILES ON C: ↵

  I saw this on my system:

```
Database Files     # Records   Last Update    Size
STEREO.DBF                10   07/10/86        748
PHONEBK.DBF                9   07/09/86       1493
CAMPLIST.DBF               7   07/10/86        358

  2599 bytes in       3 files.
38912 bytes remaining on drive.
```

  The advantage here is that you are also shown the number of records in each file.

- Secondly, you can open each file and, from the DOT prompt or the Assistant, display the structure.

```
Structure for database   : C:stereo.dbf
Number of data records  :       10
Date of last update      : 07/10/86
Field   Field Name      Type        Width    Dec
    1   CATEGORY        Character      10
    2   BRAND           Character      10
    3   MODEL           Character       6
    4   QUANTITY        Numeric         2
    5   WHOLESALE       Numeric         6      2
    6   RETAIL          Numeric         6      2
    7   LAST_ORDER      Date            8
** Total **                            49
```

- Finally, with a file open you can use the *Last update* functon. Simply type this from the Dot prompt:

```
? LUPDATE() ↵
07/10/86
```

How to Do Date Calculations

Date calculations are possible too, using the arithmetic operators. Say you wanted to know how many days it's been since you last ordered various items. You could sit down with a calendar and start counting, or you and dBASE III PLUS could do it together, faster. (Although, once again, only from the Dot prompt.)

```
LIST DATE()-LAST_ORDER FOR CATEGORY = 'RECEIVER' ↵
```

Assuming today is 7/11/86, dBASE responds

```
Record#  DATE()-LAST_ORDER
      1                180
      2                180
      3                 57
      4              12180
```

Pretty snazzy, eh? Obviously the previous owner wasn't keeping up with all the ordering. But now, since you intend to increase sales, you want to put your ordering on a regular schedule. Every thirty days you'd like to reorder each item. Assuming today is 7/13/86, you'd like to see which items have gone 30 days or more since their last order. How would you do it?

```
LIST FOR DATE()-LAST_ORDER >= 30
```

You should see

Record#	CATEGORY	BRAND	MODEL	QUANTITY	WHOLESALE	RETAIL	LAST_ORDER
1	RECEIVER	NIZO	T-33	5	225.49	350.49	01/12/86
2	RECEIVER	NIZO	T-35	4	312.00	425.25	01/12/86
3	RECEIVER	ACME	R25-MT	13	19.99	49.99	05/15/86
4	RECEIVER	NADIR	2-CHP	50	12.95	29.99	03/06/53
5	SPEAKERS	RAZCO	L-55	30	199.00	249.00	03/01/85
9	TURNTABLE	XIRTAM	25-L	5	99.99	149.99	02/29/84

This command translates to "Show the records for which today minus the last-order date is equal to or greater than 30 days."

To calculate the number of days between two typed-in dates, you have to use the CTOD function. For example, to see how many days have passed between the signing of the Declaration of Independence and the celebration of the restoration of the Statue of Liberty:

```
? CTOD("07/04/1986") - CTOD("07/04/1776")
76700
```

How to Sort and Index on Date Fields

Ordering your files according to a Date field is a frequent necessity. Both sorting and indexing on Date fields are possible for achieving this effect. Sorting may be in either ascending (earlier-to-later) order or descending order. With indexing, however, only ascending order is provided for.

To order by date, just use the *Sort* or *Index* options as outlined in Chapter 8, but use the Date field in your database as the key for the index or sort. To see a sort work with our database, execute these commands.

1. For an ascending sort by date:

```
SORT ON LAST_ORDER TO DATEUP ↵
100% Sorted          10 Records sorted
USE DATEUP ↵
LIST↵
```

Record#	CATEGORY	BRAND	MODEL	QUANTITY	WHOLESALE	RETAIL	LAST_ORDER
1	RECEIVER	NADIR	2-CHP	50	12.95	29.99	03/06/53
2	TURNTABLE	XIRTAM	25-L	5	99.99	149.99	02/29/84
3	SPEAKERS	RAZCO	L-55	30	199.00	249.00	03/01/85
4	RECEIVER	NIZO	T-35	4	312.00	425.25	01/12/86
5	RECEIVER	NIZO	T-33	5	225.49	350.49	01/12/86
6	RECEIVER	ACME	R25-MT	13	19.99	49.99	05/15/86
7	SPEAKERS	TALBEST	BG-20	6	250.00	350.88	07/13/86
8	TAPE DECK	ROLLEM	CAS-3	10	125.65	212.99	09/01/86
9	TAPE DECK	FLOWUTTER	WBL-5	5	149.33	250.77	09/15/86
10	TURNTABLE	RALURIC	RND-1	3	595.00	850.00	10/01/86

2. For descending order by date, type

SORT ON LAST_ORDER TO DATEDOWN DESCENDING ↵
100% Sorted 10 Records sorted
USE DATEDOWN ↵
LIST ↵

Record#	CATEGORY	BRAND	MODEL	QUANTITY	WHOLESALE	RETAIL	LAST_ORDER
1	TURNTABLE	RALURIC	RND-1	3	595.00	850.00	10/01/86
2	TAPE DECK	FLOWUTTER	WBL-5	5	149.33	250.77	09/15/86
3	TAPE DECK	ROLLEM	CAS-3	10	125.65	212.99	09/01/86
4	SPEAKERS	TALBEST	BG-20	6	250.00	350.88	07/13/86
5	RECEIVER	ACME	R25-MT	13	19.99	49.99	05/15/86
6	RECEIVER	NIZO	T-33	5	225.49	350.49	01/12/86
7	RECEIVER	NIZO	T-35	4	312.00	425.25	01/12/86
8	SPEAKERS	RAZCO	L-55	30	199.00	249.00	03/01/85
9	TURNTABLE	XIRTAM	25-L	5	99.99	149.99	02/29/84
10	RECEIVER	NADIR	2-CHP	50	12.95	29.99	03/06/53

One last trick

Now for one last trick. Suppose you wanted to rearrange this file so that the dates are in descending order (latest first) within each category, allowing you to zero in on the most recent orders in each case. Furthermore, you want the categories to be listed in order too, only in ascending alphabetical order (A–Z). Not only that, you want this file to replace the existing STEREO file. How could you do it?

As you will recall from Chapter 8, this qualifies as a "multilevel sort." Don't be thrown off by the fact that one sort will be ascending and the other descending. The rules you learned in Chapter 8 still apply.

Recall that the rule for multilevel sorts is to sort on the least significant key first. Since you want dates to be in order within categories, the date is less significant. Therefore, you sort on the date first. Actually we're halfway there since the DATEDOWN file is already open from the last sort, and this file is already sorted on the Date field in descending order, so we'll just use it as a starting point.

Now we just have to sort on CATEGORY in ascending order. And since we wanted to replace the existing STEREO file with the newly sorted file, we sort *to* STEREO. This will erase the old version of STEREO, replacing it with the new one.

Type in

SORT ON CATEGORY TO STEREO ↵

Now you see this message:

stereo.dbf already exists, overwrite it (Y/N?)

Answer with Y to erase the old STEREO file and replace it with the new one. This message is a thoughtful reminder from dBASE III PLUS that can be worth its weight in gold. Accidentally erasing a whole database because you didn't remember it already existed can be acutely frustrating, so dBASE asks you to verify that this is what you want to do.

Now open the new STEREO file and list it.

Record#	CATEGORY	BRAND	MODEL	QUANTITY	WHOLESALE	RETAIL	LAST_ORDER
1	RECEIVER	ACME	R25-MT	13	19.99	49.99	05/15/86
2	RECEIVER	NIZO	T-35	4	312.00	425.25	01/12/86
3	RECEIVER	NIZO	T-33	5	225.49	350.49	01/12/86
4	RECEIVER	NADIR	2-CHP	50	12.95	29.99	03/06/53
5	SPEAKERS	TALBEST	BG-20	6	250.00	350.88	07/13/86
6	SPEAKERS	RAZCO	L-55	30	199.00	249.00	03/01/85
7	TAPE DECK	FLOWUTTER	WBL-5	5	149.33	250.77	09/15/86
8	TAPE DECK	ROLLEM	CAS-3	10	125.65	212.99	09/01/86
9	TURNTABLE	RALURIC	RND-1	3	595.00	850.00	10/01/86
10	TURNTABLE	XIRTAM	25-L	5	99.99	149.99	02/29/84

14

Working with Logical Fields

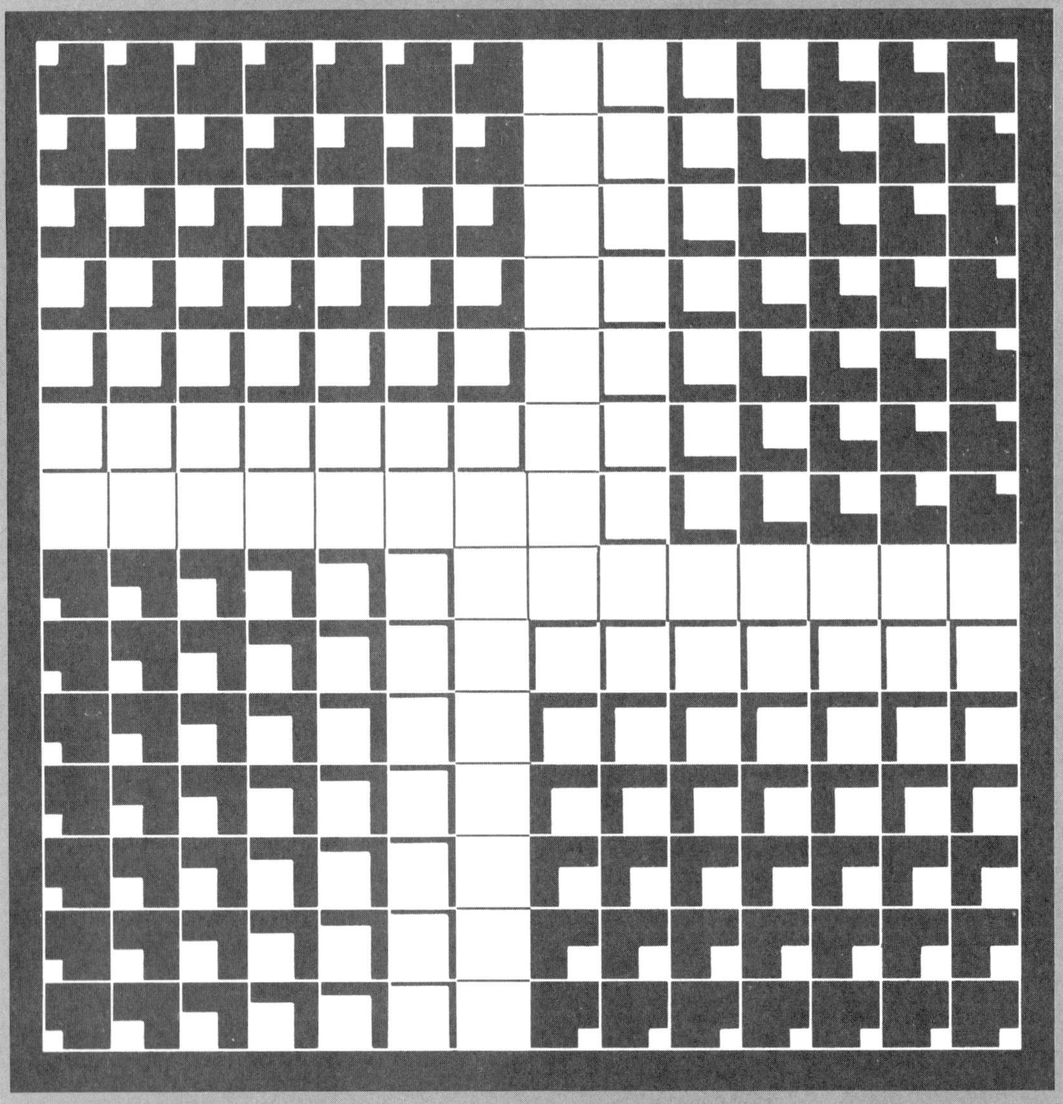

FEATURING:

Logical fields; Logical conditions for searches and calculations

The the only field type we haven't yet discussed is the Logical type, so we will take it up now. Sound logical? As you may recall, Logical fields are used exclusively for storing Yes/No (or True/False) data. Thus, Logical fields are useful for keeping track of things like "Is this donation tax-deductible?", "Did this check bounce?", "Did this recipe go over well enough at the last dinner party to bother making again?", and so on.

On the face of it, the notion of dedicating a whole field type to answers of yes and no might sound silly. You could store a yes or a no in a character field. True enough. But actually, Logical fields make retrieval of associated data much easier, because dBASE III PLUS already knows that Logical fields can only hold two values. And searching for records that meet a certain logical criterion doesn't require using quote marks, typing the word "Yes" or "No" into a search condition, or other data-entry inconveniences.

How to Add a Logical Field

To illustrate the concept and utility of Logical fields, let's add one to our STEREO store database. What will it be for? Well, let's assume there are certain items that you sell only via interstate marketing and shipping. Therefore, you don't collect state sales tax on these items. A Logical field could indicate whether or not sales tax should be added when figuring the total sales price of each product. We should also add a field to hold the total price, which would include the sales tax, where applicable. Then we can have dBASE III PLUS compute the total price and store it in that field.

1. Modify the STEREO database structure, by adding an eighth field, called TAX. Make it a Logical type.

2. Now add a ninth field, called TOTAL. Make it Numeric, six spaces wide, with two decimal places.

3. Save the new structure. Your database structure now looks like this:

	Field Name	Type	Width	Dec
1	CATEGORY	Character	10	
2	BRAND	Character	10	
3	MODEL	Character	6	
4	QUANTITY	Numeric	2	0
5	WHOLESALE	Numeric	6	2
6	RETAIL	Numeric	6	2
7	LAST_ORDER	Date	8	
8	TAX	Logical	1	
9	TOTAL	Numeric	6	2

2. Using Browse mode, fill in the TAX field with the following data, which indicates whether the item in a record is taxable or not. Incidentally, since Logical fields are only one space wide, they can only store a single letter. That letter indicates whether the field data is a yes or a no. "Yes" is represented by either a Y or a T (for True). "No" is represented by N or F (for False). You will hear a beep after each entry, because you have filled the field. Since we're only entering data into one field, make it easier on yourself by Browsing only a few fields. Use this command from the Dot prompt:

```
BROWSE FIELDS BRAND, MODEL, TAX ↵
```

Here's the data:

BRAND------	MODEL-	TAX
ACME	R25-MT	Y
NIZO	T-35	Y
NIZO	T-33	F

```
NADIR       2-CHP   T
TALBEST     BG-20   N
RAZCO       L-55    Y
FLOWUTTER   WBL-5   T
ROLLEM      CAS-3   N
RALURIC     RND-1   Y
XIRTAM      25-L    N
```

3. Notice that I intentionally used a mixture of T, F, N, and Y. You'll see why when we list the data on the screen. But since we have so many fields in the database now, listing them will cause each record to wrap around and make a bit of mess on the screen. We could modify the structure and eliminate some fields, but we might need them again later. There's another solution, the *Set fields to* command. From the Dot, type

SET FIELDS TO CATEGORY, BRAND, MODEL, RETAIL, TAX, TOTAL ↵

This tells dBASE III PLUS which fields to show with the *List, Display,* and *Browse* options. Displaying the database's structure at this point with the Display Structure command will show an arrow next to the fields that have been selected. However, the *Set fields to* command does not take hold until you enter another command to activate it. Now type

SET FIELDS ON ↵

4. The fields list is now set and turned on, so we can proceed with examining the Logical fields. Type

LIST ↵

dBASE displays

```
Record# CATEGORY   BRAND      MODEL   RETAIL  TAX  TOTAL
      1 RECEIVER   ACME       R25-MT   49.99  .T.
      2 RECEIVER   NIZO       T-35    425.25  .T.
      3 RECEIVER   NIZO       T-33    350.49  .F.
      4 RECEIVER   NADIR      2-CHP    29.99  .T.
      5 SPEAKERS   TALBEST    BG-20   350.88  .F.
      6 SPEAKERS   RAZCO      L-55    249.00  .T.
      7 TAPE DECK  FLOWUTTER  WBL-5   250.77  .T.
      8 TAPE DECK  ROLLEM     CAS-3   212.99  .F.
```

```
 9  TURNTABLE  RALURIC    RND-1   850.00  .T.
10  TURNTABLE  XIRTAM     25-L    149.99  .F.
```

5. Now look at the TAX field. Notice that there are only T's or F's there despite the Y's and N's you entered. dBASE III PLUS turns all logical values into True or False, at least for listings. In Browse or Edit mode the Y's and N's will still be there. Also, to denote logical data, a period is placed on both sides of the letter. The TOTAL field is blank because we haven't entered any data into it yet.

How to Use Logical Fields for Finding Data

Say we want a reminder of which items we have to add tax to. We would need to do a conditional listing based on the TAX field. This is how you'd do it:

1. Type

   LIST FOR TAX ↵

   dBASE responds

```
Record#  CATEGORY   BRAND      MODEL   RETAIL  TAX  TOTAL
      1  RECEIVER   ACME       R25-MT   49.99  .T.
      2  RECEIVER   NIZO       T-35    425.25  .T.
      4  RECEIVER   NADIR      2-CHP    29.99  .T.
      6  SPEAKERS   RAZCO      L-55    249.00  .T.
      7  TAPE DECK  FLOWUTTER  WBL-5   250.77  .T.
      9  TURNTABLE  RALURIC    RND-1   850.00  .T.
```

   It may help to think of the last command as saying implicitly, "List records for TAX = .T." Because TAX is a Logical field you didn't have to actually use a comparison operator (=). Similarly, from the Assistant you would build a condition just by selecting TAX from the fields box, without having to use a comparison operator.

2. What if you want to see all the items that are *not* taxable? This one's a little trickier, because it involves a new operator which we haven't covered yet: *.NOT.* The .NOT. logical operator does pretty much what its name implies. It reverses any part of a command

that you use it with. In effect it does what the word "not" does in normal English. So, to list items that are not taxable, type

LIST FOR .NOT. TAX ↵

dBASE responds

Record#	CATEGORY	BRAND	MODEL	RETAIL	TAX	TOTAL
3	RECEIVER	NIZO	T-33	350.49	.F.	
5	SPEAKERS	TALBEST	BG-20	350.88	.F.	
8	TAPE DECK	ROLLEM	CAS-3	212.99	.F.	
10	TURNTABLE	XIRTAM	25-L	149.99	.F.	

The translation might be though of as: "List records for TAX not = .T." Since "not True" is the same as "False," this amounts to "List records for TAX = .F."

How to Make File-Wide Changes Based on Logical Fields

Now let's try having dBASE III PLUS make the calculations for the TOTAL field, based on whether a record is taxable or not. Here's how it works in concept. As a first approximation, let's create a command that says: "Look at each record. If TAX is true, multiply the retail amount by 6% (assuming that's the state sales tax) and store that product in the TOTAL column." Sound hard? Actually you know all the rules necessary for figuring out this command already. Try doing it yourself. If you get stuck, look at the instructions below.

1. Type

   REPLACE ALL TOTAL WITH RETAIL * .06 FOR TAX ↵

   dBASE responds

   6 records replaced

2. Now list the file to see the replacements.

Record#	CATEGORY	BRAND	MODEL	RETAIL	TAX	TOTAL
1	RECEIVER	ACME	R25-MT	49.99	.T.	3.00
2	RECEIVER	NIZO	T-35	425.25	.T.	25.52

```
  3 RECEIVER   NIZO       T-33   350.49 .F.
  4 RECEIVER   NADIR      2-CHP   29.99 .T.    1.80
  5 SPEAKERS   TALBEST    BG-20  350.88 .F.
  6 SPEAKERS   RAZCO      L-55   249.00 .T.   14.94
  7 TAPE DECK  FLOWUTTER  WBL-5  250.77 .T.   15.05
  8 TAPE DECK  ROLLEM     CAS-3  212.99 .F.
  9 TURNTABLE  RALURIC    RND-1  850.00 .T.   51.00
 10 TURNTABLE  XIRTAM     25-L   149.99 .F.
```

Oops! Those numbers don't look right, do they? In our first approximation, we told dBASE to calculate the tax, but didn't tell it to *add* the tax to the retail price. Let's try it again.

3. Type

```
REPLACE ALL TOTAL WITH RETAIL + (RETAIL * .06)
FOR TAX ←
```

Now list again

```
Record# CATEGORY   BRAND      MODEL  RETAIL TAX  TOTAL
      1 RECEIVER   ACME       R25-MT  49.99 .T.   52.99
      2 RECEIVER   NIZO       T-35   425.25 .T.  450.76
      3 RECEIVER   NIZO       T-33   350.49 .F.
      4 RECEIVER   NADIR      2-CHP   29.99 .T.   31.79
      5 SPEAKERS   TALBEST    BG-20  350.88 .F.
      6 SPEAKERS   RAZCO      L-55   249.00 .T.  263.94
      7 TAPE DECK  FLOWUTTER  WBL-5  250.77 .T.  265.82
      8 TAPE DECK  ROLLEM     CAS-3  212.99 .F.
      9 TURNTABLE  RALURIC    RND-1  850.00 .T.  901.00
     10 TURNTABLE  XIRTAM     25-L   149.99 .F.
```

That looks better. Now, what about the nontaxable records? We'll have to use another command for those, since we asked dBASE to skip over them in the last command ("FOR TAX"). Actually, all we want to do for these items is to copy the existing retail prices into the TOTAL column.

4. Type

```
REPLACE ALL TOTAL WITH RETAIL FOR .NOT. TAX ←
```

dBASE says

```
4 records replaced
```

5. Now list everything.

Record#	CATEGORY	BRAND	MODEL	RETAIL	TAX	TOTAL
1	RECEIVER	ACME	R25-MT	49.99	.T.	52.99
2	RECEIVER	NIZO	T-35	425.25	.T.	450.76
3	RECEIVER	NIZO	T-33	350.49	.F.	350.49
4	RECEIVER	NADIR	2-CHP	29.99	.T.	31.79
5	SPEAKERS	TALBEST	BG-20	350.88	.F.	350.88
6	SPEAKERS	RAZCO	L-55	249.00	.T.	263.94
7	TAPE DECK	FLOWUTTER	WBL-5	250.77	.T.	265.82
8	TAPE DECK	ROLLEM	CAS-3	212.99	.F.	212.99
9	TURNTABLE	RALURIC	RND-1	850.00	.T.	901.00
10	TURNTABLE	XIRTAM	25-L	149.99	.F.	149.99

Additional examples

As with all the other field types and functions, you can use Logical fields as search criteria for reports, mailing labels, and other operations such as deleting or recalling records. Logical fields may also be used in conjunction with other search criteria via the .AND. and .OR. operators. Here are a couple of examples.

To list taxable receivers with a (pre-tax) retail price of over $200.00, type

LIST FOR CATEGORY = 'RECEIVER' .AND. RETAIL > 200 .AND. TAX ↵

Record#	CATEGORY	BRAND	MODEL	RETAIL	TAX	TOTAL
2	RECEIVER	NIZO	T-35	425.25	.T.	450.76

To run our Stereo report form covering only taxable items and to send the report to the printer, type

REPORT FORM STEREO FOR TAX TO PRINT ↵

Don't forget to set the fields list off before running the report. Otherwise dBASE will give you an error message because it can't find some of the fields. You do this by typing

SET FIELDS OFF ↵

15 Working with Multiple Databases

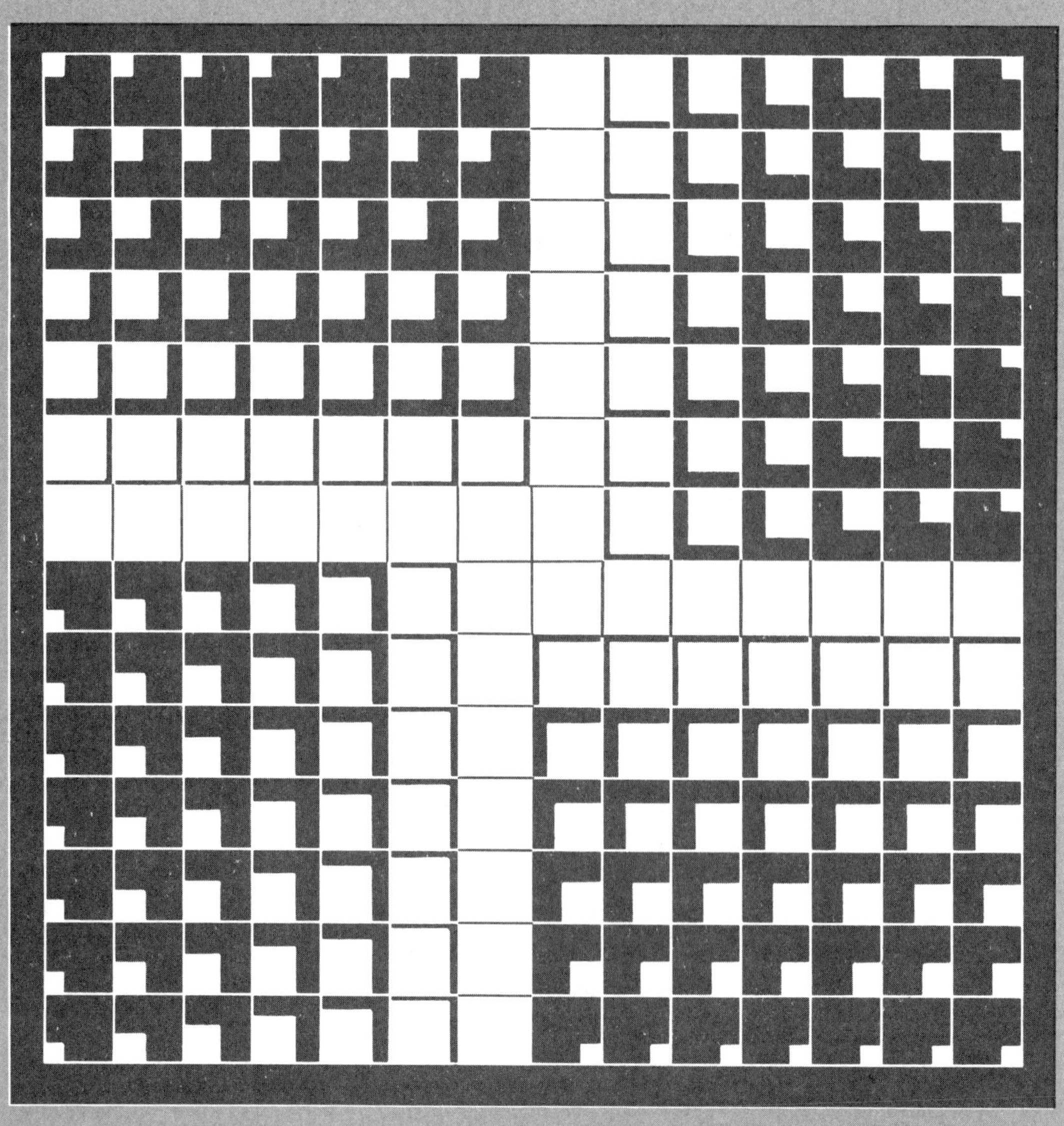

FEATURING:

merging files; multifile Views; update files

So far, all the commands you've learned and the examples we've used have dealt with only a single database at a time. However, there are situations that call for the use of several databases together. This can take the form of simply merging two or more databases into one. But it is also possible to *link* several databases together to act as one, without actually merging the data. This chapter explores multiple-database techniques and the rationale behind them. We will discuss:

- Merging data from one file into another
- Using two or more databases at the same time
- *Updating* one file with data from another

How to Append Data from Another Database

The *Append* option, while normally used for adding records to your database one at a time, also has another interesting capability. It can pull records from a second database (even a non-dBASE file) into the current file very quickly. Here's an example.

Say you've got two stores, each with its own dBASE inventory list. Both stores are doing a booming business, and space is getting cramped. One day you stumble upon a great deal on a large storefront property. Since your two stores sell similar items, you decide to buy the new space, and merge the existing operations into one big shop. Of course, it then makes sense to combine your databases as well. But do you want to pay someone to type in all the data from one file into another? Hardly. Instead you can use the *Append* command to simplify the task. (This use of *Append* only works from the Dot prompt.)

1. First, in case you didn't turn the fields list off from the last chapter, type

   SET FIELDS OFF ↵

2. Let's say the first database is the STEREO database. To start with, we'll need to create the database from the second store. Let's call it TV, since the other store sold televisions and related items. Do this from the Dot prompt by typing

   CREATE TV ↵

   Here is the structure of the TV database file:

	Field Name	Type	Width	Dec
1	CATEGORY	Character	10	
2	BRAND	Character	10	
3	MODEL	Character	6	
4	SIZE	Character	3	
5	QUANTITY	Numeric	2	0
6	RETAIL	Numeric	6	2
7	WHOLESALE	Numeric	6	2

3. Save the structure by typing ^W or ^End.
4. Now fill it with this data:

Record#	CATEGORY	BRAND	MODEL	SIZE	QUANTITY	RETAIL	WHOLESALE
1	TELEVISION	BLABBEX	K22	14″	29	249.99	189.99
2	TELEVISION	BIG-VUE	BV-45	19″	5	750.00	595.00
3	VCR	CINOSANAP	TP-120		3	345.89	540.99
4	VIDEO TAPE	MAXWELL	XX-120		45	4.99	3.49
5	VCR	THINEZ	TV-20		14	199.00	149.00

5. OK. Now we have two databases. Notice that the structures are not exactly identical. Some fields are reversed in order, others

are omitted, and the TV file has a field (SIZE) not included in the STEREO file at all.

6. Now make sure the STEREO file is open.

   USE STEREO ↵

7. To pull the TV file into the STEREO file, type

   APPEND FROM TV ↵

   dBASE responds

   5 records added

8. Now request a listing of the enlarged STEREO file

   LIST OFF ↵

   (The OFF after the *List* command suppresses the record number, so that more data can fit on the screen.) dBASE replies with

CATEGORY	BRAND	MODEL	QUANTITY	WHOLESALE	RETAIL	LAST_ORDER	TAX	TOTAL
RECEIVER	ACME	R25-MT	13	19.99	49.99	05/15/86	.T.	52.99
RECEIVER	NIZO	T-35	4	312.00	425.25	01/12/86	.T.	450.76
RECEIVER	NIZO	T-33	5	225.49	350.49	01/12/86	.F.	350.49
RECEIVER	NADIR	2-CHP	50	12.95	29.99	03/06/53	.T.	31.79
SPEAKERS	TALBEST	BG-20	6	250.00	350.88	07/13/86	.F.	350.88
SPEAKERS	RAZCO	L-55	30	199.00	249.00	03/01/85	.T.	263.94
TAPE DECK	FLOWUTTER	WBL-5	5	149.33	250.77	09/15/86	.T.	265.82
TAPE DECK	ROLLEM	CAS-3	10	125.65	212.99	09/01/86	.F.	212.99
TURNTABLE	RALURIC	RND-1	3	595.00	850.00	10/01/86	.T.	901.00
TURNTABLE	XIRTAM	25-L	5	99.99	149.99	02/29/84	.F.	149.99
TELEVISION	BLABBEX	K22	29	189.99	249.99	/ /	.F.	
TELEVISION	BIG-VUE	BV-45	5	595.00	750.00	/ /	.F.	
VCR	CINOSANAP	TP-120	3	540.99	345.89	/ /	.F.	
VIDEO TAPE	MAXWELL	XX-120	45	3.49	4.99	/ /	.F.	
VCR	THINEZ	TV-20	14	149.00	199.00	/ /	.F.	

Notice the last five records? dBASE just tacked the TV records onto the end of STEREO. It also reported to the screen the number of records which were added. Appending five records was a swift process, but a few thousand would take considerably more time as well as quite a lot of disk space. Be sure you have enough of both in such cases.

Rules for merging files with Append

Now for a few technical points. Luckily your two databases had somewhat similar structures, field names, and field lengths, otherwise the results would have been less successful. As it was, all you lost was the SIZE field information. Even though RETAIL and WHOLESALE were reversed in the TV file, dBASE recognized that and reordered those fields before pulling them into the STEREO file. The TAX field is stuffed with F's (the default Logical setting) and the LAST_ORDER and TOTAL fields are added as empty fields of course, since you haven't typed or calculated anything into them. If you wanted to include the SIZE data, you would have to modify the STEREO file's structure to add a SIZE field prior to the Append.

To understand how other discrepancies would have caused problems, let's consider what dBASE III PLUS does when given the *Append from* command. First it compares the structures of the two databases concerned. Only fields with the same names are appended. Otherwise, they are skipped over. If the data in the *from* field is too long to fit into its new field, it is shortened, or *truncated,* until it fits. So, you would lose the right-hand part of the longer entries.

OK. So much for simply appending *all* the records from another database. What about specifying some conditions which pick and choose the records to add? For example, say you only wanted to add inventory items that were TVs? This requires using the *FOR* expression, just as it's used with *List* and other commands.

1. First let's eliminate the five records we just added. Type

```
GOTO 11 ↵
DELETE NEXT 5 ↵
     5 records deleted
LIST OFF ↵
```

CATEGORY	BRAND	MODEL	QUANTITY	WHOLESALE	RETAIL	LAST_ORDER	TAX	TOTAL
RECEIVER	ACME	R25-MT	13	19.99	49.99	05/15/86	.T.	52.99
RECEIVER	NIZO	T-35	4	312.00	425.25	01/12/86	.T.	450.76
RECEIVER	NIZO	T-33	5	225.49	350.49	01/12/86	.F.	350.49
RECEIVER	NADIR	2-CHP	50	12.95	29.99	03/06/53	.T.	31.79
SPEAKERS	TALBEST	BG-20	6	250.00	350.88	07/13/86	.F.	350.88
SPEAKERS	RAZCO	L-55	30	199.00	249.00	03/01/85	.T.	263.94
TAPE DECK	FLOWUTTER	WBL-5	5	149.33	250.77	09/15/86	.T.	265.82
TAPE DECK	ROLLEM	CAS-3	10	125.65	212.99	09/01/86	.F.	212.99
TURNTABLE	RALURIC	RND-1	3	595.00	850.00	10/01/86	.T.	901.00

```
TURNTABLE    XIRTAM     25-L       5    99.99  149.99  02/29/84   .F.  149.99
*TELEVISION  BLABBEX    K22       29   189.99  249.99   /  /      .F.
*TELEVISION  BIG-VUE    BV-45      5   595.00  750.00   /  /      .F.
*VCR         CINOSANAP  TP-120     3   540.99  345.89   /  /      .F.
*VIDEOTAPE   MAXWELL    XX-120    45     3.49    4.99   /  /      .F.
*VCR         THINEZ     TV-20     14   149.00  199.00   /  /      .F.
```

2. Notice the asterisks that indicate which records are marked for deletion. Now actually remove these marked records by typing

   PACK ↵

3. Now append only Televisions from the TV file (mind your capitalization):

   APPEND FROM TV FOR CATEGORY = 'TELEVISION' ↵

   dBASE responds

   2 records added

4. Let's list things just to see the results.

   LIST OFF ↵

CATEGORY	BRAND	MODEL	QUANTITY	WHOLESALE	RETAIL	LAST_ORDER	TAX	TOTAL
RECEIVER	ACME	R25-MT	13	19.99	49.99	05/15/86	.T.	52.99
RECEIVER	NIZO	T-35	4	312.00	425.25	01/12/86	.T.	450.76
RECEIVER	NIZO	T-33	5	225.49	350.49	01/12/86	.F.	350.49
RECEIVER	NADIR	2-CHP	50	12.95	29.99	03/06/53	.T.	31.79
SPEAKERS	TALBEST	BG-20	6	250.00	350.88	07/13/86	.F.	350.88
SPEAKERS	RAZCO	L-55	30	199.00	249.00	03/01/85	.T.	263.94
TAPE DECK	FLOWUTTER	WBL-5	5	149.33	250.77	09/15/86	.T.	265.82
TAPE DECK	ROLLEM	CAS-3	10	125.65	212.99	09/01/86	.F.	212.99
TURNTABLE	RALURIC	RND-1	3	595.00	850.00	10/01/86	.T.	901.00
TURNTABLE	XIRTAM	25-L	5	99.99	149.99	02/29/84	.F.	149.99
TELEVISION	BLABBEX	K22	29	189.99	249.99	/ /	.F.	
TELEVISION	BIG-VUE	BV-45	5	595.00	750.00	/ /	.F.	

See? Only two records, and both are Televisions.

Of course, much more complex conditions can be used to stipulate which records should be appended to the database in use. The important rule to remember is that any fields referred to in your conditional expression must exist in both files. This can be confusing since the expression itself refers only to data in the *from* file. You would think that a field from the second file could be used for the purpose of picking out which records to append, but it can't.

How to Use Two or More Data Files Simultaneously

It's not uncommon in complex applications to need two files open and available for data retrieval at one time. dBASE III PLUS actually allows as many as ten files to be open at any given time, allowing you to switch between them at will, without having to close and open files all the time. How does it do this? dBASE III PLUS sets aside ten distinct *workareas,* each of which can have its own database and indexes active.

Workareas are assigned identification numbers one through ten by dBASE. To see how this works, let's try opening another database file in workarea 2, since we already have the STEREO file open in workarea 1.

1. From the Dot prompt, type

   SELECT 2 ↵
   USE PHONEBK ↵

2. Notice that the Status Line now indicates that the PHONEBK file is in use. You can surmise that this means you are in workarea 2. To see directly which workarea you are in, you can type

   DISPLAY STATUS ↵

   or simply press F6.

3. Let's switch back to workarea 1 to see the Status Line change again, indicating that you are working with the STEREO database, as before.

   SELECT 1 ↵

4. Now, close all the databases so we're back at ground zero again for the next steps.

   CLOSE ALL ↵

Incidentally, you can also call and access workareas by letter-names too, if you prefer letters to numbers. Letters A through J correspond to numbers 1 through 10.

In addition to just keeping files open at the same time, you can *link* any two of these databases temporarily, creating what appears to be one larger one. While the two files are linked, or *related,* you may work with their fields as though they were in the same datbase. This can be very handy, since it lets you, in essence, rearrange information from any of your databases to view it in a variety of ways. The linking relationship you define between the two databases is called a *View.* The relationship can even be stored for future use as what dBASE calls a *View file.*

Here's an example. For each item you sell in the stereo/TV shop, there is a salesperson whom you deal with and order from. When you look at your inventory database to see whether you'll need to order more items, you often forget the names, addresses and phone numbers of the various reps. Linking the inventory database to a second database containing the rep information can solve this problem. Here's how it's done.

Preparing the files for a View

1. Now, get back to the Assistant. We'll use the PHONEBK database for the names and addresses (I knew you were wondering who those people were!), but first we'll have to add another field that will link PHONEBK to the STEREO database. Open the PHONEBK database, and select *Modify/Database file* to alter the structure like this (use ^N to insert a new field):

Field	Field Name	Type	Width	Dec
1	FIRST_NAME	Character	10	
2	LAST_NAME	Character	15	
3	COMPANY	Character	20	
4	REP_NO	Character	2	
5	WORK_PHONE	Character	12	
6	HOME_PHONE	Character	12	
7	STREET	Character	22	
8	CITY	Character	13	
9	STATE	Character	2	
10	ZIP	Character	5	
11	NOTES	Memo	10	

2. Now, making sure the file is open, use Browse mode to enter the following ID numbers for the reps. (You may wonder if all these companies really sell electronics gear. You'll have to take my word for it.)

FIRST_NAME	LAST_NAME------	COMPANY------------	REP_NO	WORK_PHONE--
Wackford	Squeers	Ralph Nicolby Inc.	01	415-555-1212
Hank	Davies	Bass-O-Matic	02	909-549-3787
Adriator	Wegwo	Rug Flox, Inc	03	321-889-3674
Aretha	Phillipson	Soulariums-R-Us	04	908-776-5298
Randy	Batterydown	Voltaics Inc.	05	809-675-4532
Nimrod	Neverburger	Bab's Fish N Chips	06	822-991-2861
Marcel	Phillip	Feline Frenzy	07	310-563-0987
Valery	Kuletski	Literary Allusions	08	529-221-9480
MARIAN	DAVIES	CITY OPERA CO.	09	211-334-9876

3. For a View to work, the *linked* file has to be indexed on the linking field, which in this case is REP_NO. So select *Organize/Index,* type in *REP_NO* as the expression, and type in *REPS* as the index name.

   OK. That puts the reps numbers in the PHONEBK file. Now we have to add the same numbers to the STEREO inventory file.

4. Open STEREO, and modify its structure. Remove TAX and TOTAL (with ^U) since we don't need them anymore, and add REP_NO as shown:

Field	Field Name	Type	Width	Dec
1	CATEGORY	Character	10	
2	BRAND	Character	10	
3	MODEL	Character	6	
4	QUANTITY	Numeric	2	0
5	WHOLESALE	Numeric	6	2
6	RETAIL	Numeric	6	2
7	LAST_ORDER	Date	8	
8	REP_NO	Character	2	

5. Now we need to assign rep numbers to each item in the inventory. Select *Update/Browse* to enter the numbers as you see them below. And while you're editing, add dates for the last two television orders too, to complete the database:

CATEGORY--	BRAND-----	MODEL-	QUANTITY	WHOLESALE	RETAIL	LAST_ORDER	REP_NO
RECEIVER	ACME	R25-MT	13	19.99	49.99	05/15/86	09
RECEIVER	NIZO	T-35	4	312.00	425.25	01/12/86	02
RECEIVER	NIZO	T-33	5	225.49	350.49	01/12/86	02
RECEIVER	NADIR	2-CHP	50	12.00	0.00	03/06/53	01
SPEAKERS	TALBEST	BG-20	6	250.00	350.88	07/13/86	04
SPEAKERS	RAZCO	L-55	30	199.00	249.00	03/01/85	03

TAPE DECK	FLOWUTTER	WBL-5	5	149.33	250.77	09/15/86	05
TAPE DECK	ROLLEM	CAS-3	10	125.65	212.99	09/01/86	06
TURNTABLE	RALURIC	RND-1	3	595.00	850.00	10/01/86	07
TURNTABLE	XIRTAM	25-L	5	99.99	149.99	02/29/84	08
TELEVISION	BLABBEX	K22	29	189.99	249.99	10/12/86	09
TELEVISION	BIG-VUE	BV-45	5	595.00	750.00	10/12/86	09

Opening the files for a View

1. Now all you have to do is create the View that connects the databases. From the Assistant, select *Create/View.*
2. Select the data-disk drive that the STEREO and PHONEBK files are on.
3. Type in *Rep* for the View file name.
4. A new screen appears. This is the screen from which you create your multifile View.
5. The first menu, Set up, shows a list of files. dBASE wants to know which files you want to use in the View. Highlight STEREO and press ↵ until an arrow appears to the left of the name. No indexes are necessary, so press ← when the index box appears.
6. Now select the PHONEBK file, and select REPS as the index. Your screen now looks like Figure 15.1

Setting up the relationship for the View

1. Press the ← to leave the index box.
2. Type R to select the *Relate* menu.
3. Your two database names, PHONEBK and STEREO appear in a box. Now, dBASE wants to know which file is the master file. We'll be using STEREO as the main file, so select that.
4. Another box appears, with the PHONEBK file name in it. dBASE assumes it must be linking STEREO to this file, since it's the only other one you had selected for creating the View.
5. Now dBASE needs to know which field found in both databases will be used for linking, or relating, the databases. Press ↵. A little arrow appears; dBASE is ready to accept the field name.

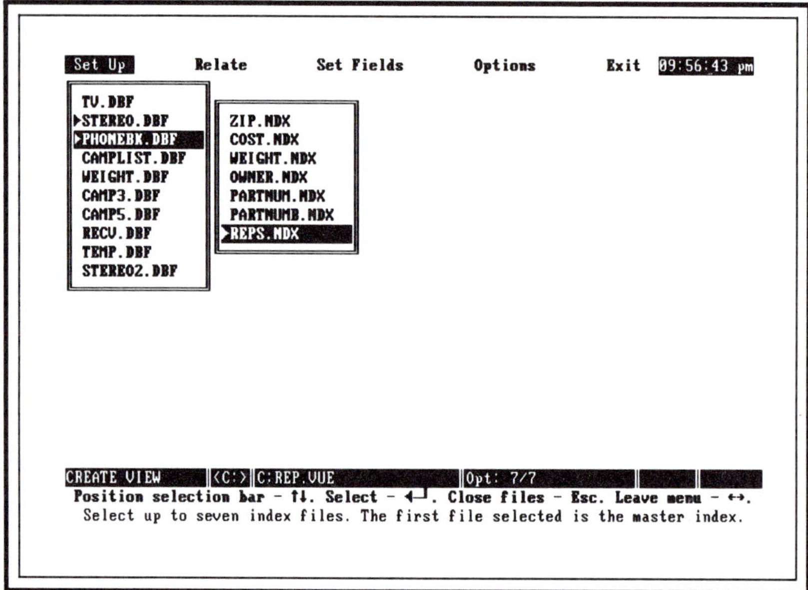

Figure 15.1: Selecting the files and indexes for a View

6. Press F10 to see a fields list. Look at the bottom of the screen. dBASE reminds you that PHONEBK is indexed on REP_NO. So, Select REP_NO from the fields list.
7. Press ↵.
8. Press →.

Selecting the fields list

1. Press → again to select the *Set Fields* menu. Now you get to select which fields you'd like to work with when your View is active. STEREO is highlighted already. Just press ↵.
2. A STEREO fields list appears, with arrows next to all the fields. This means that all of the fields will appear in the View unless you turn some off. Select BRAND, MODEL, and QUANTITY by turning the others off with the ↵ key (off = no arrows). Leave the menu with →.

3. Select PHONEBK.
4. Select FIRST_NAME, LAST_NAME, and WORK_PHONE.
5. Press → to leave the *Set Fields* menu.
6. Save the View by selecting *Exit/Save*.

Enjoying the View

1. To use the View, select *Set up/View*.
2. Choose the drive and the View name (REP.VUE).
3. Select *Retrieve/List/Execute the command* and you see

Record#	BRAND	MODEL	QUANTITY	FIRST_NAME	LAST_NAME	WORK_PHONE
1	ACME	R25-MT	13	MARIAN	DAVIES	211-334-9876
2	NIZO	T-35	4	Hank	Davies	909-549-3787
3	NIZO	T-33	5	Hank	Davies	909-549-3787
4	NADIR	2-CHP	50	Wackford	Squeers	415-555-1212
5	TALBEST	BG-20	6	Aretha	Phillipson	908-776-5298
6	RAZCO	L-55	30	Adriator	Wegwo	321-889-3674
7	FLOWUTTER	WBL-5	5	Randy	Batterydown	809-675-4532
8	ROLLEM	CAS-3	10	Nimrod	Neverburger	822-991-2861
9	RALURIC	RND-1	3	Marcel	Phillip	310-563-0987
10	XIRTAM	25-L	5	Valery	Kuletski	529-221-9480
11	BLABBEX	K22	29	MARIAN	DAVIES	211-334-9876
12	BIG-VUE	BV-45	5	MARIAN	DAVIES	211-334-9876

4. Not bad, eh? This makes checking your current inventory quantities and calling your reps to order more items almost a one-step process.
5. Now try selecting *Update/Browse* or *Update/Edit*. Notice that even editing records uses the new View, though you cannot add records while in a View. Press ^Q so that you don't make any changes though.

Note that reports may also be run with a View open, allowing you to include any of the fields in the View.

Other View options

There are some other options you may have thought of. One has to do with the Options menu on the View screen, which we haven't used. This let's you set up a condition on your View, so that only certain records show up. Suppose you wanted to show only those items whose quantity was lower than five so you could reorder in time.

1. Select *Modify/View* and select REP.VUE as the file name.
2. Select *Options/Filter.*
3. Press F10. A fields list appears.
4. Highlight QUANTITY. Your screen should look like that in Figure 15.2.
5. The message line says

   Enter a logical expression to filter the records in this View

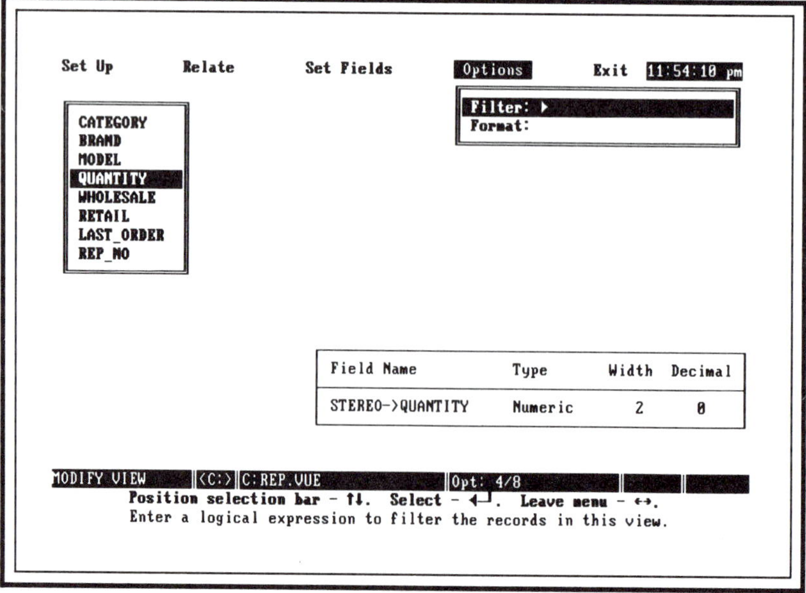

Figure 15.2: Creating a View filter

6. Press ↵. Finish the filter expression in the filter box by typing in

   <5 ↵

7. Select *Exit/Save.*
8. From the main Assistant menu, select *Retrieve/List/Execute the command.* You see

Record#	BRAND	MODEL	QUANTITY	FIRST_NAME	LAST_NAME	WORK_PHONE
2	NIZO	T-35	4	Hank	Davies	909-549-3787
9	RALURIC	RND-1	3	Marcel	Phillip	310-563-0987

These are the items of which you had only five or less.

Here are a few important points to remember when creating Views:

- You may have as many as 15 databases linked in any given View.
- Each file is linked to the next one in the chain by one (and only one) field. The linkage is declared in the same manner as you did it above.
- Fields used for each linkage must have the same name, type, width, and contents in the two databases on each side of the link.
- When linking more that two files in a chain, remember that each file can be linked "into" only once. In our example, PHONEBK was linked "into" STEREO. If you wanted to add another database to this view, it would have to link into PHONEBK, not STEREO.
- Linked files should have the same number of records to work properly.
- Each file must contain records for each entry of the common field. For example, in our case, all rep numbers appearing in the master file, STEREO, must have matching records in the linked database, PHONEBK.

Finally, how do you turn off a View once it's on? You either have to turn on another one via the *Set Up* menu or get to the Dot prompt and type

CLEAR ALL ↵

Please enter this Dot prompt command now.

How to Update a Master List from a Related File

Rather than simply adding records to a master file from a related file, as we did with the *Append from* command, more complex business applications often call for updating master file data with information contained in an associated database. The *Update* command (not to be confused with the Update menu in the Assistant) lets you do this.

Here's an example. Suppose that in addition to the stereo/TV inventory list, you want to create a receiving list to be used in your shipping and receiving department. That way, each time you receive new stock, someone in receiving could append to the receiving list a record of the items received. Later, the quantity field in your inventory could be updated from the receiving list in one fell swoop. Also, since you have to keep track of serial numbers for warrantee purposes, you can do this as each item is received.

Well, it seems that all this could be done with the STEREO inventory list you already have, with just a few modifications to the structure, such as adding a a field for the serial number—or can it? Let's think about this a moment. The serial number requires a separate record for each individual piece of equipment, like this:

Category	Brand	Model	Serial Number	Quantity	Wholesale
RECEIVER	ACME	R25-MT	1000	1	19.99
RECEIVER	ACME	R25-MT	1001	1	19.99
RECEIVER	ACME	R25-MT	1002	1	19.99

Here's the problem. The only difference between each record is the serial number. This takes up a lot of extra time typing in the same information repeatedly (inviting typos), and it takes up more disk space too—a serious consideration with large databases. Furthermore, the idea of the records in the STEREO database is to consolidate all the equipment of the same brand and model into a single quantity. It can't do that *and* keep separate records of each individual turntable with its unique serial number. Using a second database for serial numbers, which separately records each item received, is a better idea. Here's how to do it.

1. First we have to modify the structure of the main inventory database to add a part number field. The part number will serve as the "link" that connects the two databases. There must be linking field

common to both databases. So, modify the structure by adding PART. It looks like this:

	Field Name	Type	Width	Dec
1	CATEGORY	Character	10	
2	BRAND	Character	10	
3	MODEL	Character	6	
4	QUANTITY	Numeric	2	0
5	WHOLESALE	Numeric	6	2
6	RETAIL	Numeric	6	2
7	LAST_ORDER	Date	8	
8	REP_NO	Character	2	
9	PART	Character	3	

2. Now Browse the STEREO database and add the following part numbers for each record.

CATEGORY	BRAND	MODEL	QUANTITY	WHOLESALE	RETAIL	LAST_ORDER	REP_NO	PART
RECEIVER	ACME	R25-MT	13	19.99	49.99	05/15/86	09	001
RECEIVER	NIZO	T-35	4	312.00	425.25	01/12/86	02	002
RECEIVER	NIZO	T-33	5	225.49	350.49	01/12/86	02	005
RECEIVER	NADIR	2-CHP	50	12.95	29.99	03/06/53	01	007
SPEAKERS	TALBEST	BG-20	6	250.00	350.88	07/13/86	04	008
SPEAKERS	RAZCO	L-55	30	199.00	249.00	03/01/85	03	010
TAPE DECK	FLOWUTTER	WBL-5	5	149.33	250.77	09/15/86	05	004
TAPE DECK	ROLLEM	CAS-3	10	125.65	212.99	09/01/86	06	003
TURNTABLE	RALURIC	RND-1	3	595.00	850.00	10/01/86	07	011
TURNTABLE	XIRTAM	25-L	5	99.99	149.99	02/29/84	08	009
TELEVISION	BLABBEX	K22	29	189.99	249.99	10/12/86	09	006
TELEVISION	BIG-VUE	BV-45	5	595.00	750.00	10/12/86	09	012

3. Now create the receiving list database, RECV, with the following structure:

Field	Field Name	Type	Width	Dec
1	PART	Character	3	
2	SERIAL_NUM	Character	6	

4. Now add the following information for the items you received today.

Record#	PART	SERIAL_NUM
1	001	234595
2	001	234958

```
3  005    9943-T
4  012    555554
5  004    100022
6  005    399909
7  008    495891
8  010    111223
```

Good. Now there's only one more thing to do before doing the update. We have to index the master list on the linking field, PART. This field is called the *update key*. The rule is that you have to index at least the master file. You can index the other file too if you want to speed things up. Otherwise you have to add the word RANDOM to the command, as you will see. First the indexing.

1. Open the STEREO database in workarea 1 and index it like this:

   ```
   SELECT 1 ↵
   USE STEREO ↵
   INDEX ON PART TO PARTNUM ↵
   SET INDEX TO PARTNUM ↵
   ```

2. Open the RECV database in workarea 2 like this:

   ```
   SELECT 2 ↵
   USE RECV ↵
   ```

3. Now select workarea 1 again, since that's where the update is going to occur.

   ```
   SELECT 1 ↵
   ```

4. OK, now for the update. We want dBASE III PLUS to go through the RECV file, look at each record, and determine what the part number is. Then it should look for the matching record in the STEREO file and update the quantity column appropriately (add 1 for each one received.)

```
UPDATE ON PART FROM RECV REPLACE QUANTITY WITH QUANTITY + 1 RANDOM ↵
     8 records updated
LIST OFF ↵
```

CATEGORY	BRAND	MODEL	QUANTITY	WHOLESALE	RETAIL	LAST_ORDER	REP_NO	PART
RECEIVER	ACME	R25-MT	15	19.99	49.99	05/15/86	09	001
RECEIVER	NIZO	T-35	4	312.00	425.25	01/12/86	02	002

TAPE DECK	ROLLEM	CAS-3	10	125.65	212.99	09/01/86	06	003
TAPE DECK	FLOWUTTER	WBL-5	6	149.33	250.77	09/15/86	05	004
RECEIVER	NIZO	T-33	7	225.49	350.49	01/12/86	02	005
TELEVISION	BLABBEX	K22	29	189.99	249.99	10/12/86	09	006
RECEIVER	NADIR	2-CHP	50	12.95	29.99	03/06/53	01	007
SPEAKERS	TALBEST	BG-20	7	250.00	350.88	07/13/86	04	008
TURNTABLE	XIRTAM	25-L	5	99.99	149.99	02/29/84	08	009
SPEAKERS	RAZCO	L-55	31	199.00	249.00	03/01/85	03	010
TURNTABLE	RALURIC	RND-1	3	595.00	850.00	10/01/86	07	011
TELEVISION	BIG-VUE	BV-45	6	595.00	750.00	10/12/86	09	012

Well, if you typed all that in right, you should see the listing above. Notice the QUANTITY column is updated correctly. Don't forget, the RANDOM part of the command is only necessary because we didn't index the RECV database on the update key, PART.

This is one of the most complex commands in dBASE III PLUS, so don't worry if you can't grasp it immediately, or apply it to your own needs without a little trial and error. If you're baffled, it may help to divide our command into two parts. Here's the command again, divided for clarity, with the capitalization changed and with the words you fill-in in a lighter type:

UPDATE on PART **from** RECV
REPLACE QUANTITY **with** QUANTITY + 1 **random**

The first half says, "Update the current file from the file RECV, using the key, PART." The second half says, "Each time you find a match between the part numbers in the two files, add 1 to the QUANTITY column, and by the way, the FROM database isn't indexed."

Rules for updating

Here's a wrap-up of the rules to remember when doing an update:

- The database you are modifying via *Update* must be open and in the currently selected workarea. The file must be either indexed or sorted on the update-key field that links to two files.
- The other database (called the "From" database) must meet three requirements:

    1. The From file must have at least the key field in common with the "To" database (same name, size, and type).

2. If the From file is not sorted, you must add the word RANDOM to the end of the command.

3. The From file must be open in an unselected workarea.

Once you feel comfortable with the general idea, we can expand on it with further complications (or opportunities depending on your orientation).

First, although we only made a numerical adjustment to a field in our master database, it's also possible to completely replace a field's data with data from the second database. For example, you could add another field to the RECV database called PRICE to record price changes noted on the invoices which accompany the equipment you receive. These changes, along with the quantity change we already did, could be updated to the STEREO database with this more complex command:

UPDATE on PART **from** RECV **REPLACE** QUANTITY **with** QUANTITY + 1;
,WHOLESALE **with** 2->PRICE ↵

(The **;** means the command would all be typed in on one line, but we couldn't fit it all on a single line here.)

Notice that when you want *Update* to completely replace a field, you have to preface the source field with the name of the workarea it is in (such as 2->PRICE).

This chapter has shown you at least three means for using multiple databases: *Append, Create View,* and *Update.* All three commands can help eliminate unnecessary and time-consuming work for you. They are all rather complex commands and as such, offer strong dividends in flexibility and power. But becoming adept in their use will certainly require some experimentation and patience. The best approach to mastering these commands is to come up with a database application, try implementing the command on your own, and then refer back to these examples for guidance and correction.

For notes on how to append data from non-dBASE files, please refer to Appendix C, under the *Append* command.

16 Creating Customized Data-Entry and Report Screens

Screen Painter custom screens; checking for input errors

So far, when appending and editing data, you've relied on dBASE's simple built-in screen format that displays your records in a rather primitive manner. That is, the fields are stacked one on top of another, and only in the order in which they were entered when you created the database's structure. Even worse, the oddly restricted field names are the only reminder you have of what data goes where. Particularly with our inventory list, or any file with lots of cryptic field names, a data-entry person could become confused about where the data goes. This can lead to accidental entry of data into the wrong fields.

dBASE III PLUS has a built-in feature called the *Screen Painter* with which you can create customized format screens for data entry or display. Using the Screen Painter, you can design format screens that look similar to paper forms you (and perhaps your data-entry staff) are already familiar with. Fields may be placed anywhere on the screen with any names you choose, and screens can include other messages or prompts too. You can even have your screen do automatic *range checking* of data to cut down on entry of erroneous data, as when dBASE rejects month 15 in Date fields.

Once a screen is designed, it can be saved and then used whenever you like, to enter or display data. The displays can be either on screen or on paper.

How to Get Started with the Screen Painter

With no further ado, let's begin to make up a format screen for the STEREO database.

1. From the Assistant, select *Create/Format.*
2. Select the disk drive and enter STEREO as the file name of the screen format (dBASE automatically assigns the extension .SCR to the file). The screen painter presents you with a new screen, as shown in Figure 16.1.
3. From this new screen, select *Select database file/STEREO.DBF.*
4. Select *Load fields.* A fields list appears. The screen painter is asking which fields you want to include in your screen. Select them all, using the ↵ key to select, and the ↓ to move to the next field. An arrow will show up next to each field name as it is selected.
5. Press → and you will see the rather strange looking screen shown in Figure 16.2. This is called the *Blackboard,* and it is where you

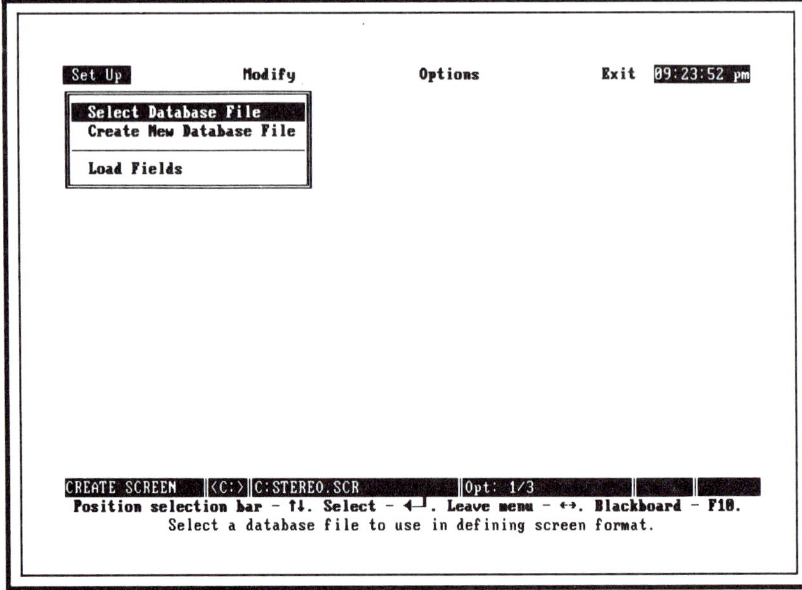

Figure 16.1: The Screen Painter main menu

construct your screen. The fields that you just selected appear in the order and format you're used to seeing them in, only on the Blackboard they have funny letters and numbers "loaded" in them. The character fields have X's in them, the numerical fields have 9s in them, and logical fields have an L in them. This is just to remind you which field type they are.

6. Now, say you want to create a screen that looks like the one in Figure 16.3, for data entry and editing.

   It's going to take a little doing, but it's not really as difficult as you might think. You simply enter the text wherever you want it to appear, and you "drag" the fields around and place them where you like. Drawing the boxes is a cinch too, as you will see.

Before going further, take a look at the list of editing keys in Table 16.1. You'll have to use these keys when working on the Blackboard.

A quick note of warning: Pressing ^V or the Ins key while the cursor is positioned on a field will result in changing the length of the field itself, something you don't want to do unless you're creating a new database from the Screen Painter (we aren't). The same goes for the Del key.

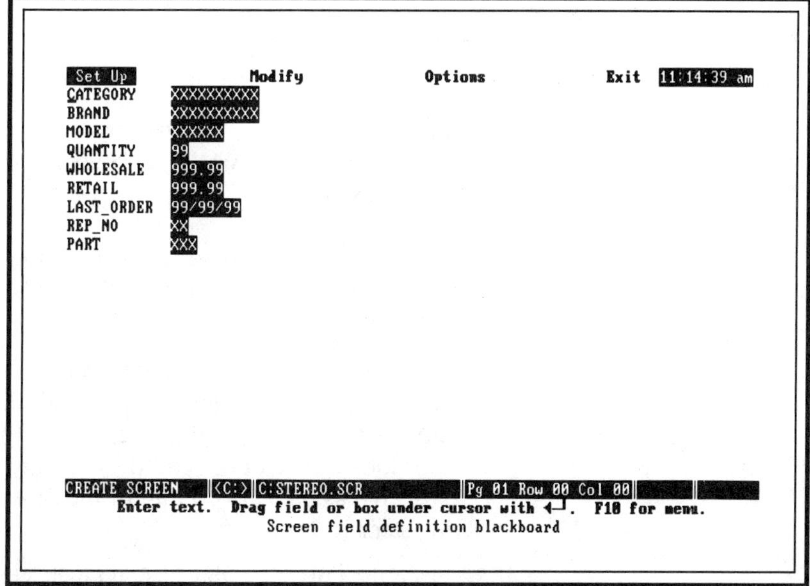

Figure 16.2: The initial Blackboard with fields loaded

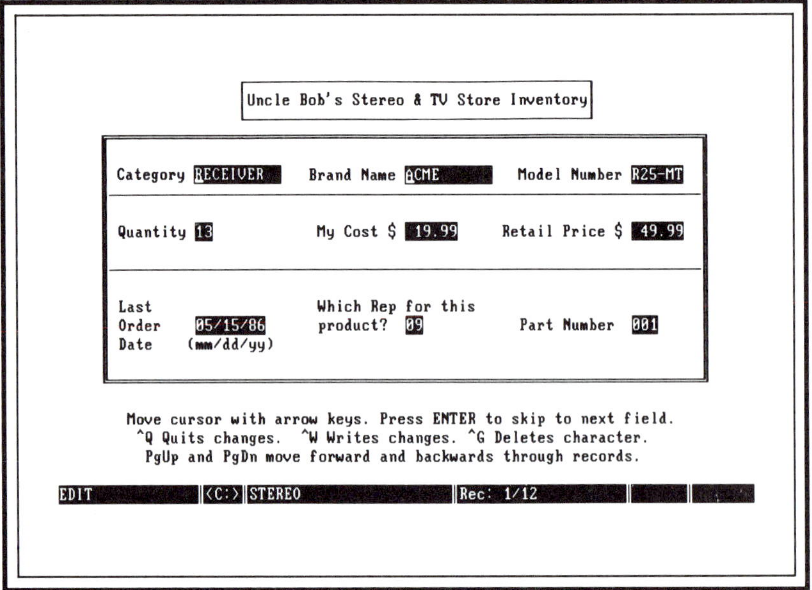

Figure 16.3: The STEREO inventory data-entry screen

How to Begin the Modifications

Obviously, if left as it is, the data-entry screen would look identical to the default screen that dBASE III PLUS uses anyway. So let's begin making changes to the screen.

1. For starters, make some room at the top of the screen by inserting blank lines to push down all the fields. Do this by pressing ^N five times.
2. Now we'll begin moving fields. You move fields by placing the cursor on a field's *highlight* (the part with the X's or the 9s). With the cursor on the highlight, press ↵. Then move the cursor to the location where you'd like the field repositioned and press ↵ again. Let's do this for the BRAND field, using the following steps.
3. Place the cursor on the BRAND highlight. Press ↵.

4. Notice the Message and Navigation Lines at the bottom of the screen. They tell you what field you are working with and how to move it. Also notice the Status Line. It tells you exactly where the cursor is at any time. This helps you line up fields and messages on the Blackboard.

Main Key	*Letter Key*	*Action*
Moving		
←,→,↑, or ↓		Moves the cursor one space in the indicated direction.
End	^F	Moves to the next word.
Home	^A	Moves to the previous word.
↵		Moves down a line. Inserts a line if insert mode is on.
PgDn	^C	Moves the cursor up 18 lines.
PgUp	^R	Moves the cursor down 18 lines.
Deleting		
Del	^G	Deletes letter at cursor position.
Backspace		Deletes letter to the left of cursor.
^T		Deletes letters up to the end of the word.
^Y		Deletes the line the cursor is on.
^U		Deletes the field or box the cursor is on.
Inserting		
Ins	^V	Turns the insert mode on/off.
^N		Inserts a blank line below the cursor.
Other		
F10		Switches between blackboard and menu mode.

Table 16.1: Screen Painter editing keys

5. Press the → key 15 times.
6. Press the ↑ key once. The Status Line should say you are at row 05, column 36.
7. Press ↵. The BRAND field jumps to the cursor position. Your screen now looks like Figure 16.4.
8. Now we'll move the MODEL field up to the same line as CATEGORY and BRAND, only further to the right. To do this, put the cursor on the MODEL highlight and press ↵.
9. Move the cursor to row 05, column 62 with the → and ↑ keys. Press ↵. The highlight should jump to the new position.

   Note: If you are having trouble getting the fields to move, before you move off the field you want to drag make sure the Navigation Line says

   Move field with ↑↓←→. Complete with ↵. Exit drag with Esc.

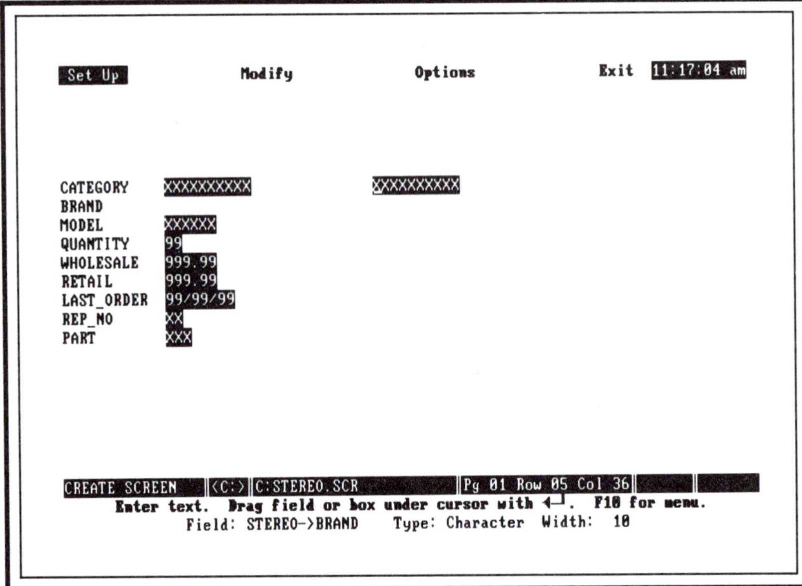

Figure 16.4: The BRAND field repositioned

If this message doesn't show, you have to hit ↵ once before you move.

10. OK. Moving right along, place all the other fields as follows, refering to Figure 16.5.

   - Move WHOLESALE to row 8, column 36.
   - Move RETAIL to row 8, column 62.
   - Move REP_NO to row 11, column 36.
   - Move PART to row 11, column 62.

   Your screen should now look like Figure 16.5.

Clearly we'll have to reposition the field names too, so that they are next to their associated highlights. But since the Blackboard allows you to replace the actual field names with more reasonable prompts, why not take advantage of this?

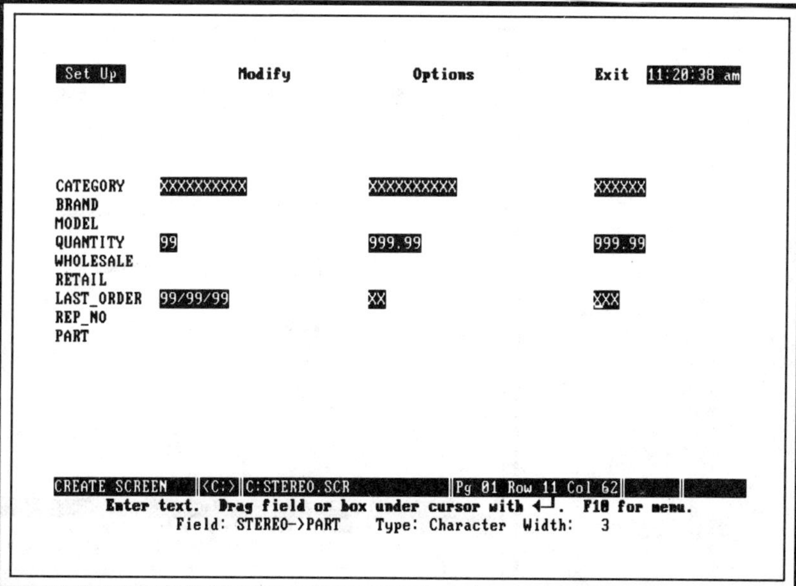

Figure 16.5: The fields repositioned

1. Make sure the cursor is not on a highlight.
2. Make sure insert mode is off. (Press ^V until the "Ins" message on the Status Line goes away.)
3. Move the cursor to the beginning of each field name on the left side of the screen, and erase each name by typing over it with spaces (pressing the space bar). Your screen should now look like Figure 16.6.
4. Let's add a few more blank lines now, to further separate the fields and to make room for what we are going to type. Place the cursor anywhere on row 6 and press ^N twice. This inserts two blank lines.
5. Now position the cursor anywhere on row 12 and press ^N twice.
6. Next, type in the prompts for the data-entry person, as you see in Figure 16.7.
7. Once that is done, let's add a title at the top. Move to row 02 column 19 and type in

Uncle Bob's Stereo & TV Store Inventory

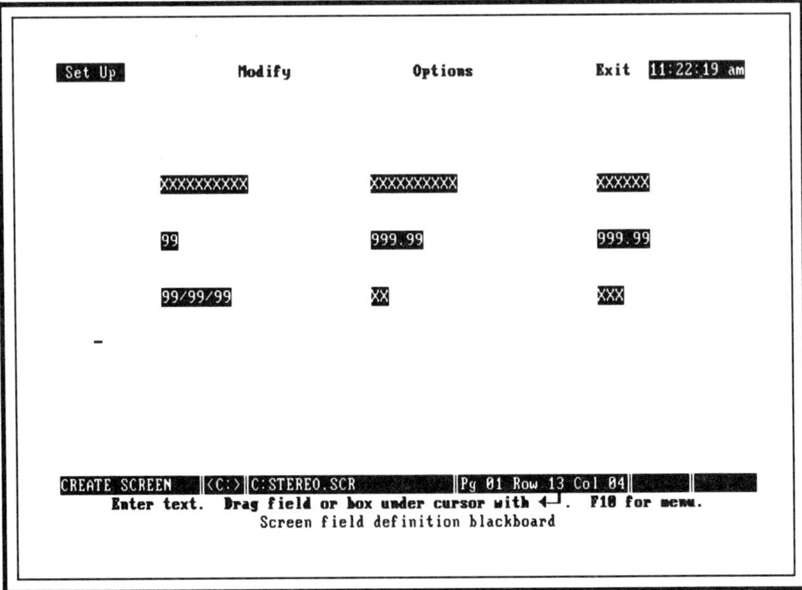

Figure 16.6: The old field names erased

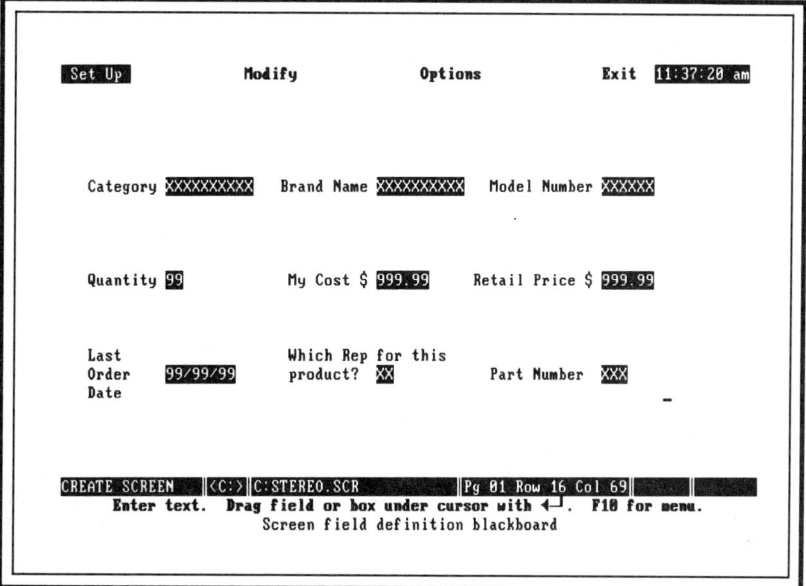

Figure 16.7: The data-entry screen with prompts added

8. Finally, let's put a nice box around the fields. To do this, press F10. Then select *Options/Double bar.*
9. Move the cursor to row 03 column 01 and press ↵. This marks the beginning of the box we're going to draw.
10. Move the cursor to row 17, column 69. This marks the opposite corner of the box. Press ↵. Voila! Not half bad. Now let's draw two horizontal lines to divide the box into sections.
11. Move the cursor to row 12 column 02. Press F10. Select *Option/Single bar.* Press ↵. This marks the beginning of the line we want to draw. Now move the cursor to row 12 column 68 and press ↵. This marks the other end of the line. Tricky, eh? You see, if you stay on the same row or column, the Blackboard draws a straight line instead of a box. (You can draw vertical lines this way too.)
12. Now repeat the above steps to draw a line across row 7. Your screen looks like Figure 16.8.
13. Now, to see how the new screen actually works, first save it by pressing F10 and selecting *Exit/Save.*

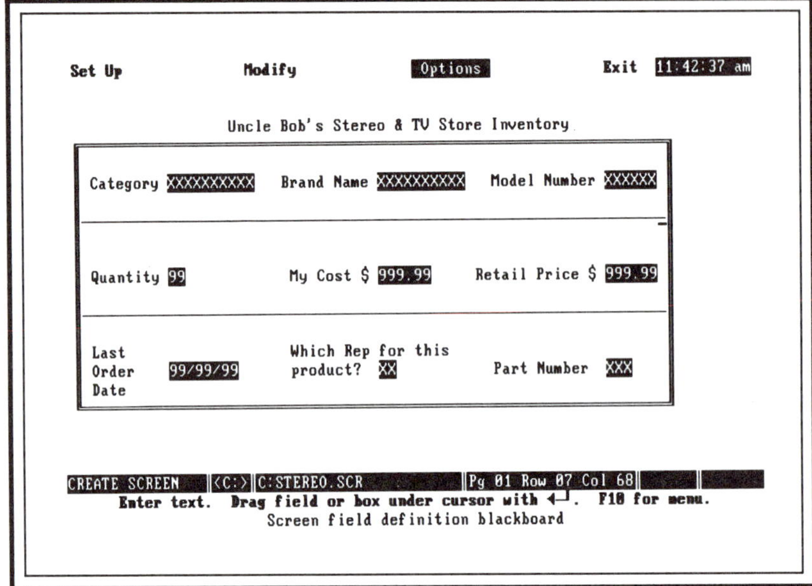

Figure 16.8: The screen with subdivisions

14. The Assistant returns. Select *Set Up/Format for screen.* Select the drive and *STEREO.FMT.* The Set Up menu reappears. It looks like nothing happened. Actually it did, though, as you'll see.
15. Make sure the STEREO database file is open, and select *Update/Edit.* Record number 1 appears magically in your new screen arrangement, as shown in Figure 16.9.

How to Modify Your Screen Format

You may have noticed that there weren't any editing commands displayed on the new screen. Pressing F1 won't make them appear either, because they would have to overwrite your formatted screen. If you think it'd be helpful to have editing commands displayed as a reminder, you'll have to type them into your format screen.

Let's do that, and while we're at it, let's add *range checking* to the Date field. Range checking ensures that data entered falls within a certain

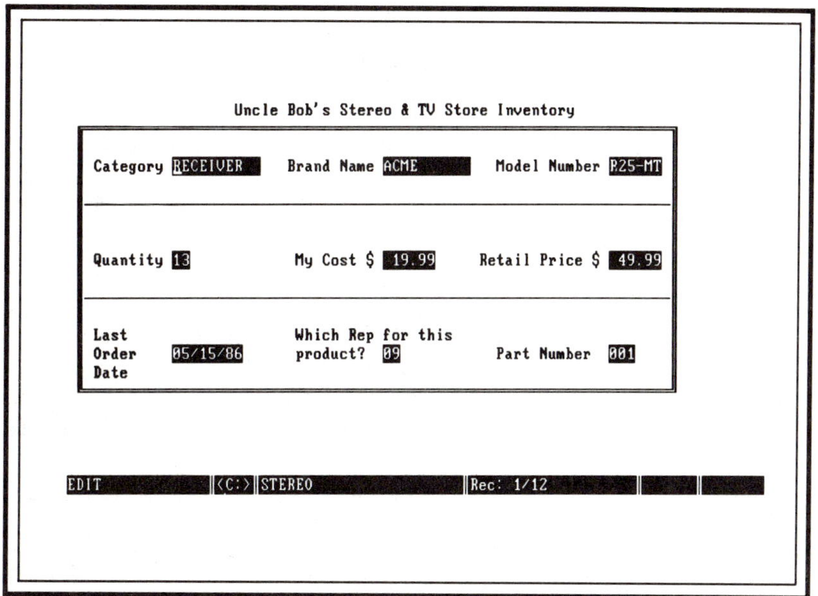

Figure 16.9: Trying out the new format file with *Edit*

range. This is particularly useful if you intend to do searches based on a field where a slight error in data entry can make a record impossible to find for reports or listings. With range checking active during data entry, the computer will beep if unacceptable data is typed in.

Another modification we could add is something to ensure that the Character fields (CATEGORY, BRAND, and MODEL) are entered into the database in uppercase only and that the Character field PART has only numbers placed in it. (This will increase the accuracy of searches using the *Seek* and *Locate* options.) These last two changes are done using the screen painter's *Picture Template* feature.

Adding Help messages

To get started making changes to the format screen,

1. Get out of Edit mode by pressing ^Q.
2. Select *Modify/Format*.

3. Select the drive and STEREO.SCR.
4. Press F10 to see your screen.
5. The cursor is at the upper left corner of the screen. Move it down to the bottom and type in some text that would help a data-entry person who is appending or editing records. Perhaps you'll want to use something similar to what I've done in Figure 16.10.

Adding range checking

OK. Now we want to add some range checking on the Date field so that only dates in the current year are acceptable.

1. Place the cursor on the *Last Order Date* highlight (technically the LAST_ORDER field). The Message Line on your screen should say

   Field: STEREO->LAST_ORDER

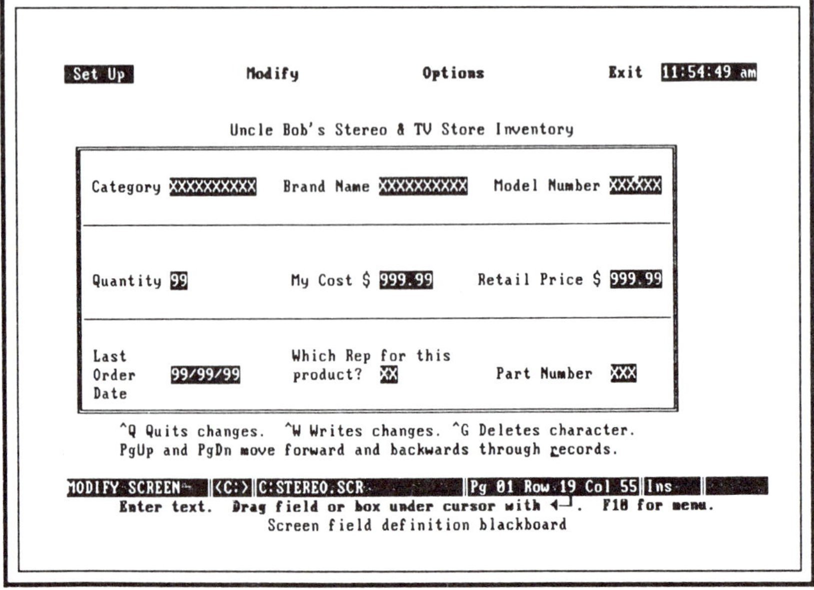

Figure 16.10: Adding Help notes to the screen

2. Press F10.
3. The *Field Definition* of the LAST_ORDER field pops up in a box. (Incidentally from this box, you can make changes to the contents and size of fields displayed on the screen, as mentioned earlier.)
4. Select *Range:*
5. Another smaller box appears now asking what the upper and lower limits of the range should be. Select *Lower.*
6. The familiar arrow appears and date slashes are typed in for you by dBASE. Since we want to allow only dates falling in the current year, type in

   01/01/87 ↵

   You'll hear a beep, and the arrow disappears.
7. Press ↓ to highlight *Upper limit.*
8. Press ↵.
9. Type in

   12/31/87

10. Press ← to exit, then F10 to get back to your screen. That finishes the range checking for the Date field. Incidentally, range checking can only be activated for Date or Numeric fields. If you want to do range checking on a field such as our Part number field, you'll have to make sure your databases structure has it listed as Numeric.

Using the Picture Template

The *Picture Template* option in the Screen Painter's Modify menu lets you format Character fields in a number of ways. By default, the Screen Painter fills all character fields with X's. But there are other options for Character fields. Here's the complete list of Picture Template options:

Symbol	*Effect*
A	Allows entry of letters only.
L	Allows entry of T, Y, N, F only.
N	Allows entry of letters and numbers only.

X Allows entry of any characters (letters, numbers, punctuation marks, etc.).

Y Allows entry of Y or N only.

Allows entry of numbers, spaces, periods, and + or – signs only.

9 Allows entry of numbers and + or – signs only.

! Allows any characters; converts all letters to uppercase.

We'll want to use the **!** symbol for each of our Character fields. I'll tell you how to do it for CATEGORY, and you can do it for the others.

1. Put the cursor on the CATEGORY highlight, then press F10.
2. Select *Picture Template.*
3. A box appears with the template options in it. Your screen now looks like Figure 16.11. Down at the bottom of the screen, a space for typing in the template for the CATEGORY field appears. This is where you change the template.
4. Type in ten **!** marks.

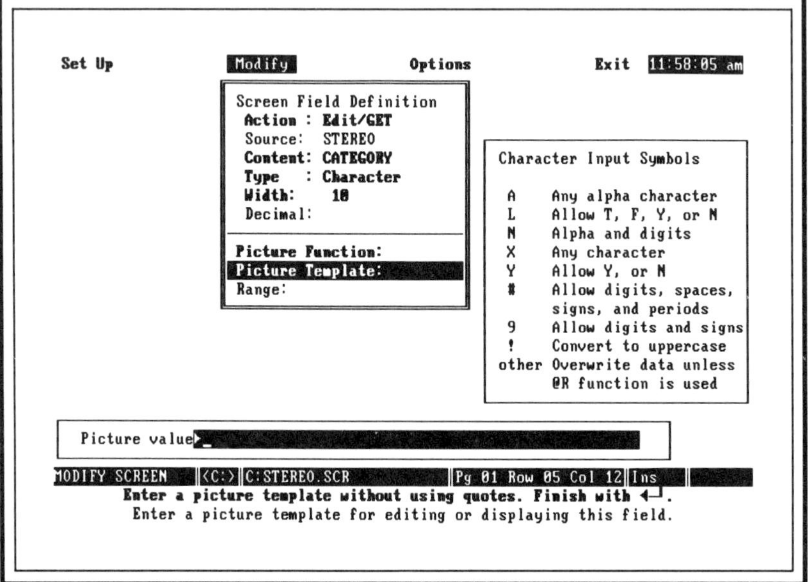

Figure 16.11: Specifying the picture template for CATEGORY

5. Press ↵ and then F10 to return to the Blackboard.
6. Now convert the BRAND and MODEL fields to **!** marks, using the same technique. Just look up in the field definition box to see how long the field is and type in that many **!** marks.
7. Finally, to ensure that the Part number and Rep number fields get only numbers placed in them, use the same technique, but type in 999 and 99 instead of the **!** marks.
8. When you're finished, your screen should look like Figure 16.12.

There is another kind of format option which can make life easier for data-entry people. You can specify certain characters to be inserted automatically in the fields of each new record you append. For example, typing in the parentheses or dashes as punctuation when entering zillions of phone numbers is a bother. Using the picture

###-###-####

in the template for a phone number field will eliminate the need to type the punctuation in each time you add a record.

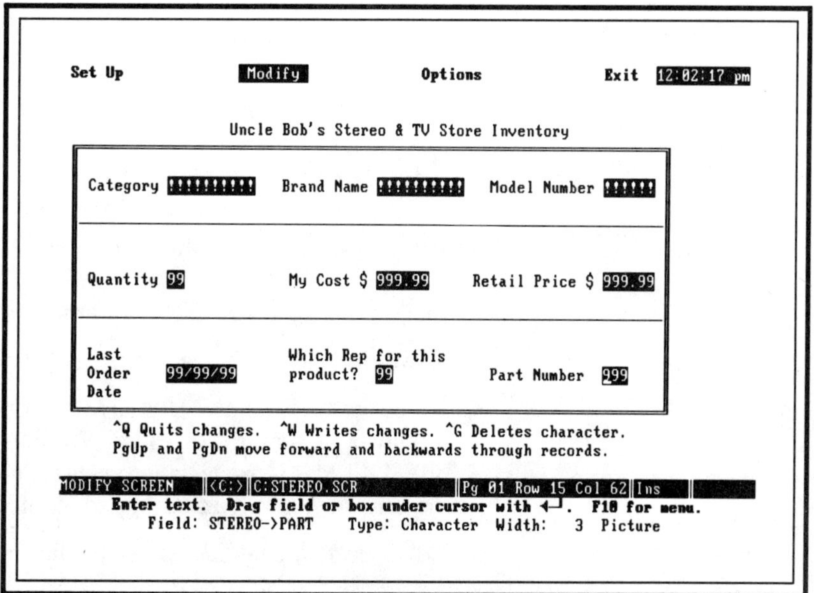

Figure 16.12: The Picture Template changes completed

Finishing touches

Great. The screen looks pretty good now. The only problem is that it's off center. Since that's a typical problem when creating screens, it's good exercise to learn how to fix it. This process would be a snap except for the fact that you cannot move a box! You have to erase it first, move the text, and then redraw the box. A word to the wise is to draw the box last!

1. To erase the box, place the cursor anywhere on the line of the box, and press ^U. The whole box disappears.
2. Now do this with each of the single lines we drew. (Actually, the cursor will be blinking just a hair below the line. You cannot get the cursor directly on the line.)
3. Make sure insert mode is on, and with the cursor at the left edge of the screen enter four spaces at the beginning of each line. This will push all the fields and text four spaces over to the right. (The word *Category* should now start on column 7.)
4. Now redraw the box and make whatever other changes you find pleasing to the eye. I made a few more changes on my screen, like eliminating a blank line or two to make things looks a little more even. Figure 16.13 shows how it finally looked when I was done. Notice the added editing instructions and the nice little box setting off the title of the screen.

Using the format screen

To use the new screen, do the following:

1. First, save it by pressing F10 and then selecting *Exit/Save*.
2. Now select *Set Up/Format for screen* from the main Assistant menu.
3. Select the drive and STEREO.FMT. (Notice that when creating or modifying a screen, it's called STEREO.SCR. When you save it, dBASE III PLUS creates another file called STEREO.FMT which is the one it actually uses during appending or editing.)
4. Now select *Update/Edit* to see the finished product.

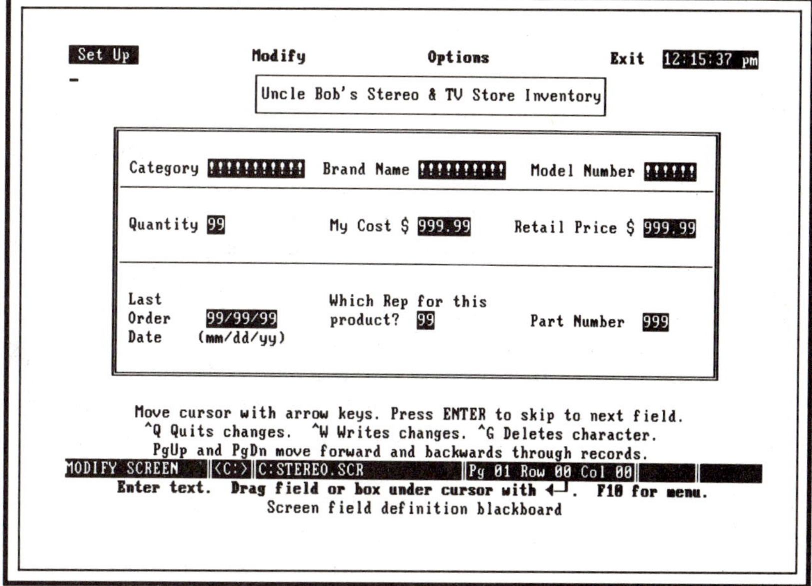

Figure 16.13: The final screen

Some additional points about format screens

There are some other options available while in the Screen Painter, such as changing the size of fields, adding new fields or even creating a whole new database. But since all of these things can be done in other ways, and with less confusion, I have not covered them in this chapter. You may want to experiment on your own.

Another possibility is to declare some fields as *display only* fields. This will prevent anyone from altering the contents of certain records while editing them. For example, we may want to protect all the fields except for Quantity and Last_Order, since none of the other fields should change from day to day. You do this by selecting the Screen Painter's Modify menu. Once you get the Blackboard up, put the cursor on the field highlight that you want to change to display-only mode. Press F10. Select *Action* from the Modify menu and press ↵. The highlighted words next to *Action* change from

Edit/GET

to

Display/SAY

Then press F10 to get back to the Blackboard. Repeat this process for each field that you want to change to display only. Then save the new form.

You're probably wondering how you can append new records, as opposed to editing old ones, if lots of the fields are display-only fields. Good question. You can't. But you *can* have as many format screens for a given database as you want. Then you can activate one for appending and one for editing, or even create customized screens for each data-entry person who uses a given database.

Unfortunately the Screen Painter doesn't let you make a few modifications and then save each new version under a different name, while retaining the original. You could make each new one from scratch, but that's a waste of time. The solution is to make as many copies of formats as you want, using the DOS *COPY* command. For example, here's how you would make three copies of our STEREO format screen for subsequent modification.

1. First you have to get out of dBASE III PLUS, using *Quit*.
2. Then from the DOS prompt type

   COPY STEREO.SCR STEREO2.SCR ↵
   COPY STEREO.SCR STEREO3.SCR ↵
   COPY STEREO.SCR STEREO4.SCR ↵

3. Now that each file has a different name, you can modify and use each one separately.

Printing your forms

You can print your forms if you like, using the *PRT SC* (print screen) key on your computer. Pressing the Shift key and this key together causes whatever is on your screen to be printed out. Make sure your printer is on and ready to print, of course. Be advised, however, that boxes and lines tend not to come out correctly on many printers. They may print as letters instead of lines. If you have this problem, and you intend to do lots of forms printing this way, you may want to just eliminate boxes and lines from your forms.

One last point. You may have noticed that the cursor moves through the fields on your new screen in order from left to right, not top to bottom. This is just how dBASE does it, and there's no altering it, without getting into complex programming. You may want to keep this in mind as you set up your screens. If it makes logical sense to separate fields into different sections on your screen, you are better off creating horizontal sections, as we did with the STEREO screen.

Appendix A

Installing dBASE III PLUS for Your Computer

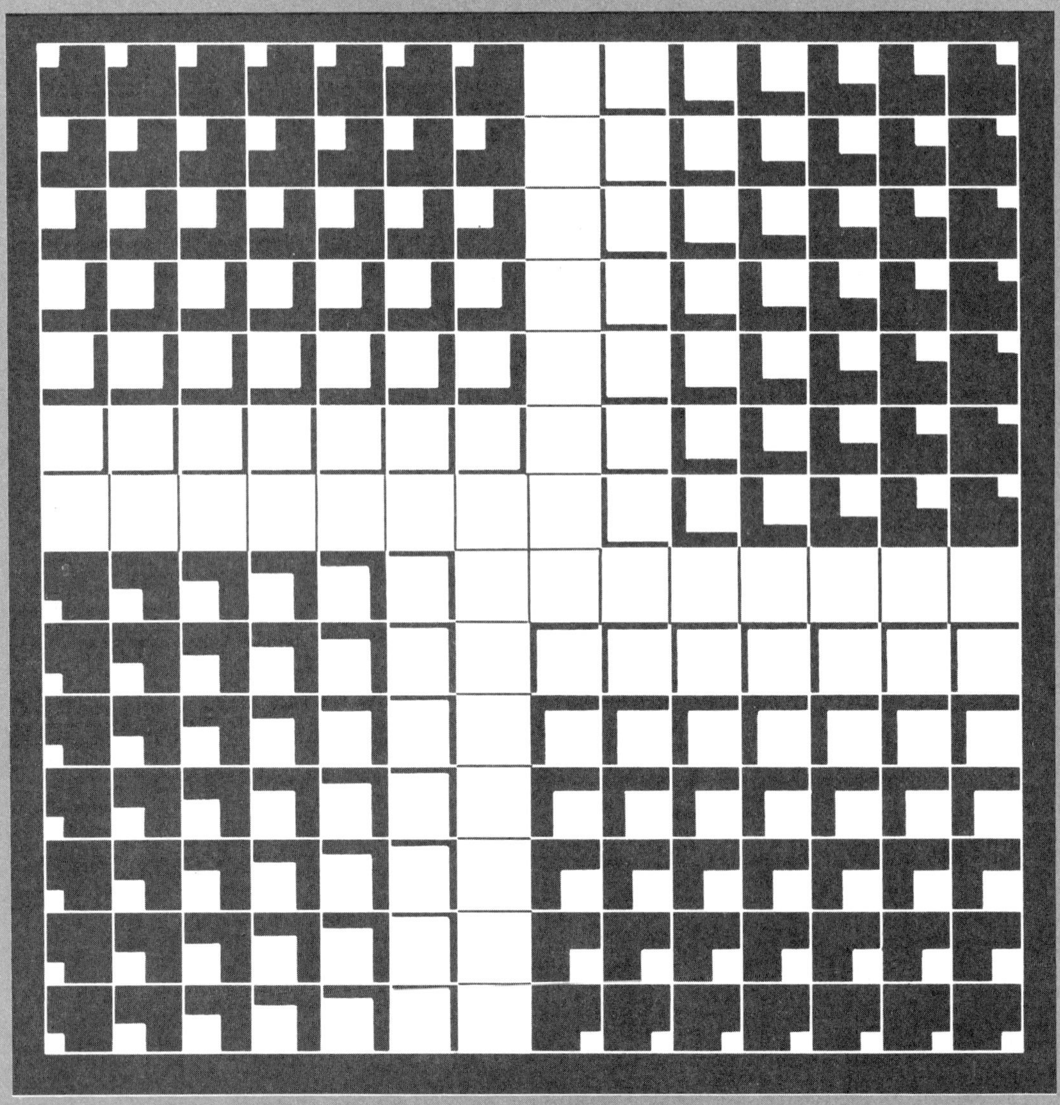

Before you can run dBASE III PLUS, you have to *install* it properly for your particular type of computer. Installation is the process of copying the dBASE III PLUS program and associated files onto new disks, and telling dBASE a few things about your computer. If you have already installed dBASE III PLUS according to the instructions that came with it, you do not need to follow the instructions in this appendix. If you have not yet installed dBASE, you should do so by following the steps described below.

Types of Computers

dBASE III PLUS can be used with three basic categories of IBM PC and compatible computers:

- Two-floppy-disk systems (generally called PC's)
- Hard-disk systems (generally called XT's)
- Two or more of the above, connected by a LAN (Local Area Network)

Installation for LANs, being rather complicated and not yet widely used, is not covered in this book. Please refer to the *Getting Started* manual included with dBASE III PLUS for installation and specific operational details for LAN systems.

If you are in doubt about whether you have a hard-disk system or a two-floppy-disk system, consult the operations manual that came with your computer, or ask your dealer.

Hardware requirements

dBASE III PLUS is designed to run on the IBM Personal Computer (PC), IBM AT, IBM XT, and the Compaq or other 100% IBM PC compatible computers, with at least 256k of RAM. Either two floppy disks or a floppy disk and a hard disk are required. If your computer is less than "100% compatible," dBASE may still run fine—it depends on the computer. Some so-called IBM compatibles are known to run dBASE without a hitch. Others, for some subtle technical reasons, don't work at all or may exhibit occassional problems with dBASE III PLUS. If in doubt, give it a try anyway. What do you have to lose? And since dBASE is such a popular program, chances are that your computer's manufacturer saw to it that it would run dBASE anyway.

There are a few hard disk computers that will not allow a normal installation, requiring a modified technique for running dBASE. These computers are listed in the hard-disk installation section.

Software requirements

In order for dBASE III PLUS to run, you must be using the following software:

1. If your computer is limited to 256k of RAM, you must have IBM PC-DOS release 2.0 or higher, or MS-DOS release 2.1 or higher. You cannot use DOS 3.0 or higher. You must also alter the CONFIG.DB and CONFIG.SYS files on your dBASE III PLUS System Disk #1 for DBASE to work in your machine. The details of this operation are covered in the addendum to the *Getting Started* manual, page 1-1. This modification basically decreases the number of "buffers" that DOS allocates to storing disk data in memory. However, if you can arrange to install more RAM in your computer, this is a better alternative to altering these files, because dBASE III PLUS will often run faster with more RAM.
2. If your computer has 384K or more, you may use PC- or MS-DOS 3.0 or higher in addition to those versions listed above.

If you have older versions of the necessary DOS operating systems (pre-2.0), acquire an upgrade before continuing the installation.

Formatting Blank Disks

Before beginning the installation, you have to make working copies of your original dBASE III PLUS disks so you're not using your master copies to run the program. This way your originals will be in good shape in case something happens to the working copies. The first step in making copies is to *format* three blank disks.

Formatting is the process required before new floppy disks are ready to store data. Here's how to format the disks:

1. Place your DOS diskette in Drive A, and get to the DOS A> prompt.

2. Type

   FORMAT ↵

   DOS responds

   Insert new diskette for drive A:
   and strike any key when ready

   Warning: Don't press any keys yet!

3. Remove the DOS disk and put the first blank disk in drive A and close the drive door.

4. Press ↵

5. When the formatting is finished, DOS will ask you if you want to format another disk. Answer Y, put the next disk in drive A, and press ↵ again. Repeat this for the third disk, then answer N to the "Format another?" question. This returns you to the DOS prompt. Now write a small F up in the upper right hand corner of the label on each of the newly formatted disks, to remind you that the disks have already been formatted. Use a felt-tip pen or something else that won't dig into the plastic diskette.

   If at any point along the way DOS tells you there was a format error, make sure that there is no gummed "write-protect" tab covering the notch on the side of the disk and that the disk is inserted in the drive correctly. Then try again. If you get a format error message again, try another disk.

Remember this technique of formatting for future use. You'll need formatted disks later for storing your databases.

The rest of this appendix is divided into two sections—one for each type of system. If you have a two-floppy-disk system, follow the instructions in the next section. If you have a hard-disk system, follow the instructions in the section "Installation on a Hard-Disk System."

Installation on a Floppy-Disk System

Now to make the working copies of your original dBASE III PLUS disks. There are three disks you'll want to make working copies of. These are

- System Disk #2 (System Disk #1 cannot be copied.)

- Sample Programs and Utilities
- On-Disk Tutorial

Here's how you do it:

1. Put System Disk #2 in drive A.
2. Put a blank, formatted disk in drive B.
3. Type

   COPY A:*.* B:/V ↵

   Wait until the DOS prompt reappears.
4. Remove the disks from both drives. Label the new disk like the original.
5. Put the Sample Programs and Utilities disk in drive A.
6. Repeat steps 2, 3 and 4.
7. Put the On-Disk Tutorial disk in drive A.
8. Repeat steps 2, 3 and 4.
9. Now put away in a safe place your original System Disk #2 and both the original and the copy of the On-Screen Tutorial and the Programs and Utilities disks. Keep the System Disk #1 and the copy of System Disk #2 out for the installation.

Now for the installation.

1. Put your DOS disk in drive A and your System Disk #1 in drive B.
2. From the A> prompt, type

   SYS B: ↵
3. When the A> prompt returns, type

   COPY COMMAND.COM B: ↵

That's it for floppy disk installation.

Installation on a Hard-Disk System

If you have a hard-disk system, it will probably have one floppy-disk drive, and one hard disk. However, some systems have two floppy-disk drives and a hard disk. If you have a hard disk system with two floppy-disk drives, you can opt to install and run dBASE III PLUS from the floppy drives. However, there isn't much sense in this unless you are strapped for room on the hard disk. If you do decide that you'd prefer not to put dBASE III PLUS on your hard disk, and you don't mind having the program run a bit slower (floppy drives transfer data to and from the computer slower than hard disks do), then follow the installation instructions above for floppy-disk systems. (You must have 2.5 million bytes free on your hard disk to install dBASE III PLUS on it.)

Hard-disk compatibility

There is a hardware compatibility problem involved in installing dBASE III PLUS on some hard disks. dBASE's copy-protection technique, called SUPERLoK, prevents you from using the DOS COPY and DISKCOPY commands to make copies of System Disk #1 either to a floppy disk or to the hard disk. If you try to do this, your copies will not work. For floppy systems, the solution is simply to use the original disk to run dBASE III PLUS.

For hard-disk use, you have to copy dBASE III PLUS, including System Disk #1, onto the hard disk, using the dBASE installation program that automates the process. This program keeps track of how many copies have been made. Once the installation program puts dBASE III PLUS on your hard disk, the original System Disk #1 is deactivated, and you cannot run dBASE from it. Nor can you install dBASE III PLUS on another computer's hard disk. However, you can *uninstall* your hard-disk copy *back* onto the floppy and then run it from there, or you can reinstall it on another hard disk if you choose. In other words, your copy of dBASE III PLUS can only be functional on one disk (floppy or hard) at any given time.

The standard installation procedure works with most hard-disk systems, including

AT&T PC 6300
IBM XT
IBM AT
ITT EXTRA

Compaq Portable and Deskpro
Ericsson PC
LEADING EDGE
SPERRY
NCR PC IV
Panasonic Senior Partner
Sanyo MBC-775
Tandy 1000—with Tandy memory expansion, DMA option installed, and running under PC-DOS.
Tandy 1200
Televideo 1605—with ROM version 2.4

However, the following systems will not allow the SUPERLoK copy-protection scheme to put System Disk #1 on the hard disk:

Data General 1 laptop portable with hard disk
GRiD Case laptop portables with hard disk
Wang with PC Emulation card.

Nonstandard hard-disk installation—without SUPERLoK

If your system is *not* in the incompatible list above, skip this section and move to "Standard hard-disk installation with SUPERLoK."
With the incompatible systems, you can copy only the System #2 disk files to the hard disk. System Disk #1 will not install on the hard disk. But you can still run dBASE III PLUS just fine. Only the startup and installation procedures are different. For these systems, you have to use a *key-disk* arrangement whereby the original, master disk has to be in drive A each time you start dBASE up. To get your disks set up, make yourself a new subdirectory on the hard disk and copy System Disk #2 to the hard disk using the DOS COPY command, like this:

1. Put System Disk #2 in drive A.
2. Get to drive C by typing

   C: ↵

3. Create a dBASE subdirectory called DBASE by typing

   MD DBASE ↵

4. Move to the new directory by typing

   CD DBASE ↵

5. Copy all of System Disk #2 to the new directory by typing:

   COPY A:*.* C: ↵

6. Put all of your disks except for System Disk #1 in a safe place for storage.

Now you have to add the DOS system files and the COMMAND.COM file to System Disk #1. To do this

1. Put your DOS disk in drive A.
2. Type

   COPY A:SYS.COM C: ↵

   COPY A:COMMAND.COM C: ↵

3. Remove the DOS disk from drive A and replace it with System Disk #1.
4. Type

   C:SYS A: ↵
   COPY C:COMMAND.COM A: ↵

Running dBASE on a hard disk without SUPERLoK

Now to run the program.

1. Put System Disk #1 in drive A.
2. Reset the computer either by turning it off or by pressing Ctrl, Alt, and Del at the same time.
3. Then to start up the program you must first get to your DBASE directory on the hard disk. Type

   CD DBASE ↵

and then start the program up by typing

A:DBASE ↵

4. After the program loads, you can remove System Disk #1 from drive A.

Standard hard-disk installation with SUPERLoK

Before beginning the installation, you should make backup copies of your dBASE III PLUS disks to work with so you're not using your master copies to run dBASE. This way you'll have unmodified master copies to resort to in case something happens to the working copies. (*Note:* If your hard-disk system has two floppy drives, the easiest way to make these copies is to follow instructions 1–8 at the beginning of the section above "Installation on a Floppy-Disk System." Then return to this section for installation.)

For those of you with hard-disk systems that have only one floppy drive, here's how to make the backup copies, there are three disks you'll want to make backups of. These are

- System Disk #2 (System Disk #1 cannot be copied.)
- Sample Programs and Utilities
- On-Disk Tutorial

Follow these steps to make the copies:

1. Get to drive C (your hard disk) by typing

   C: ↵

2. Create a new subdirectory for storing dBASE III PLUS and associated files by typing

   CD\ ↵
   MD DBASE ↵

3. Move to that subdirectory by typing

   CD DBASE ↵

4. Type

   DIR ↵

   IMPORTANT! DOS should say there are only *two* files in this subdirectory! They will appear to have the names

   . <DIR>
   .. <DIR>

   (This amounts to the directory being empty.) You must be in the DBASE subdirectory, and it must be empty before you continue, because we will be erasing any files in this directory later in the installation process. If there are additional files already there, then you must create a different subdirectory of the main directory, with a different name of your choice. Use that name instead of DBASE in the following steps.

5. To begin making copies, put System Disk #2 in drive A.

6. Type

   COPY A:*.* /V ↵

7. When the copying process is over, put a blank, formatted disk in drive A.

8. Type

   COPY *.* A: /V ↵

   Wait until the DOS prompt reappears.

9. Remove the disk from drive A. Label the new disk like the original.

10. Erase the files in the DBASE subdirectory by typing

    ERASE \DBASE*.* ↵

11. Put the Sample Programs and Utilities disk in drive A.

12. Repeat steps 6 through 10.

13. Put the On-Disk Tutorial disk in drive A.

14. Repeat steps 6 through 10.
    Note: If at any point along the way DOS tells you there was a copying error, refer to your DOS manual for appropriate action.

You may have to try another blank floppy disk and start the copying process for that disk over again. Sometimes it helps just to remove the disk from the drive and reinsert it. Then try again.

15. Now put away in a safe place your original System Disk #2 and both the original copy of the On-Screen Tutorial and the Programs and Utilities disks. Keep the System Disk #1 and the copy of System Disk #2 out for the installation.

16. Now put System Disk #1 in drive A and get to that drive by typing

    A: ↵

17. Begin the automated installation process by typing

    INSTALL C: ↵

18. You should see the dBASE III PLUS installation screen.

19. Follow the prompts to complete the installation. *Notes:* If you get error messages on the screen and the installation process comes to a halt, please refer to page GS-51 in the *Getting Started* manual supplied with dBASE III PLUS.

20. When the installation is complete, you will see the DOS A> prompt again. dBASE is now installed on your hard disk, in the DBASE subdirectory.

Uninstalling dBASE III PLUS

You may want to remove dBASE III PLUS from your hard disk for any of the following reasons:

- You want to install it on another machine.
- You want to run dBASE from floppies to save space on your hard disk.
- Your hard disk has failed.
- You want to run the DOS BACKUP and RESTORE programs for the files in the root directory. (See more on this below)

Doing this requires running the UNINSTAL program. Please refer to the *Getting Started* manual supplied with dBASE III PLUS, page GS-17 for instructions in the use of this program.

Warning! Before using BACKUP and RESTORE

Be advised that the DOS BACKUP and RESTORE procedures, if performed on the entire hard disk or even just on the root directory (\), will destroy your copy of dBASE III PLUS. SUPERLoK stores "invisible" files on the root directory which, once backed up and restored, will no longer work, rendering your copy of dBASE III PLUS nonfunctional. If you want to use BACKUP and RESTORE, make sure to use them only on selected subdirectories, *not* on the root directory, unless you uninstall dBASE III PLUS first. Alternatively, you can use BACKUP with the option that restricts the backup to files stored or changed after a date you specify. If you specify a date after you installed dBASE, BACKUP will leave the dBASE program files alone. See your DOS manual for details on BACKUP options.

Note that, although you cannot make a functioning backup copy of System Disk #1, a backup copy is provided with the program. For floppy-disk systems, this serves simply as a "spare" in case something happens to the first disk. For hard-disk installations, using the backup disk is somewhat more complicated. Refer to the dBASE *Getting Started* pamphlet for details.

There are two other disks provided with dBASE III PLUS that we have not covered in this book. These are the Administrator disks, which are mainly concerned with network installations and with restricting access to files (using "passwords"). Refer to the dBASE manual for instructions on using the Administrator.

Appendix B

Additional Options with the Report Generator

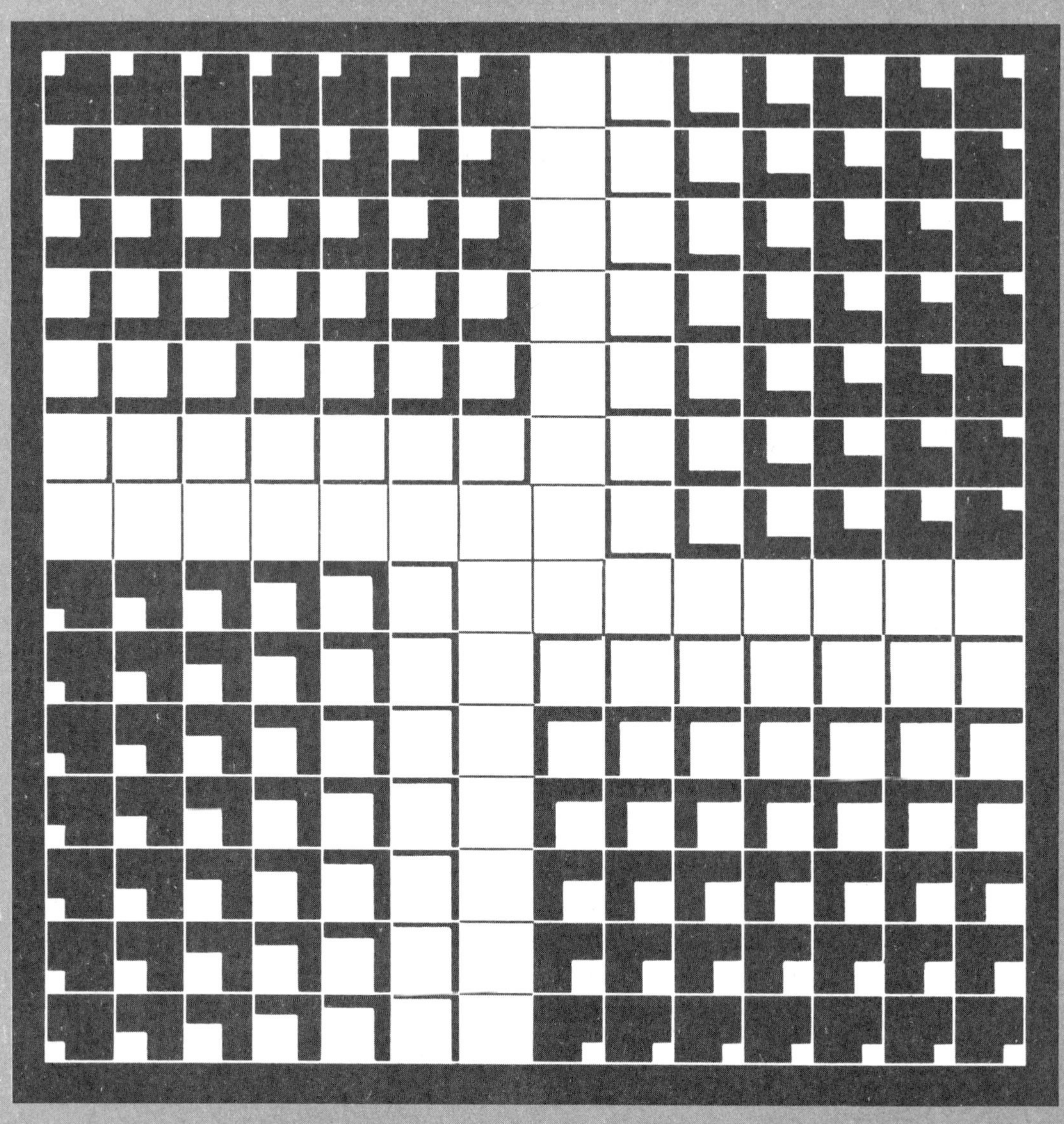

The report generator offers several options that weren't covered in Chapter 10, "Making Professional-Looking Reports." These other options are selectable from the *Options* and *Groups* menus of the report generator, when either creating or modifying a report form. For ease of reference, all the selections from both menus are explained below, including those already discussed in Chapter 10.

Options menu selections

Page title

Lets you type in the title you'd like to have at the top of each page of your report. You can have as many as four lines in a title, with each line up to 35 characters long.

Page width

The maximum width of your printed page, measured in characters (columns). The default is 80. The range is anywhere from 1 to 500. Keep in mind that the part of the page width that you devote to left and right margins will decrease the width of the actual printing, so unless you set the margins to 0, you will not get a full 80-character printed line.

Left margin

The number of blank spaces between the left edge of the page and the first column of printed data. The default left margin is 8, and the range is from 0 up to the total page width.

Right margin

This is the same as the left margin, only on the right side of the page. The default is 0, however, rather than 8.

Lines per page

This figure indicates the maximum number of printed lines per page. This defaults to 58. The range is from 30 to 100. You would alter this to adapt a report to shorter or longer forms.

Double space report

Selecting double spaced report simply prints out your report with a blank line between each record in the report. The default is single spaced.

Page eject before printing

If page eject is set to Yes, the printer will advance one blank page before it begins printing the report. Setting this to Off will save you a sheet of paper each time. The default is Yes.

Page eject after printing

If set to Yes, this option causes the printer to advance one blank sheet of paper after the last page of a report. This is often handy for letter quality printers using tractors, because it rolls the last page of your report up far enough for you to tear it off. The default is No.

Plain page

Setting this to No suppresses the printing of the system date and the page number on each page. It also prevents the report title from printing after the first page. If you want the pages numbered, and you want your title printed on each page, leave this set to No.

Group menu selections

Group on expression

If you want subtotals in your report, you have to fill in this option. It tells dBASE what expression (i.e. field) to use for grouping records. Your database file must be either indexed on this field (with the index active) or sorted on this field. The word *expression* is used in this option to indicate that the grouping can be based on something more complex than merely a field. Any valid dBASE field expression may be used, so long as the data file is indexed or sorted on that field expression. For example, if you indexed the file on a combination of two fields (e.g. CATEGORY+WHOLESALE), the same expression could be used as the basis for grouping.

Group heading

For each subtotal grouping, dBASE can print an explanatory note, or heading. This heading can be up to four lines long. The heading itself will be identical for each subgrouping, but in each case it will have added to it the field data that the group had in common. For example, in the sample report from Chapter 10 of this book, the heading was "Figures for all." The group expression was the field CATEGORY. The records in the file contained the words

RECEIVER
TURNTABLE
SPEAKERS

and so on. So the subtotals came out with the actual headings:

Figures for all RECEIVER
Figures for all TURNTABLE
Figures for all SPEAKERS

Summary report only

Selecting Yes to this option suppresses the details of each of the records within a group. Only the subtotal lines will appear. The default is No.

Page eject after group

Selecting Yes to this option causes each subtotal group to be printed on a separate page. The default is No.

Sub-group on expression

Within the normal groupings, you may elect to separate records further—into sub-groups. Enter on this line the field expression that should be used to divide records into sub-groups. This expression must be based on an active index field.

Sub-group heading

For each subgrouping, a heading can be printed. See Group Heading, above.

Appendix C

dBASE III PLUS Commands and Functions

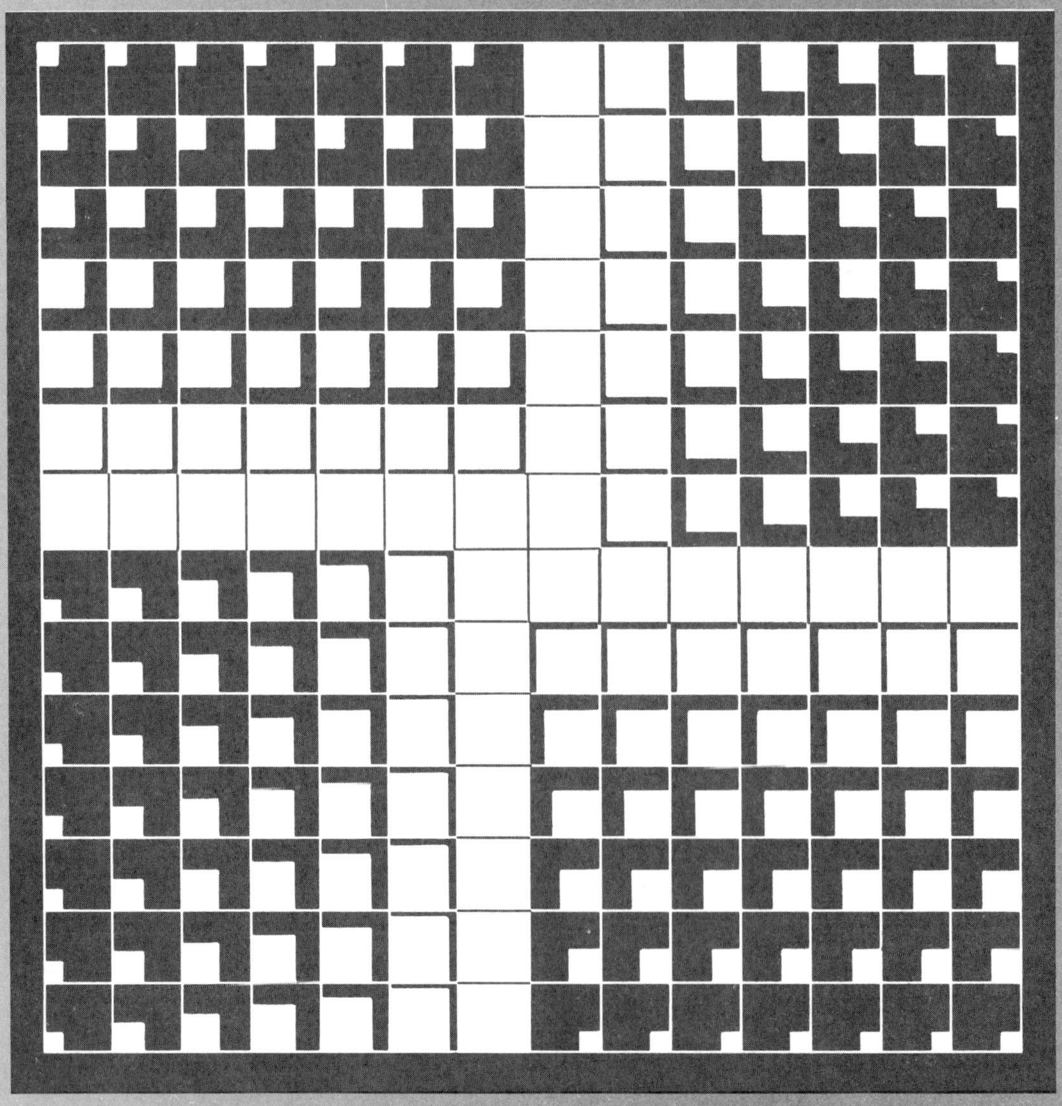

The following is a complete list of dBASE III PLUS commands and functions and the meaning of each one. Due to the scope of this book, many of the commands described here were not dealt with in the exercises you have completed. Thus, you may occassionally encounter some confusing terminology. For a more in-depth discussion of such commands, you may want to refer to the following books as resource material:

- The dBASE III PLUS manual, particularly the *Using III PLUS* section.
- Simpson, Alan. *Understanding dBASE III PLUS.* Berkeley, CA: SYBEX, 1986.
- Townsend, Carl. *Mastering dBASE III PLUS: A Structured Approach.* Berkeley, CA: SYBEX 1986.

A great deal of useful information is also to be found in the monthly publication *Databased Advisor,* which deals exclusively with database management on PC's, particularly with dBASE. The address is 1975 Fifth Avenue, San Diego, CA 92101. Phone number: (619) 236-1182.

Conventions

The following conventions are used in this summary to show the correct form (syntax) for each command:

Convention	***Meaning***
[ ]	Optional parameter.
<condition>	Specifies a limited range for the command (Example: <LNAME="Asarnow">).
<conditionlist>	A list of two or more conditions.
<scope>	Expression to specify how much of the database to use in the command (Examples: NEXT 10, REST, ALL, RECORD 3. NEXT and REST start at the current pointer location.)
uppercase letters	Indicate a command keyword.
/	Indicates when either of several commands may be used (Example: FOR/WHILE).

<prompt>	Displayed character string; delimiters required (Example: "Test").
<memvar>	Memory variable.
<memvarlist>	A list of one or more memory variables.
<row,col>	Row and column combination (Example: 2,3).
<expression>	File variables, memory variables, literals, functions, and operators.
<expressionlist>	A list of one or more memory variables and operators.
<fieldlist>	A list of one or more data fields.
<filename>	The name of a file including drive designator.
<template>	Characters used to control output format.
<commands>	One or more dBASE III PLUS commands.
<keyword>	A verb recognized by dBASE III PLUS or a dBASE III PLUS parameter (Examples: GOTO, ON, ALIAS).

Commands

? <expression list>

Displays the expression list on the next line.

?? <expression list>

Displays the expression list on the current line.

**@ <row,col> [SAY <exp> [PICTURE <clause>]]
[[GET <variable> [PICTURE <clause>]]
[RANGE <exp,exp>]] [CLEAR]**

Displays and gets formatted data lines. This is used in programming for creating screens for interactive data input.

@ <row1,col1> [CLEAR] TO <row2,col2> [DOUBLE]

Draws and erases boxes and lines, from the Dot prompt or within a program.

ACCEPT [<prompt>] TO <memvar>

Stores an inputted character string to a memory variable.

APPEND [BLANK]

Adds a record to the end of a database file. BLANK causes an empty record to be added.

APPEND FROM <filename> [FOR <condition>] [TYPE] [<filetype>]

Adds records to the end of a database file from another file. Using the TYPE clause lets you input data from non-dBASE files as well. The file types are:

Delimited	Syntax: **[with<delimiter>/BLANK]** Standard ASCII files, with no delimiters, with delimiters, or with a blank (space) as a delimiter. Carriage return and line feed at end of each record.
SDF	System Data Format. Fixed-length records. ASCII files. Carriage return and line feed at end of each record.
DIF	VisiCalc file format. Each VisiCalc row converts to a dBASE record. Each column converts to a field.
SYLK	Multiplan spreadsheet format. Arrangement same as for DIF.
WKS	Lotus 1-2-3 spreadsheet format. Arrangement same as for DIF.

Note: for PFS files, use the IMPORT command.

ASSIST

Switches dBASE III PLUS to the menu-driven mode.

AVERAGE [<expressionlist>] [<scope>] [WHILE <condition>] [FOR <condition>] [TO <memvarlist>]

Computes the arithmetic mean to the screen or to a memory variable.

BROWSE [FIELDS <fieldlist>] [LOCK<exp>] [FREEZE <field>] [NOFOLLOW] [NOMENU] [NOAPPEND] [WIDTH<exp>]

Menu-driven full-screen database edit.

CALL <module> [WITH<exp>/<memvar>]

Executes a binary program file loaded with LOAD, for programmers to run customized utilities within a dBASE program.

CANCEL

Aborts execution of a dBASE program.

CHANGE [<scope>] [FIELDS <fieldlist>] [WHILE <condition>] [FOR <condition>]

Edits specified fields in a database. Useful particularly for editing a Memo field from a program.

CLEAR

Erases the screen.

CLEAR ALL

Closes all database, index, and format files. Clears relations. Releases all memory variables and selects first workarea.

CLEAR FIELDS

Clears fields set with SET FIELDS command.

CLEAR GETS

Releases pending GET variables so they won't be processed by the next READ. In dBASE III PLUS this is done automatically by the READ command.

CLEAR MEMORY

Erases all current memory variables.

CLEAR TYPEAHEAD

Empties typeahead buffer.

CLOSE ALL <filetype>

Closes specified file types: Alternate, Database, Format, Index, Procedure.

CONTINUE

Continues to search for next record using conditions specified by a LOCATE command.

COPY FILE <filename> TO <filename>

Duplicates any type of file. Be sure to indicate the file extension.

COPY STRUCTURE [EXTENDED] TO <filename>
[FIELDS <fieldlist>]

Creates a dBASE III PLUS database file structure from an existing file structure. The resulting database will contain no records, only the structure (and header). If the EXTENDED clause is used, a database file is created containing a header and one data record. The data field variables in this one record will contain the names of the fields in the source file.

COPY TO <filename> [<scope>] [FIELDS <fieldlist>] [WHILE <condition>] [FOR <condition>] [TYPE <filename>]

Copies database file in use to another file.

COUNT [<scope>] [WHILE <condition>] [FOR <condition>]
[TO <memvar>]

Tallies the number of records that meet the condition specified.

CREATE <filename>

Defines a new dBASE III PLUS database file.

CREATE <filename> FROM <structure extended file>

Creates a new database file from a file created by COPY STRUCTURE EXTENDED.

CREATE LABEL <filename>

Creates a file to define a form for printing mailing labels.

CREATE QUERY <filename>

Creates a filter condition and stores it in a query file.

CREATE REPORT <filename>

Creates a file used to define a report.

CREATE SCREEN <filename>

Creates a screen format file (.FMT) and custom screen format file (.SCR).

CREATE VIEW <filename>

Creates a relation between files as a working environment and saves it to a file.

CREATE VIEW <filename> FROM ENVIRONMENT

Creates a View file from the current working environment. If you have already set up a View, using several workareas and relations, this saves it all as a View.

DELETE [<scope>] [WHILE <condition>] [FOR <condition>]

Marks for deletion records in a database that meet the specified conditions.

DIR [<drive>] [<path>] [<filename>]

Displays the names of the files that meet the specified drive, path, and template description. In other words, it works just like the DOS DIR command.

DISPLAY [OFF] [<scope>] [<expressionlist>] [WHILE <condition>] [FOR <condition>] [TO PRINT]

Displays the records and fields in the current database. Pauses between screen displays. OFF suppresses the record numbers from the display.

DISPLAY HISTORY [LAST <exp>] [TO PRINT]

Displays previously executed commands.

DISPLAY MEMORY [TO PRINT]

Displays the current active memory variables.

DISPLAY STATUS [TO PRINT]

Displays current status information about active databases, indexes, alternative files, and system parameters.

DISPLAY STRUCTURE [TO PRINT]

Displays the structure of the current active database.

DO <filename> [WITH <parameter list>]

Executes a program or procedure. Parameters can be passed to the called routine.

DO CASE . . . CASE <conditionlist> [CASE <conditionlist>] . . . [OTHERWISE <condition>] ENDCASE

Executes one of several alternate program paths. Used in place of IF, ELSE, ENDIF structures.

DO WHILE <condition> <commands> ENDDO

Executes a loop within the program until a specified condition is met.

EDIT [<scope>] [FIELDS <fieldlst>] [WHILE <condition>] [FOR <condition>]

Edits the contents of a database record.

EJECT

Executes a form feed on the printer.

ERASE <filename>

Deletes the specified file from the directory.

EXIT

Escapes from a DO WHILE loop in a dBASE program without regard to the specified condition.

EXPORT TO <filename> [TYPE <filetype>]

Creates PFS files from dBASE III files.

FIND <string> <number>

Positions record pointer in an indexed database to the first record that meets the specified condition.

GO/GOTO <expression>/[BOTTOM/TOP]

Positions record pointer in a database to a specified record.

HELP [<keyword>]

Switches to dBASE III PLUS' menu-driven Help mode.

IF <condition> <commands> [ELSE <commands>] ENDIF

Permits execution of the specified commands if a particular condition is met.

IMPORT FROM <filename> [TYPE <filetype>]

Creates dBASE III PLUS files from PFS files.

INDEX ON <keyexpression> TO <filename>

Creates an index for a database on a specified key.

INPUT [<prompt>] TO <memvar>

Permits entry of data to a specified memory variable.

INSERT [BLANK] [BEFORE]

Inserts a new record at the specified position in the database.

JOIN WITH <alias> TO <filename>
FOR <condition> [FIELDS <fieldlist>]

Combines records and fields from two databases to a third database. This is a complex and powerful command. Be sure to read more in the dBASE III PLUS manual before using.

LABEL FORM <filename> [<scope>] [SAMPLE] [TO PRINT]
[WHILE <condition>] [FOR <condition>]
[TO FILE <filename>]

Prints labels using the specified label form file. The SAMPLE clause prints a sample of the label format so you can check paper alignment.

LIST [OFF] [<scope>] [<expressionlist>] [WHILE <condition>]
[FOR <condition>] [TO PRINT]

Lists records from the database meeting the specified conditions.

LIST HISTORY [LAST <exp>] [TO PRINT]

Lists current history (last commands executed).

LIST MEMORY [TO PRINT]

Lists current active memory variables.

LIST STATUS [TO PRINT]

Lists current status of databases and system parameters.

LIST STRUCTURE [TO PRINT]

Lists structure of current active database.

LOAD **<filename>**

Places binary file in memory to execute from the CALL command.

LOCATE [<scope>] [FOR <condition>] [WHILE <condition>]

Positions record pointer to first record in a database meeting the specified condition. Uses unindexed files, scanning the file until the match is found. Operates rather slowly on large files.

LOOP

Skips all commands from the current command to the end of the DO loop.

MODIFY COMMAND <filename>

Modifies a program using dBASE III PLUS' internal editor or, if specified in the CONFIG.DB file, an external word processor.

MODIFY LABEL <filename>

Modifies a file that defines a label.

MODIFY QUERY <filename>

Modifies specified query file.

MODIFY REPORT <filename>

Modifies a report form file.

MODIFY SCREEN <filename>

Modifies specified screen file.

MODIFY STRUCTURE [<filename>]

Modifies the structure of a database, if possible without losing the data within the database.

MODIFY VIEW <filename>

Modifies specified View file.

NOTE/* && [<text>]

Indicates nonexecuting commment line in a dBASE program. The **&&** can be used on the same line as a command, off to the right.

ON ERROR/ESCAPE/KEY <dBASE command>

Executes specified dBASE command when error occurs, the Escape key is pressed, or any key is pressed.

PACK

Removes all records in the database that are marked for deletion. If the database is open with an index, the index will be updated. This will change the record numbers in the database of all records after any records that were marked for deletion.

PARAMETERS <memvarlist>

Specifies memory variables to be used with the DO . . . WITH command.

PRIVATE [ALL [LIKE/EXCEPT <expression>]] [<memvarlist>]

Specifies memory variables that are to be considered local to the program and not passed to higher-level programs.

PROCEDURE <name>

Identifies an executable procedure in a procedure file.

PUBLIC <memvarlist>

Defines variables to be available to all programs at any level (global variables).

QUIT

Closes all files and exits dBASE III PLUS.

READ [SAVE]

Permits user to enter data to all pending GETs. Used in programs for full screen entry of data. Using SAVE prevents dBASE from automatically clearing the pending GETs after the READ.

RECALL [<scope>] [WHILE <condition>] [FOR <condition>]

Unmarks specified records that were previously marked for deletion (cannot be used if the database has been packed since the records were marked).

REINDEX

Rebuilds all currently open indexes automatically.

RELEASE [ALL [LIKE/EXCEPT <template>]]/[<memvarlist>] [MODULE <name>]

Erases specified memory variables except those declared public or initialized in a nested command file. Used in programs.

RENAME <old filename> TO <new filename>

Changes the name of any file. You have to stipulate the extension.

REPLACE [<scope>] <field> WITH <expression> [,<field> WITH <expression> . . . . .] [WHILE <condition>] [FOR <condition>]

Changes the contents of the specified database fields. (STORE will not change a database field.)

REPORT FORM <filename>[<scope>] [FOR <condition>] [WHILE <condition>] [PLAIN] [HEADING <string>] [NOEJECT] [TO PRINT] [TO FILE <filename>] [SUMMARY]

Creates a report using a previously created report form from the current database.

RESTORE FROM <filename> [ADDITIVE]

Retrieves saved memory variables (see SAVE TO).

RESUME

Resumes a suspended program.

RETRY

Ends a command file and executes the same statement in the calling program.

RETURN [TO MASTER]

Returns to the calling program or the main menu.

RUN <command>

Runs a program external to dBASE III PLUS.

SAVE TO <filename> [ALL LIKE/EXCEPT <template>]

Saves current memory variables to a memory file.

SEEK <expression>

Positions the record pointer to the first record in an indexed file with a key value matching the specified expression. Searches on character fields require single or double quotes around the expression.

SELECT <workarea>/<alias>

Switches dBASE III PLUS between active work areas. Up to 10 work areas can be defined with the USE command.

SET

Menu-driven command to set environment switches.

SET ALTERNATE on/OFF

Switches output to alternate file on or off. See next command.

SET ALTERNATE TO <filename>

Defines an alternate file name that can be used to save whatever data dBASE displays on the screen. The display is stored as a text file that can be used in a word processor. The extension is .TXT by default, though you may specify it differently. You must SET ALTERNATE ON before data capture begins, and then SET ALTERNATE OFF and CLOSE ALTERNATE before reading the file into a word processor.

SET BELL ON/off

Turns on the bell during data entry when the data field has been filled.

SET CARRY on/OFF

Copies data from a prior record to a new record when APPEND or INSERT is used. Very useful if many records have identical data in some fields.

SET CATALOG ON/off

Adds file opened to catalog file (see next command). Catalogs are used to store the names of related files, such as database files, label files, format files, etc.

SET CATALOG TO <filename>

Creates a catalog file and opens it in workarea 10.

SET CENTURY on/OFF

Controls the display of the century in data displays.

SET COLOR TO <standard> [<enhanced>..][<border>..]

Sets selection of colors for color monitors, or display-screen attributes for monochrome. Blinking, inverse, and high intensity are available. Consult the manual for details.

SET CONFIRM on/OFF

Requires carriage return on data entry.

SET CONSOLE ON/off

Sends or suspends output to the screen.

SET DATE AMERICAN/ANSI/BRITISH/ITALIAN/FRENCH/GERMAN

Determines format of date display.

SET DEBUG on/OFF

Controls whether the SET ECHO ON output is sent to the printer or not.

SET DECIMALS TO <expression>

Sets the number of decimal places displayed after a calculation.

SET DEFAULT TO <drive>

Defines the default drive for all programs and databases, and all file access.

SET DELETED on/OFF

Determines whether commands see records marked for deletion.

SET DELIMITERS on/OFF

Selects optional delimiter to appear on each end of a data field on the screen.

SET DELIMITERS TO [<string>]/[DEFAULT]

Specifies delimiters to use for displays. The default is colons (:).

SET DEVICE TO printer/SCREEN

Determines if formatted output will be sent to screen or printer.

SET DOHISTORY on/OFF

Controls the saving of command lines executed from a program. Normally on.

SET ECHO on/OFF

Determines if command lines in a dBASE III PLUS program are echoed on the output device as they are being executed.

SET ESCAPE ON/off

Controls whether pressing the ESCAPE key can abort a command file execution.

SET EXACT on/OFF

Controls whether exact matching is necessary in a string comparison.

SET FIELDS on/OFF

Accepts or ignores fields set with SET FIELDS TO.

SET FIELDS TO <fieldlist>/ALL

Specifies fields for access.

SET FILTER TO [<condition>]/[FILE <filename>]

Controls filter or template used as a condition by other commands in retrievals. The database will then appear to contain only records that meet the filter condition.

SET FIXED on/OFF

Controls whether the number of displayed decimal places is fixed or floating.

SET FORMAT TO [<filename>]

Opens a format (.FMT screen) file used for formatted input and editing.

SET FUNCTION <expression> TO <expression>

Sets a function key value. Example: To set function key 1 to display the structure: SET FUNCTION 1 TO 'DISPLAY STRUCTURE;' The semicolon acts like the ↵ key.

SET HEADING ON/off

Controls the display of the heading with LIST and DISPLAY commands.

SET HELP ON/off

Determines whether the query *Do you want some help? (Y/N)* will appear in response to an error.

SET HISTORY ON/off

Controls line editing at Dot prompt from history file.

SET HISTORY TO <exp>

Specifies number of lines to save in history. Default is 20.

SET INDEX TO [<filelist>]

Opens the specified index file(s).

SET INTENSITY ON/off

Turns the reverse video attribute on and off. It's normally on, so fields appear in bright reverse video.

SET MARGIN TO <expression>

Defines the left margin for the printer.

SET MEMOWIDTH TO <exp>

Defines width of memo field output. Default is 50.

SET MENUS ON/off

Controls the display of the function key prompt menu.

SET MESSAGE TO [<cstring>]

Displays specified message at bottom of screen.

SET ORDER TO [<exp>]

Specifies which of several open index files are used to control the FIND and SEEK commands. This is faster than using the SET INDEX TO command. Example: If you opened three indexes, X,Y, and Z in that order, they are assigned the numbers 1,2, and 3 by dBASE. Issuing the command SET INDEX TO 3,2,1 reverses the order. Z is now the master index.

SET PATH TO [<pathlist>]

Specifies a path for file searches.

SET PRINT on/OFF

Directs unformatted output to the printer.

SET PRINTER TO <DOS device>

Redirects output of printer to devices such as COM1, LPT2, etc.

SET PROCEDURE TO [<filename>]

Opens the specified procedure file.

SET RELATION TO [<expression>/RECNO() INTO <alias>]

Links two databases on the key expression. If the RECNO() expression is used, the files are linked by record number, rather than by a field.

SET SAFETY ON/off

If on, causes dBASE warns you before overwriting a file.

SET SCOREBOARD ON/off

Suppresses the display of certain status information, permitting the user to use line zero on the display.

SET STATUS ON/off

Controls display of Status Line at bottom of screen.

SET STEP on/OFF

Halts execution of a program after each instruction.

SET TALK ON/off

Displays the result of each command after execution.

SET TITLE ON/off

Controls prompt for descriptive title when a file is added to the catalog with SET CATALOG ON.

SET TYPEAHEAD TO <expression>

Controls size to typeahead buffer. Default is 20.

SET UNIQUE on/OFF

Controls whether all records with a given key appear in the index file. Default is off. With unique on, only the first of several identical records will be recorded in the index. This is useful for effectively eliminating duplicate records.

SET VIEW TO <filename>

Opens a View file.

SKIP [<expression>]

Moves the current record pointer backward or forward by the amount specified in the expression.

SORT TO <filename> ON <field> [/A] [/D] [/C]
[<field> [/A] [/D] [/C] . . .] [<escape>] [FOR <condition>]
[WHILE <condition>]

Creates a database with records sorted in the specified sort order.

STORE <expression> TO <memvarlist>

Stores an expression or value to a memory variable.

SUM [<scope>][<expressionlist>] [TO <memvarlist>]
[WHILE <condition>] [FOR <condition>]

Computes the sum of an expression.

SUSPEND

Halts execution of a command file for debugging.

TEXT **<text> ENDTEXT**

Displays a block of text from a command file.

TOTAL ON **<keyfield> TO <filename> [<scope>]
[FIELDS <fieldlist>] [WHILE <condition>]
[FOR <condition>]**

Creates a summary database of a presorted file containing totals.

TYPE **<filename> [TO PRINT]**

Displays or prints a file. (*Note:* TYPE( ), unlike this command, is a function and is used to test an expression.)

UPDATE ON **<keyfield> FROM <alias> REPLACE <field> WITH
<expression> [<field> WITH <expression> . . .]
[RANDOM]**

Allows modification of a file from a batch file.

USE **[<filename>] [INDEX <filename list] [ALIAS <alias>]**

Opens the specified database in the current work area.

WAIT **[<prompt>] [TO <memvar>]**

Suspends program execution until any key is pressed.

ZAP

Equivalent to a DELETE ALL followed by a PACK. It erases all records in the current database. *Be careful with this command.* If SAFETY is set on, dBASE will ask for verification before ZAPping your database.

Functions by Category

CATEGORY	*FUNCTION*	*DESCRIPTION*
Date and Time	CDOW	Converts Date variable to day of week (Character string)
	CMONTH	Converts Date variable to month (Character string)

	CTOD	Converts Character string to Date variable
	DATE	System date
	DAY	Day of month (Numeric)
	DOW	Day of week (Numeric) from Date variable
	DTOC	Date to Character conversion
	MONTH	Month (Numeric) from Date variable
	TIME	System time
	YEAR	Year (Numeric) from Date variable
Character	&	Macro substitution
	AT	Substring search
	LEFT	Substring select from left
	LOWER	Converts to lowercase
	LTRIM	Removes leading blanks
	REPLICATE	Repeats character expression
	RIGHT	Substring select from right
	RTRIM	Removes trailing blanks
	SPACE	Outputs spaces
	STUFF	Replaces portion of string
	SUBSTR	Creates substring
	TRANSFORM	Character/number in picture format
	TRIM	Removes trailing blanks
	UPPER	Converts to uppercase
Mathematical	ABS	Absolute value
	EXP	Exponential
	INT	Integer

	LOG	Logarithm
	MAX	Greater of two values
	MIN	Smaller of two values
	MOD	Modulus
	ROUND	Round off
	SQRT	Square root
Conversion	ASC	Converts Character to ASCII code
	CHR	Converts ASCII code to Character
	STR	Converts Numeric to Character
	VAL	Converts Character to Numeric
Miscellaneous	BOF	Beginning of file
	COL	Current screen column
	DELETED	Deleted record
	DISKSPACE	Free space on disk
	EOF	End of file
	ERROR	Number of ON ERROR condition
	FILE	Tests for file existence
	FOUND	Result of database file search
	IIF	One expression or another
	ISALPHA	Evaluates for letter
	ISCOLOR	Evaluates for color mode
	ISLOWER	Evaluates for lowercase
	ISUPPER	Evaluates for uppercase
	LEN	Length of character string
	LUPDATE	Last update of database file
	MESSAGE	ON ERROR message string
	PCOL	Printer column position
	PROW	Printer row position

	RECCOUNT	Number of records in database
	RECNO	Current record number in file
	RECSIZE	Size of record
	ROW	Current screen row
	TYPE	Validates an expression
Identification	DBF	Name of database file in use
	FIELD	Names of fields in database
	FKLABEL	Names of function keys
	FKMAX	Maximum number of function keys
	GETENV	Gets DOS environment variables
	NDX	Names of open index files
	OS	Name of operating system
	VERSION	dBASE III PLUS version number
Input	INKEY	Keypress during program execution
	READKEY	Full-screen exiting keypress

INDEX

Note: Entries in italics are dBASE III PLUS commands or menu options.

Selections from The SYBEX Library

Software Specific

DATABASE MANAGEMENT SYSTEMS

UNDERSTANDING dBASE III PLUS
by Alan Simpson
415 pp., illustr., Ref. 349-X
Emphasizing the new PLUS features, this extensive volume gives the database terminology, program management, techniques, and applications. There are hints on file-handling, debugging, avoiding syntax errors.

ADVANCED TECHNIQUES IN dBASE III PLUS
by Alan Simpson
500 pp., illustr., Ref. 369-4
The latest version of what ***Databased Advisor*** called "the best choice for experienced dBASE III programmers." Stressing design and structured programming for quality custom systems, it includes practical examples and full details on PLUS features.

MASTERING dBASE III PLUS: A STRUCTURED APPROACH
by Carl Townsend
350 pp., illustr., Ref. 372-4
This new edition adds the power of PLUS to Townsend's highly successful structured approach to dBASE III programming. Useful examples from business illustrate system design techniques for superior custom applications.

UNDERSTANDING dBASE III
by Alan Simpson
250 pp., illustr., Ref. 267-1
The basics and more, for beginners and intermediate users of dBASEIII. This presents mailing label systems, bookkeeping and data management at your fingertips.

ADVANCED TECHNIQUES IN dBASE III
by Alan Simpson
505 pp., illustr., Ref. 282-5
Intermediate to experienced users are given the best database design techniques, the primary focus being the development of user-friendly, customized programs.

MASTERING dBASE III: A STRUCTURED APPROACH
by Carl Townsend
338 pp., illustr., Ref. 301-5
Emphasized throughout is the highly successful structured design technique for constructing reliable and flexible applications, from getting started to advanced techniques. A general ledger program is used as the primary illustration for the examples.

SIMPSON'S dBASE III LIBRARY
by Alan Simpson
362 pp., illustr., Ref. 300-7
Our bestselling dBASE author share his personal library of custom dBASE III routines for finance, graphics, statistics, expanded databases, housekeeping, screen management and more.

UNDERSTANDING dBASE II
by Alan Simpson
260 pp., illustr., Ref. 147-0
Learn programming techniques for mailing label systems, bookkeeping, and data management, as well as ways to interface dBASE II with other software systems.

ADVANCED TECHNIQUES IN dBASE II

by Alan Simpson

395 pp., illustr. Ref., 228-0

Learn to use dBASE II for accounts receivable, recording business income and expenses, keeping personal records and mailing lists, and much more.

MASTERING Q&A

by Greg Harvey

350 pp., illustr., Ref. 356-2

An experienced consultant gives you straight answers on every aspect of Q&A, with easy-to-follow tutorials on the write, file, and report modules, using the Intelligent Assistant, and hundreds of expert tips.

MASTERING REFLEX

by Robert Ericson and Ann Moskol

336 pp., illustr., Ref. 348-1

The complete resource for users of Borland's Reflex: The Analyst, with extensive examples and templates for practical applications.

POWER USER'S GUIDE TO R:BASE 5000

by Alan Simpson

350 pp., illustr., Ref. 354-6

For R:BASE 5000 users who want to go beyond the basics, here is an in-depth look at design and structured programming techniques for R:BASE 5000—packed with expert tips and practical, usable examples.

UNDERSTANDING R:BASE 5000

by Alan Simpson

413 pp., illustr., Ref. 302-3

This comprehensive tutorial is for database novices and experienced R:BASE newcomers alike. Topics range from elementary concepts to managing multiple databases and creating custom applications.

INTEGRATED SOFTWARE

MASTERING 1-2-3

by Carolyn Jorgensen

466 pp., illustr., Ref. 337-6

Here is a thorough, lucid treatment of 1-2-3, including Release 2, with emphasis on intermediate to advanced uses—complex functions, graphics and database power, macro writing, and the latest add-on products.

SIMPSON'S 1-2-3 MACRO LIBRARY

by Alan Simpson

298 pp., illustr., Ref. 314-7

Share this goldmine of ready-made 1-2-3 macros for custom menus, complex plotting and graphics, consolidating worksheets, interfacing with mainframes and more. Plus explanations of Release 2 macro commands.

ADVANCED BUSINESS MODELS WITH 1-2-3

by Stanley R. Trost

250 pp., illustr., Ref. 159-4

If you are a business professional using the 1-2-3 software package, you will find the spreadsheet and graphics models provided in this book easy to use "as is" in everyday business situations.

THE ABC'S OF 1-2-3 (2nd Edition)

by Chris Gilbert and Laurie Williams

245 pp., illustr., Ref. 355-4

A complete introduction to 1-2-3, featuring Release 2—for first-time users who want to master the basics in a hurry. With comprehensive tutorials on spreadsheet, database, and graphics. ". . . an easy and comfortable way to get started on the program."

—*Online Today*

MASTERING SYMPHONY (2nd Edition)

by Douglas Cobb

817 pp., illustr., Ref. 341-4

"*Mastering Symphony* is beautifully organized and presented . . . I recommend it," says *Online Today*. *IPCO Info* calls it "the bible for every Symphony user . . . If you can buy only one book, this is definitely the one to buy." This new edition includes the latest on Version 1.1

ANDERSEN'S SYMPHONY TIPS AND TRICKS

by Dick Andersen

321 pp., illustr., Ref. 342-2

Hundreds of concise, self-contained entries cover everything from software pitfalls to time-saving macros—to make working with Symphony easy, efficient and productive. Includes version 1.1. and new Add-in programs.

FOCUS ON SYMPHONY DATABASES

by Alan Simpson

350 pp., illustr., Ref. 336-8

An expert guide to creating and managing databases in Symphony—including version 1.2—with complete sample systems for mailing lists, inventory and accounts receivable. A wealth of advanced tips and techniques.

FOCUS ON SYMPHONY MACROS

by Alan Simpson

350 pp., illustr., Ref. 351-1

Share Symphony expert Alan Simpson's approach to planning, creating, and using Symphony macros—including advanced techniques, a goldmine of ready-made macros, and complete menu-driven systems. For all versions through 1.1.

BETTER SYMPHONY SPREADSHEETS

by Carl Townsend

287 pp., illustr., Ref. 339-2

For Symphony users who want to gain real expertise in the use of the spreadsheet features, this has hundreds of tips and techniques. There are also instructions on how to implement some of the special features of Excel on Symphony.

MASTERING FRAMEWORK

by Doug Hergert

450 pp., illustr. Ref. 248-5

This tutorial guides the beginning user through all the functions and features of this integrated software package, geared to the business environment.

ADVANCED TECHNIQUES IN FRAMEWORK

by Alan Simpson

250 pp., illustr. Ref. 257-4

In order to begin customizing your own models with Framework, you'll need a thorough knowledge of Fred programming language, and this book provides this information in a complete, well-organized form.

MASTERING THE IBM ASSISTANT SERIES

by Jeff Lea and Ted Leonsis

249 pp., illustr., Ref. 284-1

Each section of this book takes the reader through the features, screens, and capabilities of each module of the series. Special emphasis is placed on how the programs work together.

DATA SHARING WITH 1-2-3 AND SYMPHONY: INCLUDING MAINFRAME LINKS

by Dick Andersen

262 pp., illustr., Ref. 283-3

This book focuses on an area of increasing importance to business users: exchanging data between Lotus software and other micro and mainframe software. Special emphasis is given to dBASE II and III.

MASTERING PARADOX (2nd Edition)

by Alan Simpson

463 pp., illustr., Ref. 375-9

Total training in Paradox from our bestselling database author: everything from basic functions to custom programming in PAL, organized for easy reference and illustrated with useful business-oriented examples.

JAZZ ON THE MACINTOSH

by Joseph Caggiano and Michael McCarthy

431 pp., illustr., Ref. 265-5

Each chapter features as an example a business report which is built on throughout the book in the first section of each chapter. Chapters then go on to detail each application and special effects in depth.

MASTERING EXCEL

by Carl Townsend

454 pp., illustr., Ref. 306-6

This hands-on tutorial covers all basic operations of Excel plus in-depth coverage of special features, including extensive coverage of macros.

APPLEWORKS: TIPS & TECHNIQUES

by Robert Ericson

373 pp., illustr., Ref. 303-1

Designed to improve AppleWorks skills, this is a great book that gives utility information illustrated with every-day management examples.

MASTERING APPLEWORKS

by Elna Tymes

201 pp., illustr., Ref. 240-X

This bestseller presents business solutions which are used to introduce AppleWorks and then develop mastery of the program. Includes examples of balance sheet, income statement, inventory control system, cash-flow projection, and accounts receivable summary.

PRACTICAL APPLEWORKS USES

by David K. Simerly

313 pp., illustr., Ref. 274-4

This book covers a breadth of home and business uses, including combined-function applications, complicated tasks, and even a large section on interfacing AppleWorks with the outside world.

SPREADSHEETS

UNDERSTANDING JAVELIN

by John R. Levine, Margaret H. Young, and Jordan M. Young

350pp., illustr., Ref. 358-9

A complete guide to Javelin, including an introduction to the theory of modeling. Business-minded examples show Javelin at work on budgets, graphs, forecasts, flow charts, and much more.

MASTERING SUPERCALC 3

by Greg Harvey

300 pp., illustr., Ref. 312-0

Featuring Version 2.1, this title offers full coverage of all the sophisticated features of this third generation spreadsheet, including spreadsheet, graphics, database and advanced techniques.

DOING BUSINESS WITH MULTIPLAN

by Richard Allen King and Stanley R. Trost

250 pp., illustr., Ref. 148-9

This book will show you how using Multiplan can be nearly as easy as learning to use a pocket calculator. It presents a collection of templates for business applications.

MULTIPLAN ON THE COMMODORE 64

by Richard Allen King

250 pp., illustr. Ref. 231-0

This clear, straightforward guide will give you a firm grasp on Multiplan's function, as well as provide a collection of useful template programs.

WORD PROCESSING

INTRODUCTION TO WORDSTAR (3rd Edition)

by Arthur Naiman

208 pp., illustr., Ref. 134-9

A bestselling SYBEX classic. "WordStar is complicated enough to need a book to get you into it comfortably. Naiman's **Introduction to WordStar** is the best."

—***Whole Earth Software Catalog***

". . . an indispensable fingertip guide, highly recommended for beginners and experienced users."

—***TypoWorld***

PRACTICAL WORDSTAR USES

by Julie Anne Arca

303 pp., illustr. Ref. 107-1

Pick your most time-consuming office tasks and this book will show you how to streamline them with WordStar.

SYBEX Computer Books are different.

Here is why . . .

At SYBEX, each book is designed with you in mind. Every manuscript is carefully selected and supervised by our editors, who are themselves computer experts. We publish the best authors, whose technical expertise is matched by an ability to write clearly and to communicate effectively. Programs are thoroughly tested for accuracy by our technical staff. Our computerized production department goes to great lengths to make sure that each book is well-designed.

In the pursuit of timeliness, SYBEX has achieved many publishing firsts. SYBEX was among the first to integrate personal computers used by authors and staff into the publishing process. SYBEX was the first to publish books on the CP/M operating system, microprocessor interfacing techniques, word processing, and many more topics.

Expertise in computers and dedication to the highest quality product have made SYBEX a world leader in computer book publishing. Translated into fourteen languages, SYBEX books have helped millions of people around the world to get the most from their computers. We hope we have helped you, too.

For a complete catalog of our publications: